Cars

gettyimages

Cars

The Early Years
Die Anfänge des Automobils
Les Premières Années de l'Automobile

Text by Brian Laban

Picture research by
Alex Linghorn
and Ali Khoja

h.f.ullmann

The birth process of the Beetle. The German 'people's car' was designed before World War II by Dr Ferdinand Porsche. It went into full production after the war, and eventually overtook Ford's Model T for the highest production numbers of any car.

Die Stunde des Käfers. Noch vor dem Zweiten Weltkrieg hatte Dr. Ferdinand Porsche den »Volkswagen« konstruiert. Die eigentliche Fertigung begann jedoch erst nach dem Krieg, und am Ende sollte der VW das T-Modell von Ford als meistproduziertes Auto aller Zeiten ablösen.

La naissance de la Coccinelle. La « voiture du peuple » allemande fut dessinée par le Dr Ferdinand Porsche. Construite en série après la guerre, elle battit les records de production détenus jusque là par la Ford Model T.

Frontispiece: In 1907 Talbot cars recorded 109 competition wins and were advertised as the 'Invincible Talbot', as typified by this four-cylinder model, seen at speed during a 1908 trial.
Front cover photo: see page 297
Back cover photo: see page 17

Frontispiz: Im Jahr 1907 konnte die Firma Talbot 109 Rennsiege verbuchen, und die Werbung pries den Wagen als »den unbesiegbaren Talbot« an. Hier ein Vierzylinder von 1908 in voller Fahrt.
Vorderes Coverfoto: siehe S. 297
Hinteres Coverfoto: siehe S. 17

Frontispice: En 1907, les voitures Talbot, comme ce modèle quatre-cylindres photographié lors d'une épreuve en 1908, totalisent 109 victoires en compétition et se voient qualifiées d'invincibles.
1re de couverture : voir p. 297
4e de couverture : voir p. 17

© 2005 h.f.ullmann publishing GmbH

Photographs © 2000 Getty Images

This book was produced by Getty Images, Unique House, 21–31 Woodfield Road, London W9 2BA

Original title: *Cars*
Original ISBN: 978-3-8331-1333-6

For the publisher:
Managing editor: Sally Bald
Assistant editor: Monika Dauer
German translation: Manfred Allié
French translation: Arnaud Dupin de Beyssat

For Getty Images:
Art director: Michael Rand
Design: B+B
Project manager: Alex Linghorn
Editor: Richard Collins
Proof-reader: Elisabeth Ihre
Production: Tea McAleer
Scanning: Antonia Hille
Special thanks to: Ian Denning, Deidre McGale, Jonathon Anderson, Steve Jacobs, Leon Meyer

© 2011 for this edition: h.f.ullmann publishing GmbH

Special edition

Cover design: Simone Sticker

Overall responsibility for production:
h.f.ullmann publishing GmbH, Potsdam, Germany

ISBN 978-3-8480-0517-8

Printed in China, 2013

10 9 8 7 6 5 4 3 2 1
X IX VIII VII V IV III II I

www.ullmann-publishing.com
newsletter@ullmann-publishing.com

Contents

Inhalt

Sommaire

Prologue

Entering the twenty-first century, it is difficult to imagine a world without the automobile, a world without the mobility and personal freedom it offers, or the virtually unrestricted horizons it has created. At the same time, it is increasingly difficult to ignore the less positive sides of the automobile's influence, in a world which has come to regard personal mobility as a right. We love and defend the pleasures of motoring, while deep down we worry about its consequences. We drive more cars over more miles than ever before, yet we worry about their impact on our environment, our health and safety; we worry about conserving energy and finite natural resources, are concerned about creating pollution; we worry about traffic congestion, noise and accidents. But we motor on, and, looking back over these early years of the motor car, it seems clear that none of the above is really new; the relationship was always a volatile one.

The fact is that the world has had to learn to live with the automobile because it cannot live without it. That became true from the moment of its birth, more than a century ago. Since then, the story of the automobile has been a constant battle between passion and conscience, spiced by speed, style and extraordinary personalities.

The automobile may be a defining icon of the twentieth century but it was actually a product of the late nineteenth century, an age when technical revolution seemed to know few boundaries. The first practicable automobiles, built by Karl Benz and Gottlieb Daimler in Germany, stuttered into life within weeks of each other in 1885, calling on all the materials and methods of what was then the cutting edge of technology, in an era obsessed with invention. Only 60 years earlier, the transport revolution had been led by the railways. In 1825 George Stephenson's Stockton and Darlington line pioneered steam trains for passenger transport, and from there the railways spread across the globe. They gave the public a first taste of long-distance travel, which in turn gave men like Daimler and Benz their vision of another degree of freedom, in the automobile.

In the beginning, there was no single blueprint, only innovation. There would be steam cars and electric cars, but ultimately the gasoline version would dominate. At its heart was the lightweight internal combustion engine, the majority of whose individual designers would adhere to the 'four-stroke' cycle patented by Nikolaus August Otto in Germany in 1877. These power units would use 'petroleum spirit' (distilled from heavier oil) as their fuel, mixing it with air in variations of the 'carburettor' invented by Daimler in 1876. Some would ignite the fuel mixture in their cylinders with a glowing 'hot-tube', as patented by Leo Funk in Germany in 1879. Others, including Benz, would use electric sparks, variously fed by magnetos, or high-voltage induction circuits using developments of the 'batteries' invented by Alessandro Volta in Italy at the turn of the nineteenth century. Eventually, when oil and gas lamps were no longer bright enough for the motor car's increasing speed, batteries would power the electric lights developed by Thomas Alva Edison in 1879. The new automobiles borrowed technology wherever they could, and when necessary invented more of their own.

They would improve rapidly and continuously. The earliest models would run on solid rubber tyres, pioneered in 1846 by an Englishman, Thomas Hancock, adopting the hard 'vulcanised' rubber developed in America in 1841 by Charles Goodyear. In 1895, in France, following the inventions of Scotsman John Boyd Dunlop in 1888, André and Édouard Michelin would make motoring life more comfortable, with the first pneumatic automobile tyres – and so the improvements and refinements went on.

An industry was born, and also a motoring fraternity. From Germany, the motor car spread to France, Britain, around Europe and, most significantly, by the early 1890s to America. So soon after the birth and boom of the bicycle industry in the second half of the nineteenth century, it was no surprise that many early car manufacturers, from Rover in Britain to Peugeot in France and Opel in Germany, grew out of bicycle building. No surprise, either, that builders of other kinds of precision machinery joined the motor makers – from the White Company in America, which made sewing machines before it launched its steam cars, to Wolseley, which made sheep-shearing equipment.

At first, the enthusiasts clubbed together as much to defend their interests as to share and enjoy them, because the new form of transport was not universally welcomed. In November 1895 a weekly journal, now the world's oldest surviving motoring magazine, was launched in Britain to report on and promote the 'horseless carriage'. It was called *The Autocar*, and, although its subject was already some ten years old, there were still notes of caution: 'Every new movement meets with a certain amount of senseless opposition from prejudiced individuals in this country, and the autocar is not likely to be an

exception to the rule.' It wasn't, and not only in Britain. But gradually it overcame the prejudices and by the turn of the century it was clearly here to stay.

It changed the world, in peacetime and in war. It began as a rich man's toy and had it stayed that way it might never have had the influence it had. But eventually it became a universal workhorse – largely thanks to the less class-dominated social structure of America, and more than anything else to the vision of one man, Henry Ford. It was Ford who decided to put the ordinary world on wheels and Ford who achieved it, with his seminal creation the Model T and his adoption of real mass production. His philosophy and methods turned a small industry into a global one, with a market to match. It created a new social order, where the richest men in the world were no longer aristocrats or traders, but the new industrialists, the motor makers – and appropriately enough the one-time farmboy Henry Ford was the world's first dollar billionaire.

The automobile shared its infancy with other 'modern' inventions – the telephone, invented in 1876 by Alexander Graham Bell; the gramophone, by Edison in 1878; and wireless telegraphy, pioneered by Marconi in 1894. By happy coincidence, it also grew up alongside one other great invention of the nineteenth century, photography. In 1835, in France, Louis Daguerre created the process of producing a silver image on a copper plate, and in 1837 made his first permanent pictures. Over the next fifty years, William Fox Talbot pioneered paper negative images for reproducing multiple prints; wet plates and waxed paper processes followed, and with better films and better lenses, 'high speed' photography, with exposures of only a few seconds, was possible by the 1850s. By 1885, at the automobile's birth, the state of the art was dry glass plates with 'panchromatic' emulsions, and magnesium flash-powder for high speed exposures. Then in 1888, George Eastman in the USA introduced his first Kodak roll-film box camera, popularising photography and guaranteeing that the history of the motor car was recorded in detail at all social levels. This is its story through the first 75 years, from Benz's first car, through two world wars, prosperity, depression, resistance and acceptance to the end of the 1950s and the coming, with the Mini, of a new generation.

Heute, am Anfang des 21. Jahrhunderts, kann man sich eine Welt ohne Automobile kaum noch vorstellen, eine Welt ohne die Mobilität und die Freiheit des Einzelnen, die das Auto mit sich bringt, ohne die fast grenzenlos offenen Horizonte, die wir ihm verdanken. Zugleich wird es aber auch immer schwieriger, die unerfreulicheren Seiten einer Kultur, in der uneingeschränkte Bewegung als Recht angesehen wird, außer Acht zu lassen. Wir lieben das Autofahren und verteidigen es gegen die Kritiker, doch in unserem Innersten machen uns die Folgen Sorgen. Wir fahren von Jahr zu Jahr mehr Kilometer, aber wir sorgen uns um Umwelt, Gesundheit und Sicherheit; wir wollen Energie und Rohstoffe sparen, die Umweltverschmutzung eindämmen, wir leiden am Lärm, an den Verkehrsstaus und dem Unfallrisiko. Aber trotzdem fahren wir weiter, und wenn wir in die Anfangsjahre des Automobils zurückschauen, wird uns bald klar , dass keine dieser Sorgen wirklich neu ist – das Zwiespältige in unserer Beziehung zum Auto gab es vom ersten Tage an.

Die Welt musste lernen, mit dem Automobil zu leben, weil sie nicht ohne es leben kann. Das gilt im Grunde, seit vor über hundert Jahren die ersten Autos auf die Straße kamen. Seitdem ist die Geschichte des Automobils ein ständiger Kampf zwischen Leidenschaft und Gewissen, angefeuert von Geschwindigkeit, Eleganz und großen Persönlichkeiten.

Kaum etwas anderes hat das 20. Jahrhundert so geprägt wie das Automobil, doch eigentlich ist es ein Kind des späten 19. Jahrhunderts, einer Zeit, in der die Entwicklungsmöglichkeiten der Technik fast grenzenlos schienen. Die ersten beiden funktionstüchtigen Motorfahrzeuge, von Karl Benz und Gottlieb Daimler in Deutschland gebaut, nahmen nur wenige Wochen nacheinander im Jahr 1885 Gestalt an und nutzten alle Materialien und Methoden der fortschrittlichsten Technologien der Zeit – und es war eine Zeit, die vom Fortschritt geradezu besessen war. Nur sechzig Jahre zuvor hatten die Eisenbahnen die Revolution des Transportwesens in Gang gebracht. 1825 fuhr George Stephensons erster, von einer Dampflokomotive gezogener Passagierzug von Stockton nach Darlington, und von da breitete sich das Eisenbahnnetz um den ganzen Erdball aus. Eisenbahnen gaben einen ersten Begriff davon, was Reisen über eine längere Entfernung bedeuten konnte, und daraus bezogen wiederum Männer wie Daimler und Benz ihre Vision einer noch viel weiter gehenden Freiheit, der Freiheit des Automobils.

Anfangs gab es keine etablierten Formen und Techniken, und alle Möglichkeiten standen offen. Man experimentierte mit Dampf- und Elektrowagen, doch nach und nach setzte sich der leichtere Verbrennungsmotor durch, dessen Konstrukteure sich dabei meist an das Viertaktprinzip hielten, das Nikolaus August Otto sich 1877 in Deutschland patentieren ließ. Bei diesem Motor wird das aus schweren Ölen raffinierte Benzin in verschiedenen Varianten des Vergasers, den Daimler 1876 vorgestellt hatte, mit Luft zum eigentlichen Brennstoff gemischt. Einige entzündeten das Gemisch in den Zylindern mit einem Glührohr, 1879 in Deutschland für Leo Funk patentiert. Andere, darunter auch Benz, zogen elektrische Zündkerzen vor, die den erforderlichen Strom durch Magnete oder Hochspannungsinduktoren erhielten, und als Speicher dienten Weiterentwicklungen der Batterien, die der Italiener Alessandro Volta an der Wende zum 19. Jahrhundert erfunden hatte. Als nach einer Weile die Öl- und Gaslampen für die immer schneller werdenden Fahrzeuge nicht mehr hell genug waren, traten an ihre Stelle die 1879 von Thomas Alva Edison ersonnenen, aus Batterien gespeisten elektrischen Lampen. Die Ingenieure der frühen Automobile nahmen an Techniken von überall her, was sie brauchen konnten, und wo etwas fehlte, erfanden sie es selbst.

Die Technik ging in Riesenschritten voran. Die frühesten Wagen fuhren auf Vollgummireifen, die seit 1846 nach einem Verfahren des Engländers Thomas Hancock aus dem 1841 von Charles Goodyear in Amerika entwickelten vulkanisierten Gummi hergestellt wurden. 1895 sorgten André und Édouard Michelin in Frankreich mit den ersten luftgefüllten Reifen (auf Grundlage der Erfindung des Schotten John Boyd Dunlop von 1888) dafür, dass das Fahren ein gutes Stück komfortabler wurde – so kam eine Verbesserung zur anderen.

Eine Industrie entstand, und zugleich entstand die Gemeinschaft der Autofahrer. Von Deutschland breitete sich der Motorwagen nach Frankreich, Großbritannien und über ganz Europa aus, und besonders wichtig war, dass ihm Anfang der 1890er Jahre auch der Sprung nach Amerika gelang. Die zweite Hälfte des 19. Jahrhunderts war die Blütezeit der Fahrradindustrie gewesen, und so wundert es nicht, dass viele frühe Autohersteller vom Fahrradbau her kamen, von Rover in England und Peugeot in Frankreich bis zu den deutschen Opel-Werken. Überhaupt erweiterten Betriebe, die bereits Präzisionsmaschinen herstellten, ihre Palette oft um Motorfahrzeuge, von der White Company in Amerika, die Nähmaschinen baute, bevor sie ihre Dampfwagen auf den Markt brachte, bis zum britischen Hersteller Wolseley, der sich seinen Ruf mit Schafschermaschinen erworben hatte.

Die Enthusiasten taten sich in Clubs zusammen, anfangs ebenso sehr, um ihre Interessen zu verteidigen wie um den Enthusiasmus miteinander zu teilen, denn das neue Transportmittel war nicht überall gern gesehen. Im November 1895 kam in England die erste Nummer der Wochenzeitung *The Autocar* heraus, der ältesten heute noch erscheinenden Autozeitschrift. Die Zeitung war eigens gegründet, um die Verbreitung der »pferdelosen Kutsche« zu fördern, und auch wenn die Erfindung mittlerweile zehn Jahre alt war, fanden die Herausgeber ein Wort der Warnung angebracht: »In diesem Lande hat jede Neuerung mit der gedankenlosen Opposition konservativer Kreise zu rechnen, und da wird der Motorwagen keine Ausnahme sein.« Das sollte sich bewahrheiten, und nicht nur in England. Doch der Widerstand wurde gebrochen, und als das neue Jahrhundert kam, konnte niemand mehr daran zweifeln, dass das Automobil sich durchsetzen würde.

Es veränderte die Welt, in Friedens- wie in Kriegszeiten. Es begann als Spielzeug für Reiche, und wäre es dabei geblieben, hätte es wohl nie den Einfluss bekommen, den es schließlich errang. Doch binnen kurzem wurde das Auto zum Arbeitspferd für die ganze Menschheit – was hauptsächlich der fast klassenlosen Gesellschaft der Vereinigten Staaten und insbesondere der Vision eines einzigen Mannes zu verdanken ist: Henry Ford. Ford war der Mann, der sich vornahm, die ganze Welt auf Räder zu stellen, und es sollte ihm gelingen, mit seinem Epoche machenden T-Modell und der ersten echten Massenproduktion. Sein Ehrgeiz und seine neuen Produktionsverfahren machten aus Manufakturen eine Schlüsselindustrie der Weltwirtschaft und schufen den Markt dafür gleich mit. Es entstand eine neue Sozialstruktur, und die reichsten Männer der Welt waren nun nicht mehr Aristokraten oder Kaufleute, sondern die neuen Industriemagnaten, die Autoproduzenten – und so war es nur angemessen, dass der erste Dollarmilliardär der Welt niemand anderer war als der ehemalige Farmerjunge Henry Ford.

Das Automobil wuchs gemeinsam mit anderen großen Erfindungen der modernen Zeit auf – dem Telefon, das Alexander Graham Bell 1876 präsentierte, dem 1878 von Edison erfundenen Grammophon und der drahtlosen Telegrafie, deren erste Übermittlung Marconi im Jahr 1894 gelang. Und es ist eine glückliche Fügung, dass das Auto gemeinsam mit einer anderen bedeutenden Errungenschaft des 19. Jahrhunderts groß wurde, der Fotografie. 1835 hatte Louis Daguerre in Frankreich das Verfahren ersonnen, ein Bild mit Silberiodid auf eine Kupferplatte zu bannen, und 1837 hatte er die ersten haltbaren Daguerrotypien produziert. Binnen der nächsten fünfzig Jahre erfand William Fox Talbot das Negativverfahren, es folgten Kollodiumverfahren und gewachstes Papier, bessere Emulsionen und Objektive und schnellere Verschlüsse – schon in den 1850er Jahren waren Belichtungszeiten von nur wenigen Sekunden möglich. Als 1885 das Automobil zur Welt kam, waren trockene Glasplatte, panchromatische Emulsion und der Magnesiumblitz für Hochgeschwindigkeitsaufnahmen schon zum Standard geworden. 1888 stellte schließlich George Eastman in den USA seine Kodak-Boxkamera mit Rollfilm vor – die Fotografie wurde zum Volksmedium, und das war die Garantie dafür, dass der Siegeszug des Automobils in allen gesellschaftlichen Schichten und in allen Einzelheiten festgehalten wurde. Dies ist die Geschichte der ersten 75 Jahre, vom Benz-Motorwagen über zwei Weltkriege, Wohlstand und Wirtschaftskrise, Kampf und Triumph der Motorisierung bis zum Ende der fünfziger Jahre, als mit dem Mini eine neue Ära begann.

Lines of cars in Detroit, Michigan. Detroit became the home of the American motor industry and car-building capital of the world. Its workers could also afford cars of their own, here out in force on the first day of a public transport strike in the 1940s.

Autoverkehr in Detroit, Michigan. Detroit wurde zur Heimat der amerikanischen Autoindustrie, zur Auto-Hauptstadt der Welt. Die Arbeiter konnten sich auch einen eigenen Wagen leisten, und hier sind sie in den 1940er Jahren in Massen unterwegs, am ersten Tag eines Streiks der öffentlichen Verkehrsbetriebe.

Ces files de voitures à Detroit (Michigan) témoignent de l'importance de la ville comme centre de l'industrie mécanique américaine et capitale mondiale de l'automobile. Les ouvriers, qui peuvent alors s'offrir leur propre voiture, se retrouvent ici dans les embouteillages le premier jour d'une grève des transports publics, dans les années 1940.

À l'aube du XXIᵉ siècle, il est difficile d'imaginer un monde sans automobile, sans la liberté et les déplacements qu'elle offre à l'individu et sans les horizons presque infinis qu'elle lui permet d'atteindre désormais. Il est en même temps de plus en plus difficile d'ignorer des aspects beaucoup moins positifs de l'automobile dans ce monde qui en est venu à considérer comme un droit la mobilité individuelle. Si nous apprécions et défendons certes les plaisirs que nous procure l'automobile, nous ne pouvons qu'en regretter profondément les conséquences. Et pourtant ! Alors que nous nous inquiétons de l'impact de l'automobile sur notre environnement, notre santé et notre sécurité ; que nous nous préoccupons d'économiser l'énergie et des ressources naturelles limitées et que nous craignons la pollution ; que nous nous alarmons de la congestion de la circulation, du bruit et de l'augmentation des accidents, nos voitures sont chaque jour plus nombreuses à parcourir des distances de plus en plus grandes et nous continuons malgré tout à rouler. Il est vrai que, si nous jetons un coup d'œil en arrière sur les premières années de l'automobile, il semble clair qu'aucun de ces problèmes ne soit vraiment nouveau et que la relation entre l'homme et l'automobile a toujours été explosive.

Il faut bien admettre que le monde a dû apprendre à vivre avec l'automobile – et à s'en accommoder – parce qu'il n'a pas pu ou su vivre sans elle. Et ce dès sa naissance, il y a plus d'un siècle. De ce jour, l'histoire de l'automobile est une bataille constante entre la passion et notre conscience, que viennent épicer le besoin de vitesse, l'envie de style et qu'animent d'extraordinaires personnalités.

Si l'automobile est un symbole du XXᵉ siècle, il s'agit en réalité d'une création de la fin du XIXᵉ siècle, une époque où l'évolution technique repoussait sans cesse les limites de l'invention. C'est en effet en 1885 que, faisant appel à des matériaux et à des méthodes qui étaient alors à la pointe de la technologie, Karl Benz et Gottlieb Daimler construisirent presque simultanément en Allemagne les premières véritables automobiles. Soixante ans plus tôt seulement, en 1825, la locomotive avait déjà provoqué la révolution des transports lorsque George Stephenson inaugure la ligne de chemin de fer à vapeur Stockton-Darlington pour le transport des passagers. Le train, qui se répand alors à travers le monde et donne au public un avant-goût des longs voyages, ouvre à son tour la voie à des hommes comme Daimler et Benz pour réaliser leur vision d'un nouveau degré de liberté : l'automobile.

Au départ, il n'y a aucun plan défini mais seulement le goût d'innover. Après la naissance de voitures mues par la vapeur ou fonctionnant à l'électricité, seule subsistera finalement l'automobile à essence, équipée d'un moteur léger à combustion interne, pour lequel la majorité des concepteurs optera pour le cycle à quatre temps breveté en 1877 en Allemagne par Nikolaus August Otto. Ces moteurs utilisent pour carburant un « esprit de pétrole » (distillat de pétrole lourd) mélangé à de l'air grâce à différentes variantes du carburateur inventé par Daimler en 1876. Certains, comme lui, utilisent un tube chauffé au rouge, système breveté par Leo Funk en Allemagne en 1879, pour enflammer le mélange dans les cylindres ; d'autres, notamment Benz, préfèrent un allumage par étincelle électrique, soit alimenté par une bobine, soit par un circuit à induction haute tension utilisant des améliorations de la batterie inventée en Italie par Alessandro Volta au tournant du XIXᵉ siècle. Ce sont ces mêmes batteries qui alimenteront les ampoules électriques développées par Thomas Alva Edison en 1879 lorsque l'on jugera insuffisant pour la vitesse de l'automobile l'éclairage dispensé par les lampes à gaz et à huile. Comme on le voit, les constructeurs de ces nouvelles machines n'hésitent pas à utiliser la technologie moderne et, si besoin est, à inventer de nouveaux procédés.

L'automobile va ainsi s'améliorer rapidement et en permanence. Les premiers modèles sont équipés de pneus à bandage de caoutchouc, système inventé en 1846 par un Anglais, Thomas Hancock, qui adopte pour cela le caoutchouc vulcanisé durci obtenu aux États-Unis en 1841 par Charles Goodyear. En 1895, s'appuyant sur les inventions de 1888 de l'Écossais John Boyd Dunlop, les Français André et Édouard Michelin rendent la conduite plus confortable en créant les premiers pneumatiques gonflables pour automobile.

Une véritable industrie automobile – presque une communauté –se développe alors rapidement. Partie d'Allemagne, l'automobile se répand en France, en Grande-Bretagne puis dans toute l'Europe et, enfin, de manière considérable, aux États-Unis dans les années 1890. Il n'est pas étonnant que, si tôt après la naissance et le boom de l'industrie du cycle dans la seconde moitié du XIXᵉ siècle, nombre des premiers constructeurs d'automobiles, de Rover en Grande-Bretagne à Peugeot en France et Opel en Allemagne, soient à l'origine des fabricants de bicyclettes. Il est également peu surprenant que beaucoup de constructeurs de machines de précision produisent des moteurs – comme la White Company aux États-Unis, qui fabriquait des machines à coudre avant de construire des auto-mobiles à vapeur, ou Wolseley, spécialisée dans le matériel de tonte pour moutons.

Les premiers partisans enthousiastes de l'automobile commencèrent à se regrouper et à s'organiser autant d'ailleurs pour défendre leur intérêts que pour faire partager et profiter les autres de leur passion, ce nouveau mode de transport n'étant pas encore très bien accueilli partout. C'est en novembre 1895 qu'est lancé en Grande-Bretagne le premier hebdomadaire automobile (aujourd'hui le plus ancien magazine automobile du monde) pour informer et promouvoir la « voiture sans cheval » auprès du public : *The Autocar*. On peut d'ailleurs y lire une note d'avertissement (qui ne concernera d'ailleurs pas que la Grande-Bretagne) : « Toute nouvelle activité rencontre dans ce pays une certaine opposition stupide de la part d'individus de parti pris, et il est peu probable que l'automobile fasse exception à la règle. » Les gens finissent pourtant par surmonter leurs réticences face à l'automobile qui, au tournant du siècle, tient désormais une place indispensable dans la société.

L'automobile a effectivement réussi à transformer le monde. Mais si elle était restée ce « jouet » pour riches qu'elle était à ses débuts, elle n'aurait sans doute jamais pu avoir autant d'influence sur notre comportement ni devenir cette « machine » universelle que nous connaissons. Ceci est certes dû en grande partie à la structure sociale américaine, moins dominée par les classes et plus démocratique d'esprit, mais surtout à la vision d'un homme : Henry Ford. C'est Ford qui décida d'offrir l'automobile aux gens ordinaires et qui y parvint en créant le Model T et en adoptant un système de véritable production de masse. C'est grâce à ses idées et à ses méthodes que l'artisanat des débuts put devenir une industrie mondiale, disposant d'un vaste marché à satisfaire et auquel s'adapter. Il fit alors naître un nouvel ordre social où les hommes les plus riches du monde n'étaient plus ni des aristocrates ni des marchands mais ces nouveaux industriels du XXe siècle : les constructeurs de moteurs – et l'ancien garçon de ferme qu'était Henry Ford devint le premier milliardaire en dollars du monde.

L'automobile a partagé son enfance avec bien d'autres inventions « modernes » – le téléphone, inventé en 1876 par Alexander Graham Bell ; le gramophone par Edison en 1878 ; et le télégraphe sans fil, inauguré par Marconi en 1894. Par une heureuse coïncidence, elle se développe en même temps qu'une autre grande invention du XIXe siècle : la photographie. En 1835, le Français Louis Daguerre découvre comment obtenir une image argentique sur une plaque de cuivre et produit en 1837 ses premières photographies durables. Les améliorations se succéderont au cours des cinquante années suivantes : William Fox Talbot met au point le procédé des images sur papier négatif permettant de reproduire à l'infini des épreuves positives, puis divers procédés sur plaques humides et papier ciré. Disposant de films et d'optiques de meilleure qualité, la photographie « instantanée » – c'est-à-dire une exposition de quelques secondes seulement – devient possible dans les années 1850. En 1885, à la naissance de l'automobile, on en est déjà aux plaques de verre à émulsions « panchromatiques » et flash à la poudre de magnésium pour les expositions instantanées. En 1888, George Eastman commercialise aux États-Unis le premier appareil à rouleau de film, le « Kodak », qui démocratise la photographie et permet à tout un chacun de fixer désormais, en temps de paix comme en temps de guerre, l'histoire de l'Automobile. Ce sont ses 75 premières années, de la première voiture de Benz jusqu'à la fin des années 1950 et l'arrivée, avec la Mini, d'une nouvelle génération de voitures, que racontent les images de cet ouvrage.

America wasn't the only home of exceptional automobile styling. These are the hands of two of the most famous stylists of all – Sergio Farina and son, in Italy, better known as Pininfarina.

Nicht immer kamen Stiltendenzen aus Amerika. Hier sehen wir die Hände zweier der berühmtesten Automobildesigner aller Zeiten, in Italien aufgenommen – Sergio Farina und Sohn, besser bekannt als Pininfarina.

Les États-Unis ne sont pas le seul centre du stylisme automobile. On voit ici les mains italiennes de deux des plus célèbres stylistes du monde : Sergio Farina et son fils, deux Italiens plus connus sous le nom de Pininfarina.

1
Entering the Automobile Age

In 1886 the world entered a new age – the automobile age. On 29 January that year, Karl Benz was granted German Patent No. 37435. Rather than covering only the components of its subject, Patent No. 37435 described the idea of a motor vehicle as a total concept. It defined 'a vehicle with gas-engine drive', where the engine was one 'whose gas fuel derives from volatile substances to be processed by an apparatus to be included as part of the mechanism'. The outcome of the patent would be Karl Benz's first practicable automobile – in fact the *world's* first practicable automobile. By the time the historic patent was granted, the vehicle was already under construction.

Benz was born on 25 November 1844 in Mühlberg, a suburb of Karlsruhe. His father, Hanns Georg, was a locomotive engineer in the early days of the railway; his mother, Josephine, had worked in a household in Karlsruhe. His father died before Karl was two, but Karl had inherited a love of mechanical things, and a desire to travel.

That craving for mobility drove the experimenting and tinkering by Benz and dozens like him around the world. So far, man had been restricted either to walking or using animals for transport and carriage. The dreamers believed that mechanical power could one day take the place of the horse or oxen, and for centuries they had tried to achieve it. There were carts pulled by kites or driven by windmills, vehicles powered by springs, clockwork and treadmills. Most promisingly, there were experiments with steam, and the first successful full-sized steam-powered cart, a three-wheeled artillery 'fardier' designed by Nicholas Joseph Cugnot, ran in the Paris arsenal in November 1770.

Later, steam carriages and coaches – like Cornish engineer Richard Trevithick's carriage of 1803, Walter Hancock's carriages of the 1830s, and those of the Bollée brothers of Le Mans in the 1870s – made regular long-distance journeys carrying fare-paying passengers. But they would have a short reign. The steam era gave us the word 'chauffeur', which originally referred to the stoker of the boiler, but the real role of steam would be in powering the railways. The railways ran on their own tracks, but the key to producing a mechanically-propelled vehicle on a smaller scale, capable of running on the abysmal roads of the day, was a different kind of engine, a smaller, lighter, more efficient mechanism – the gas engine, or internal combustion engine.

Experimenters had been working with explosive engines since the advent of illuminating gas in the eighteenth century, and through the nineteenth century the idea of an engine as we know it today, with reciprocating pistons and a rotating crankshaft, powered by the combustion of an air and fuel mixture, began to develop.

Early engines were powered by coal or other explosive gases, later ones by the flammable vapours given off by volatile liquids, such as what we now know as gasoline. Working in France, Belgian inventor Jean-Joseph Étienne Lenoir patented a 'two-cycle' gas engine, which he put into a heavy carriage in 1863. In Germany a clerk, Nikolaus August Otto, working with an engineer, Eugen Langen, began building engines of their own design. That led to Otto working on engines fuelled by petroleum vapour, and what he patented in August 1877 as the seminal four-stroke cycle, which is still dominant today.

The Otto cycle, German Patent No. 532, was vital to the automobile but initially it had a restrictive effect, because any engine builder using its principles had to pay a licence fee to Otto. That led to many experimenters, Benz included, wasting much time and effort on alternative designs, before the Otto patent was cancelled in 1886.

This was the break Benz needed. Around 1872 he had set up a workshop in Mannheim and in 1877, after years on the edge of bankruptcy, he committed himself to building engines – initially two-stroke types to avoid the Otto patent issue. He ran his first on New Year's Eve 1879, the company expanded and Benz gained several patents of his own. Until the cancellation of Otto's patent his business struggled, but once Benz could build the lightweight four-cycle engines he had always wanted to build, he prospered. In 1885 he adapted one of his engines to what was to become his, and the world's, first truly practical gasoline-powered automobile, the Benz 'Patent Motorcar'.

It had a light and simple tubular steel frame, solid-tyred, wire-spoked wheels, tiller steering to the single front wheel, and a single-cylinder 954cc four-stroke engine driving the rear wheels through a system of leather belts and chains. Its 0.8hp gave the three-wheeler a top speed of around 10mph, and Benz tested it in secret, often at night. By summer 1886 it was appearing in public and on 3 July a local newspaper reported, 'a velocipede driven by Ligroin gas, built by the Rheinische Gasmotorenfabrik of Benz et Cie, already reported in these pages on 4 June, was tested this morning early on the Ringstraße, during which it operated satisfactorily'. The automobile age had begun.

Benz had been in a race to be first on the road. Another German pioneer, Gottlieb Daimler (who had visited Lenoir in 1860 and worked for Otto in the 1870s), patented his own engine in 1883 and in November 1885 tested a single-cylinder 0.5hp version in a crude, wooden-framed boneshaker bicycle. Once satisfied that it would run, he started work on a four-wheeler, taking a large, high-wheeled carriage, throwing away the shafts for the horse, and installing one of his engines. But by the time it was ready for testing, in autumn 1886, Benz had already made the headlines.

Now the challenge was to turn the automobile into a commercial proposition, and to see it accepted into a society which was initially hostile to this noisy, smelly, largely unwanted monster that frightened the horses. The struggle would be plagued by outdated laws such as the one in Britain that restricted 'locomotives' on the road to 4mph, and (in theory at least) required them to be preceded by an attendant on foot, originally carrying a red flag as a warning, but there could be no stopping the automobile now.

In 1888 Benz exhibited his improved car in Munich and offered examples for sale, at 2,000 marks – this was the world's first 'production' car. Also in 1888 Benz's wife, Bertha, struck a blow for the automobile's credibility when she, with two of her sons, took one of the cars on its first long trip, from Mannheim to Pforzheim. It was an adventure which led to improvements, including more power to cope with the hills.

This was how the motor car developed – empirically and through experience. It has often been said that, if Germany was the birthplace of the motor car, France was the nursery. One of Benz's first sales (which were slow to start) was to his agent in Paris, Émile Roger, who bought a Benz four-wheeler in 1887 and left the car for a while in the factory of Panhard et Levassor, French agent for Daimler's engines. Panhard supplied engines to another French pioneer, Armand Peugeot, and in 1890 built their own first complete car. In 1891, in an age where every possible mechanical layout was being tried, they devised the one that most cars would follow for decades to come, the Système Panhard. That had the engine vertically at the front of the car, under a 'bonnet', driving the rear wheels through a sliding-pinion gearbox, of whose early versions Émile Levassor famously said, 'C'est brutal, mais ça marche': 'it's crude but it works'.

Already the automobile was becoming more sophisticated, more refined and more reliable. Trials were fashionable, at first

simply to prove that the car could do the basics like climb hills and stop efficiently, later to pit one car against another, which inevitably led to the birth of motor racing, with great inter-city road races being held even before the turn of the century. The roads were still mostly awful but the adoption of pneumatic tyres in the mid-1890s improved comfort, if not durability, while bigger and more powerful engines were also giving more touring ability and, of course, more speed. In 1899 Camille Jenatzy became the first man ever to exceed 100kph in a motor vehicle, and perversely it was an electrically powered vehicle, because although the petrol engine would ultimately win through, this was a time for investigation of alternative power sources, and those would still, for many years, include steam as well as electricity.

As the product developed so did the industry. In 1894 Benz sold 67 cars, but the early sales leader was De Dion Bouton in France, which sold some 1,500 cars up to April 1901, contributing to France being the biggest automobile producing country in the world by the turn of the century. The industry was already expanding around the globe. In 1896 the Daimler Company became the first in Britain formed specifically to build petrol motor cars, but even more significantly two years earlier the Duryea Motor Wagon Company had taken on the same role in America. The scene was set.

In 1887 a 'race' from Neuilly to Versailles was contested by only one competitor, one of the steam quadricycles built by Count de Dion and Georges Bouton – which did at least complete the course.

Dieses »Rennen« von Neuilly nach Versailles im Jahre 1887 hatte nur einen einzigen Teilnehmer, ein Dampf-Vierrad, gebaut vom Grafen de Dion und Georges Bouton – immerhin erreichte es das Ziel.

En 1887 se déroula une « course » entre Neuilly et Versailles à laquelle ne participa qu'un seul concurrent, le comte de Dion, à bord de la quatre-roues à vapeur qu'il avait construite avec Georges Bouton.

Im Jahr 1886 begann für die Welt eine neue Ära – das Automobilzeitalter. Am 29. Januar jenes Jahres wurde Carl Benz das Reichspatent Nr. 37435 gewährt. Diese Patentschrift bezog sich nicht nur auf einzelne Bauteile, sondern patentierte die Idee eines Motorfahrzeugs insgesamt. Es definierte einen »selbstfahrenden Motorwagen«, dessen Antrieb »durch ein Gas bewirkt wird, welches aus flüssigen Substanzen mittels eines Apparates aufbereitet wird, der selbst Teil des Antriebs ist«. Diese Schrift beschrieb Carl Benz' erstes fahrtüchtiges Automobil – genauer gesagt das erste fahrtüchtige Automobil der Welt. Als das historische Patent gewährt wurde, befand sich das Fahrzeug bereits im Bau.

Benz kam am 25. November 1844 in Mühlberg zur Welt, einem Vorort von Karlsruhe. Sein Vater Hanns Georg war Bahningenieur in den Anfangstagen der Eisenbahn, seine Mutter Josephine Hausangestellte in Karlsruhe. Der Vater starb, als Carl noch nicht einmal zwei Jahre alt war, doch der Junge hatte von ihm eine Liebe zu allem Mechanischen ebenso wie die Reiselust geerbt.

Diese Sehnsucht nach Mobilität trieb den Bastler Benz an, und rund um die Welt Dutzende andere wie ihn. Bis dahin hatten Menschen entweder zu Fuß gehen müssen, oder sie ritten auf Tieren oder ließen sich von ihnen in Wagen ziehen. Die Träumer glaubten daran, dass eines Tages mechanische Kraft an die Stelle von Pferd oder Ochse treten könnte, und schon seit Jahrhunderten war die Idee im Schwange. Es gab Wagen, die von Flugdrachen oder Windmühlen gezogen werden sollten, Fahrzeuge, deren Antrieb Federn, Uhrwerke oder Treträder waren. Am viel versprechendsten waren die Experimente mit Dampfantrieb, und das erste ausgewachsene Dampfgefährt, eine von Nicholas Joseph Cugnot entworfene dreirädrige Zugmaschine für die Artillerie, lief im Pariser Arsenal im November 1770.

Später gab es Dampfkutschen im regelmäßigen Passagierdienst – gebaut von Richard Trevithick in Cornwall, 1803, von Walter Hancock in den 1830er Jahren und von den Brüdern Bollée in Le Mans in den 1870ern. Doch diese Blütezeit war kurz. Geblieben aus der Dampfära ist uns das Wort »Chauffeur«, ursprünglich der Heizer der Dampfkessel – doch ihren wahren Platz sollten die Dampfmaschinen in den Lokomotiven der Eisenbahn finden. Die Eisenbahnen hatten ihre eigenen Schienen; entscheidend für ein mechanisches Fahrzeug im kleineren Maßstab, das auf den entsetzlichen Straßen der damaligen Zeit fahren konnte, war jedoch eine neue Form des Antriebs, ein leichterer Motor mit höherem Wirkungsgrad: der benzinbetriebene Verbrennungsmotor.

Mit Explosionsmotoren wurde schon experimentiert, seit im 18. Jahrhundert das Leuchtgas in die Städte kam, und im Laufe des 19. Jahrhunderts nahm der Motor, wie wir ihn heute kennen, mit beweglichen Kolben und einer rotierenden Kurbelwelle, angetrieben von einem Luft-Brennstoff-Gemisch, allmählich Gestalt an.

Frühe Exemplare wurden mit Kohle- oder anderen explosiven Gasen betrieben, spätere mit den entzündlichen Dämpfen flüchtiger Flüssigkeiten, etwa jener, die wir heute als Benzin kennen. Der in Frankreich tätige belgische Erfinder Jean-Joseph Étienne Lenoir ließ sich einen Zweitaktmotor patentieren, den er 1863 in eine schwere Kutsche montierte. In Deutschland begann der Büroangestellte Nikolaus August Otto zusammen mit dem Ingenieur Eugen Langen Motoren nach eigenen Entwürfen zu bauen. Auf diese Weise kam Otto schließlich zu einem Antrieb, der mit Petroleumdämpfen betrieben wurde, und diesen ließ er im August 1877 als den Epoche machenden Viertaktmotor patentieren, der auch heute noch den Motorenbau bestimmt.

Der Ottomotor, Reichspatent Nr. 532, war entscheidend für das Entstehen des Automobils, doch anfangs behinderte er die Entwicklung eher, denn jeder, der seinen Motor nach Ottos Prinzipien konstruierte, musste dafür Lizenzgebühren an ihn entrichten. Das führte dazu, dass viele, darunter auch Benz, viel Zeit und Mühen für die Suche nach alternativen Antrieben vergeudeten, bis das Patent 1886 gelöscht wurde.

Das kam Benz wie gerufen. Um das Jahr 1872 hatte er in Mannheim eine Werkstatt eröffnet, und nach Jahren am Rande des Bankrotts verlegte er sich 1877 auf den Motorenbau – anfangs mit Zweitaktmotoren, um die Lizenzgebühren an Otto zu sparen. Der erste Motor lief am Sylvestertag 1879, und von da an baute Benz den Betrieb aus und erwarb etliche eigene Patente. Bis zur Aufhebung von Ottos Patent kam er auf keinen grünen Zweig, doch von da an konnte Benz die leichten Viertaktmotoren bauen, die er immer gewollt hatte, und es ging aufwärts mit der Firma. 1885 baute er einen seiner Motoren in den »Benz-Patent-Motorwagen« ein, sein erstes wirklich fahrtüchtiges Automobil mit Verbrennungsmotor – und das erste weltweit.

Das Dreirad hatte einen leichten und einfachen Stahlrohrrahmen, Speichenräder mit massiven Reifen, wobei das vordere über einen Hebel gesteuert wurde, und im Heck einen 954 ccm großen Einzylinder-Viertakter, der über ein System von Lederriemen und Ketten die Hinterräder trieb. Mit seinen 0,8 PS erreichte das Gefährt eine Geschwindigkeit von etwa 15 km/h, und Benz machte seine ersten Versuchsfahrten im Geheimen, oft nachts. Im Sommer 1886 tat er jedoch den Schritt an die Öffentlichkeit, und am 3. Juli stand in der Lokalzeitung zu lesen: »In den frühen Morgenstunden des heutigen Tages wurde auf der Ringstraße eine Versuchsfahrt mit dem mit Ligroin-Gas betriebenen Velociped der Rheinischen Gasmotorenfabrik Benz et Cie. unternommen, von welchem wir bereits am 4. Juni berichteten. Die Fahrt verlief zufriedenstellend.« Das war der Beginn des Automobilzeitalters.

Es war ein Wettrennen um den ersten fahrtüchtigen Wagen zwischen Benz und einem weiteren deutschen Pionier, Gottlieb Daimler. Daimler ließ seinen eigenen Motor im Jahr 1883 patentieren und testete im November 1885 einen 0,5-PS-Einzylinder in einem einfachen hölzernen Fahrradrahmen. Als er sich vergewissert hatte, dass er lief, begann er die Arbeit an einem vierrädrigen Fahrzeug; er nahm eine große Kutsche mit hohen Rädern, montierte die Deichsel ab und baute seinen Motor hinein. Doch als der Wagen im Herbst 1886 zur ersten Testfahrt bereit war, hatte Benz das Rennen bereits gewonnen.

Die nächste Herausforderung war, das Automobil so weit zu entwickeln, dass es sich gewinnbringend verkaufen ließ, und es überhaupt in einer Gesellschaft durchzusetzen, die diesem lärmenden, stinkenden, lästigen Monstrum, das nur die Pferde scheu machte, zunächst feindselig gegenüberstand. Veraltete Gesetze erschwerten den Erfolg, etwa jenes in Großbritannien, das die Geschwindigkeit von »Lokomotiven« auf der Straße auf 4 Meilen pro Stunde beschränkte und (zumindest theoretisch) vorschrieb, dass ein Mann mit einer roten Flagge zur Warnung voranging.

1888 stellte Benz ein verbessertes Modell in München aus und bot es für 2000 Reichsmark zum Verkauf – das erste »kommerzielle« Auto der Welt. Im selben Jahr tat Benz' Frau Bertha viel für die Glaubwürdigkeit der neuen Maschine, als sie mit zweien ihrer Söhne die erste längere Fahrt unternahm, von Mannheim nach Pforzheim. Das Abenteuer führte zu weiteren Verbesserungen, unter anderem einem stärkeren Motor, der die Steigungen besser bewältigen konnte.

Durch solche Erfahrungen entwickelte sich der Motorwagen weiter. Es heißt, dass Deutschland zwar der Geburtsort des Automobils war, doch Frankreich seine Kinderstube. Einer der ersten Wagen, die Benz verkaufte (das Geschäft lief nur sehr schleppend an), ging an seinen Agenten in Paris,

Émile Roger, der 1887 einen vierrädrigen Benz-Wagen erwarb und ihn eine Weile in der Fabrik von Panhard et Levassor ließ, des französischen Vertriebspartners für die Daimler-Motoren. Panhard lieferte Daimler-Motoren auch einem anderen französischen Pionier, Armand Peugeot, und baute im Jahr 1890 seinen ersten eigenen Wagen. 1891, zu einer Zeit, als alle erdenklichen Grundkonzepte erprobt wurden, entstand hier der Bauplan, dem jahrzehntelang die meisten Autos folgen sollten, das »Système Panhard«. Dieser Wagen hatte unter der Motorhaube am Vorderende einen senkrecht stehenden Motor, der über eine Welle die Hinterräder trieb, und dazwischen lag das Zahnrad-Wechselgetriebe, dessen frühe Exemplare Émile Levassor mit dem berühmten Satz kommentierte: »C'est brutal, mais ça marche« – das ist nicht fein, aber es funktioniert.

Schon wurden die Automobile anspruchsvoller, technisch ausgeklügelter und zuverlässiger. Testfahrten kamen in Mode, anfangs nur, um zu beweisen, dass ein Wagen die Grundanforderungen erfüllte, bergauf fahren und ohne Schwierigkeiten anhalten konnte, doch schon bald gab es Vergleichsfahrten, und daraus entwickelte sich der Motorsport wie von selbst, und schon vor der Jahrhundertwende gab es Straßenrennen zwischen den großen Städten. Die Straßen waren größtenteils noch in kläglichem Zustand, doch die Luftreifen, die Mitte der 1890er Jahre aufkamen, verbesserten den Komfort, auch wenn sie weniger haltbar waren, und größere und stärkere Motoren sorgten nicht nur für mehr Tempo, sondern auch für bessere Reisetauglichkeit. 1899 überschritt Camille Jenatzy als Erster die 100-Kilometer-Marke, kurioserweise in einem Elektrowagen, denn auch wenn sich schließlich der Verbrennungsmotor durchsetzen sollte, war dies noch die Zeit, in der auch mit anderen Antrieben experimentiert wurde, und noch viele Jahre lang gab es neben den benzinbetriebenen auch Elektro- und Dampfautos.

Mit der Entwicklung des Produktes entwickelte sich auch die Industrie. 1894 verkaufte Benz 67 Wagen, doch am erfolgreichsten waren in jenen frühen Jahren die französischen De Dion-Bouton, von denen bis April 1901 bereits an die 1500 Stück verkauft waren; Frankreich war zur Jahrhundertwende der größte Automobilproduzent weltweit. Andere Länder kamen hinzu: In England wurde 1896 als erste britische Firma ausdrücklich für den Bau von benzinmotorgetriebenen Fahrzeugen die Daimler Company gegründet, und zwei Jahre zuvor war, wichtiger noch, in Amerika die Duryea Motor Wagon Company entstanden. Die Bühne war bereit.

Billancourt 1898, Marcel Renault in the 1897 quadricycle on the left, brother Louis at the wheel of the 1898 voiturette in the centre, Paul Hugé at the wheel of the prototype 1899 Renault, on the right.

Billancourt 1898, links Marcel Renault in einem Vierradwagen aus dem Vorjahr, in der Mitte sein Bruder Louis am Steuer einer 1898er Voiturette, rechts Paul Hugé mit einem Renault-Prototypen für das Jahr 1899.

Billancourt, 1898 : Marcel Renault conduit son quatre-roues de 1897 (à gauche) tandis que son frère Louis est au volant d'une voiturette de 1898 (au centre) et que Paul Hugé pilote le prototype Renault de 1899 (à droite).

L'année 1886 marque le passage du monde dans une nouvelle ère : celle de l'automobile. C'est en effet le 29 janvier que Karl Benz obtient le brevet allemand n° 37435 qui, au lieu de détailler tous les éléments du projet, définit le concept global d'un véhicule à moteur en décrivant « un véhicule propulsé par un moteur à gaz ... dont le combustible gazeux est fourni par des substances volatiles traitées par un appareil faisant partie du mécanisme ». De ce brevet va naître le premier véhicule de Karl Benz : en réalité, la première véritable automobile du monde, d'ailleurs déjà en construction à l'époque où ce brevet historique fut accordé.

Karl Benz est né le 25 novembre 1844 à Mühlberg, aux environs de Karlsruhe (Allemagne). Son père, Hanns Georg Benz, était conducteur de locomotive aux premiers temps du chemin de fer et sa mère, Josephine, a travaillé comme femme de ménage à Karlsruhe. Karl héritera de son père, mort avant qu'il ait deux ans, une passion certaine pour la mécanique et le goût des voyages.

Jusqu'à présent l'homme a dû se contenter de marcher à pied ou d'employer des animaux pour se déplacer ou transporter des charges. C'est leur désir de plus grande mobilité qui pousse Benz et des douzaines d'inventeurs comme lui dans le monde, depuis des siècles, à se lancer dans des expériences et des réalisations plus ou moins bricolées. Ces « rêveurs » sont en effet persuadés qu'une énergie mécanique pourra un jour remplacer le cheval ou le bœuf. On connaîtra des chars tractés par des cerfs-volants ou mus par des moulins à vent, des véhicules actionnés par des ressorts, des horloges et des plateaux rotatifs. Plus prometteuses furent les expériences avec la vapeur ; le premier chariot « automobile » mû par la vapeur fut un fardier d'artillerie à trois roues conçu par Nicholas Joseph Cugnot, qu'il fait circuler à l'arsenal de Paris en novembre 1770.

Des chariots et des diligences à vapeur – comme la locomotive routière de l'ingénieur cornouaillais Richard Trevithick de 1803, les voitures de Walter Hancock dans les années 1830 ou celles des frères Bollée, du Mans, dans les années 1870 – furent régulièrement utilisés pour emmener des passagers payants sur des distances plus ou moins longues. Si aucune de ces machines n'eut de véritable succès dans les transports routiers, la vapeur joua cependant un rôle essentiel dans les chemins de fer. De cet âge de la vapeur est resté, dans le domaine de l'automobile, le mot « chauffeur », qui désignait l'homme chargé d'alimenter la chaudière. Alors que le train

circule sur des voies qui lui sont propres, il fallait trouver un véhicule à propulsion mécanique plus petit, capable de rouler sur les exécrables routes de l'époque. Cela impliquait d'inventer une machine d'un genre différent et disposant d'une énergie mécanique de volume réduit, plus léger et plus efficace : le moteur à gaz, ou moteur à combustion interne.

Des expérimentateurs ont déjà travaillé sur le moteur à explosion depuis l'invention du gaz d'éclairage au XVIIIe siècle mais c'est au cours du XIXe siècle que commence à naître l'idée du moteur tel que nous le connaissons aujourd'hui, c'est-à-dire à pistons alternatifs et vilebrequin rotatif, alimenté par la combustion d'un mélange d'air et de carburant.

Les premiers moteurs furent alimentés au gaz de charbon ou d'autres gaz explosifs, puis par les vapeurs inflammables de liquides volatils (comme l'essence que nous connaissons maintenant). L'inventeur français d'origine belge Jean-Joseph Étienne Lenoir fait ainsi breveter un moteur à gaz « deux-temps » qu'il installe sur un chariot lourd en 1863. En Allemagne, Nikolaus August Otto, un employé de bureau, s'associe avec l'ingénieur Eugen Langen pour construire des moteurs de leur conception alimentés par de l'essence de pétrole. De leurs recherches résulte le moteur à « quatre-temps », dont le cycle de fonctionnement est le même que les moteurs produits aujourd'hui, dont Otto dépose le brevet en août 1877 sous le n° 532.

Si cette invention est capitale, elle ralentit au départ un temps le développement de l'automobile dans la mesure où l'existence du brevet oblige tout constructeur de moteur voulant utiliser ce principe à payer une licence à Otto. Nombre d'inventeurs ainsi handicapés, à l'instar de Benz, perdent alors du temps et de l'énergie à rechercher un système différent de conception, libre de droits, pour fabriquer leurs moteurs. La situation se débloque en 1886, lorsque le brevet d'Otto est annulé.

C'est le moment que Benz attendait pour se développer. Après plusieurs années de vaches maigres dans l'atelier mécanique qu'il a ouvert à Mannheim vers 1872, Benz se lance en 1877 dans la construction de moteurs deux-temps pour voiture, dont le premier fonctionne la veille du Nouvel An 1879, et dépose plusieurs brevets de son invention. L'annulation des brevets d'Otto permet à Benz de construire librement un petit moteur quatre-temps qu'il adapte en 1885 à ce qui devient la première « voiture automobile brevetée » à essence.

Le véhicule, un tricycle, est un simple cadre tubulaire en acier monté sur des roues à rayons fils garnies de bandages en caoutchouc plein, avec une direction à colonne actionnant

French pioneer Louis Renault at the lathe in his first workshop, in the gardens of his parents' house in Billancourt, where he built his first De Dion powered car, in 1898.

Der französische Pionier Louis Renault an der Drehbank seiner Werkstatt im Garten des elterlichen Hauses in Billancourt, wo er 1898 seinen ersten Wagen baute, mit einem Motor von De Dion.

Louis Renault, l'un des pionniers de l'automobile française, travaille au tour dans son premier atelier, aménagé dans le jardin de la maison de ses parents à Billancourt, où il construisit en 1898 sa première voiture à moteur De Dion.

l'unique roue avant, propulsé par un moteur monocylindre quatre-temps de 954 cm³, d'une puissance de 0,8 ch, qui entraîne l'essieu arrière par un système de chaînes et de courroies en cuir à la vitesse maximum de 16 km/h. Benz procède secrètement à ses essais, la nuit de préférence. Il présente enfin son véhicule au public et obtient, le 3 juillet 1886, un article dans le journal local qui annonce « le vélocipède mû au gaz d'éther de pétrole, construit par la Rheinische Gasmotorenfabrik de Benz et Cie, déjà présenté dans ces pages le 4 juin, a été testé tôt ce matin dans la Ringstraße et a fonctionné de manière satisfaisante. » L'ère de l'automobile démarrait.

En fait, Karl Benz est arrivé de justesse le premier dans la course entre constructeurs. En effet, un autre inventeur allemand, Gottlieb Daimler, a fait breveter son moteur en 1885 et, en novembre 1885, en a testé une version monocylindre de 0,5 ch monté sur un bicycle à cadre de bois. L'engin fonctionnant de manière satisfaisante, il se lance alors dans la construction d'un quatre-roues sur la base d'une charrette à hautes roues, de laquelle il enlève le timon pour installer un moteur. Il est prêt à faire ses essais à l'automne 1886 ... juste quelques mois après que Benz eut fait les gros titres des journaux !

Mais l'aventure de l'automobile n'est pas terminée. Il faut maintenant qu'elle devienne une réalité commerciale et soit acceptée dans une société au départ hostile à ces monstres bruyants, malodorants et gênants qui effraient les chevaux. Le combat est également rendu plus difficile par des lois dépassées comme celle en vigueur en Grande-Bretagne qui limite la vitesse des « locomotives » sur route à 6,5 km/h et oblige – au moins en théorie – les conducteurs à se faire précéder par un homme à pied portant un drapeau rouge.

En 1888, Benz expose à Munich une version améliorée de sa première voiture, qu'il vend 2 000 mark, ce qui en fait la première voiture de « production » du monde. Cette même année, Bertha Benz, la femme de Karl, emprunte la voiture de son mari pour se rendre avec deux de ses fils de Mannheim à Pforzheim, soit un premier long trajet. Cette escapade permit de procéder à quelques améliorations, notamment l'augmentation de la puissance du moteur pour franchir les côtes. La voiture automobile se développe ainsi progressivement, de manière empirique et par l'expérience.

On a souvent dit que, si l'Allemagne avait été le berceau de la voiture automobile, la France lui a servi de crèche. L'une des premières ventes d'automobile que réalise Benz est, en 1887, celle d'une quatre-roues à Émile Roger. Ce dernier, qui devient ensuite l'agent Benz à Paris, laisse la voiture quelque temps à l'atelier de Panhard et Levassor, représentants français des moteurs Daimler – qu'ils fournissent notamment à un autre pionnier français, Armand Peugeot. Ils construisent leur première voiture complète en 1890 et conçoivent l'année suivante, à une époque où l'on essayait toutes les combinaisons mécaniques possibles, le Système Panhard : le moteur, protégé par un capot, est disposé verticalement à l'avant de la voiture et entraîne l'essieu arrière grâce à un système d'engrenages coulissants à pignons. Parlant de la première version du système, Émile Levassor prononça cette phrase célèbre : « C'est brutal, mais ça marche ».

L'automobile est alors déjà plus sophistiquée, plus raffinée et plus fiable. Les compétitions deviennent à la mode, non seulement pour prouver que la voiture peut, tout simplement, gravir une colline et s'arrêter efficacement, mais aussi pour le plaisir d'affronter d'autres voitures. De ce subit engouement sportif naquirent avant même le tournant du siècle de nombreuses courses automobiles entre deux villes sur des distances plus ou moins grandes. Les routes étaient encore assez mauvaises mais l'adoption de pneumatiques gonflables au milieu des années 1890 améliora le confort, voire la solidité, des voitures tandis que l'adoption de moteurs plus gros et plus puissants facilitait le tourisme automobile et améliorait naturellement la vitesse. En 1899, Camille Jenatzy devient le premier homme à dépasser les 100 km/h mais, assez ironiquement, dans un véhicule électrique ; en effet, s'il est assez probable qu'un moteur à pétrole l'aurait également permis, les recherches se poursuivent encore activement sur les sources d'énergie alternatives à l'essence, en particulier la vapeur et l'électricité.

Les progrès de la voiture entraînent parallèlement le développement de l'industrie automobile. Alors que Benz a vendu 67 voitures en 1894, De Dion-Bouton contribue à faire de la France le plus grand pays producteur d'automobiles du monde au début du XXᵉ siècle en totalisant près de 1 500 ventes jusqu'en avril 1901. Les fabricants d'automobiles ne se cantonnent plus à l'Europe continentale mais se répandent dans le monde entier. Si la Daimler Company devient en 1896 la première firme de Grande-Bretagne créée spécifiquement pour construire des automobiles à essence, la Duryea Motor Wagon Company a déjà joué le même rôle aux États-Unis deux ans plus tôt. Le décor est planté, le rideau peut se lever !

The Bollée family were bell founders in Le Mans who began to build steam carriages in the 1870s. This is Amédée junior's light two-seater steamer, built in 1885.

Die Familie Bollée, Glockengießer in Le Mans, bauten seit den 1870er Jahren Dampfkutschen. Das Bild zeigt den leichten Dampf-Zweisitzer von Amédée junior, 1885.

Les Bollée étaient fondeurs de cloches au Mans et commencèrent à construire des voitures à vapeur dans les années 1870. On voit ici la voiturette à vapeur biplace d'Amédée Bollée fils, construite en 1885.

In the beginning

The first practical gasoline-engined automobile (above).
Karl Benz started building the 0.8hp single-cylinder
three-wheeler in 1885, patented the automobile as
a complete concept in January 1886, and developed his
'patent motor car' through that year. By 1891 Benz was
working on four-wheelers (right). In 1893 he patented
a new steering system and began to build the Viktoria.
This trip in 1894 included Benz, in the light suit, his
family, including wife, Bertha, in the car on the left, and
friend Theodor von Liebieg in the Viktoria on the right.

Das war der Anfang

Das erste praktikable Fahrzeug mit Benzinmotor
(oben). Karl Benz begann den Bau seines Dreirads mit
0,8-PS-Einzylinder 1885, ließ sich das Automobil als
Ganzes im Januar 1886 patentieren und entwickelte
seinen »Patent-Motorwagen« im Laufe jenes Jahres.
1891 folgte der Benz-Vierradwagen (rechts). 1893 patentierte er eine neue Art der Lenkung und brachte den
Viktoria auf den Markt. Das Bild bei einem Ausflug
1894 zeigt Benz (im hellen Anzug) mit seiner Familie
einschließlich Ehefrau Bertha im Wagen links und
seinen Freund Theodor von Liebieg rechts im Viktoria.

Au début

Ce tricycle monocylindre de 0,8 ch (ci-dessus), construit en 1885 par Karl Benz, est considéré comme la
première véritable automobile à essence. Il fit breveter
ses caractéristiques en janvier 1886 et développa cette
année-là sa « voiture automobile brevetée ». En 1891,
Benz se lance dans la construction d'une quatre-roues
(à droite). Il fait breveter un nouveau système de direction
en 1893 et commence à construire la Viktoria. Cette
photographie, prise en 1894 au cours d'une excursion,
montre Benz, en blanc, avec sa femme Bertha et ses
enfants installés dans la voiture de gauche, accompagné
de son ami l'industriel Theodor von Liebieg, dans la
Viktoria, à droite.

Electricity has its moment

In the early days, electricity was widely tried as an alternative to gasoline. The first car to exceed 100kph (60mph) was the electric Jamais Contente (above) driven by Belgian 'Red Devil' Camille Jenatzy to an official record of 105.85kph (65.79mph) at Achères in April 1899. Inventor of the light bulb, Thomas Alva Edison, with his Baker electric car (right) was a pioneer of electric power with his nickel-alkali battery.

Sternstunde der Elektrizität

Am Anfang gab es Versuche mit einem Elektroantrieb als Alternative zum Verbrennungsmotor. Der erste Wagen, der die 100-Kilometer-Tempomarke überschritt, war der elektrische Jamais Contente (oben), mit dem der belgische »Rote Teufel« Camille Jenatzy im April 1899 in Achères einen offiziellen Rekord von 105,85 km/h fuhr. Thomas Alva Edison (rechts), der Erfinder der Glühbirne, hier in seinem Baker-Elektrowagen, zählte mit seiner Nickel-Alkali-Batterie zu den Pionieren des Elektroantriebs.

À l'heure de l'électricité

Au début certains voulurent utiliser l'électricité plutôt que l'essence dès les débuts de l'automobile. La première voiture électrique à dépasser les 100 km/h fut la Jamais Contente (ci-dessus), conduite par le belge « Diable rouge » Camille Jenatzy et chronométré officiellement à Achères en avril 1899 à la vitesse de 105,85 km/h. Thomas Alva Edison (à droite), l'inventeur de l'ampoule électrique, à côté de sa voiture électrique Baker, fut un des pionniers de l'électricité automobile grâce à sa batterie nickel-alcaline.

Pioneers in America and Britain

In 1895, Charles and Frank Duryea (above) set up the first company in America to build cars commercially. That year their second prototype won America's first motor race, sponsored by the Chicago Times Herald, and production started in 1896. Sir David Salomons, seated left, in his Peugeot (right), staged Britain's first 'motor show' in 1895, in Tunbridge Wells, where he was mayor.

Anfänge in England und Amerika

1895 gründeten Charles und Frank Duryea (oben) die erste Firma, die in den Vereinigten Staaten kommerziell Automobile herstellte. Im selben Jahr gewann ihr zweiter Prototyp das erste Autorennen Amerikas, veranstaltet vom Chicago Times Herald, und 1896 begann die Fertigung. Sir David Salomons, im Bild links in seinem Peugeot (rechts), veranstaltete 1895 in Tunbridge Wells, wo er Bürgermeister war, den ersten britischen »Autosalon«.

Les pionniers en Amérique et en Grande-Bretagne

Charles et Frank Duryea (ci-dessus) créèrent en 1895 la première société commerciale américaine de construction d'automobiles. Leur second prototype (dont la production démarra en 1896) remportait la première course automobile organisée aux États-Unis, que sponsorisait le Chicago Times Herald. En 1895 sir David Salomons, assis à gauche dans sa Peugeot (à droite), organisa la première exposition automobile de Grande-Bretagne à Tunbridge Wells.

Motoring for ladies and gentlemen

In its infancy, the motor car was disliked by much of the gentry, but only the upper classes like the chauffeured gentlemen (left) could afford it. Dressed more for town than dusty countryside (right), two ladies in a 3,5hp De Dion Bouton four-wheeler of around 1900. De Dion was Europe's biggest car maker by the turn of the century, and France the world's largest car maker. Comte de Dion also founded the Automobile Club de France, in 1895.

Für die Dame, für den Herrn

Anfangs verachteten große Teile des Adels den Motorwagen, doch nur wohlhabende Herrschaften, wie sie sich hier (links) chauffieren lassen, konnten ihn sich leisten. Zwei Damen (rechts), eher für die Stadt als für eine Fahrt auf staubigen Landstraßen gekleidet, in einem vierrädrigen 3,5-PS-De Dion-Bouton, um 1900. Um die Jahrhundertwende war De Dion der größte Hersteller in Europa, und Frankreich fertigte weltweit die meisten Automobile. Der Comte de Dion gründete auch den Automobile Club de France, 1895.

L'automobile du grand monde

Si la gentry anglaise bouda l'automobile à ses débuts, seules les classes supérieures avaient les moyens d'en posséder, comme ces hommes que conduit un chauffeur (à gauche) ou ces deux ladies, vêtues pour la ville plus que pour les chemins poussiéreux de la campagne (à droite), qui se promènent dans un vis-à-vis De Dion-Bouton de 3,5 ch datant de 1900 environ. Au tournant du siècle, De Dion était le fabricant d'automobiles le plus important d'Europe et la France le plus grand pays de construction. Le comte De Dion fonda également en 1895 l'Automobile Club de France.

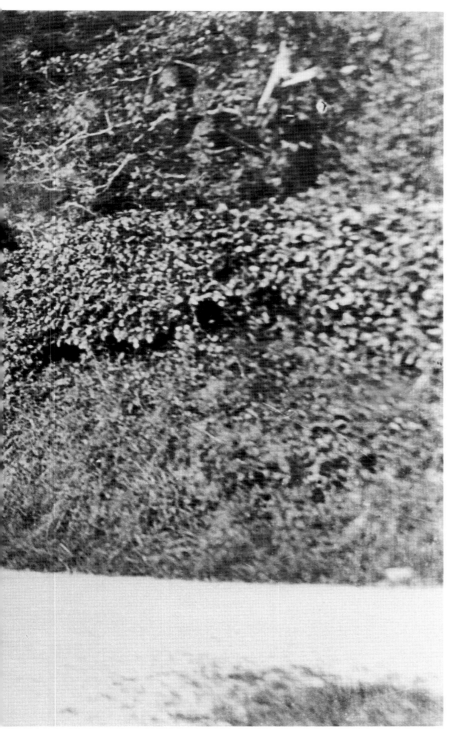

Birth of an industry

In April 1894 Benz introduced the Velo, a smaller, lighter, less expensive model than their first four-wheeler, the Viktoria. The Velo became the world's first 'mass-produced' car and in 1895, of the 135 cars of various types that Benz built, 62 were Velos. They were widely exported, and Velo-based cars were built in many countries, including, as here, in Britain.

Geburt einer Industrie

Im April 1894 stellte Benz den Velo vor, ein kleineres, leichteres, preisgünstigeres Modell als sein erster Vierradwagen Viktoria. Der Velo war das erste »serien-produzierte« Automobil, und 1895 waren von den 135 Fahrzeugen, die Benz baute, 62 Velos. Sie wurden in viele Länder exportiert und vielfach auch nach-gebaut, wie dieses britische Exemplar.

Naissance d'une industrie

En avril 1894, Benz présente la Velo, un modèle plus petit, plus léger et moins cher que la Viktoria, sa première voiture à quatre roues. Son succès en fait la première automobile produite en série : sur 135 voitures de différents modèles construites par Benz en 1895, 62 furent des Velo. Ce modèle s'exporta égale-ment très bien et on construisit des voitures imitées de la Velo dans de nombreux pays, notamment comme ici en Grande-Bretagne.

The three-wheel alternative

Three-wheelers always had an enthusiastic following. In 1898
British motoring pioneer Charles Jarrott (above) drove this
French Léon Bollée tandem, with 650cc 2.5hp engine and
a maximum speed of more than 50kph. The Léon Bollée was
one of the more successful tricat offerings; others, like the
Eagle (right), built in Altrincham (Cheshire) from 1901 as a near
copy of the contemporaneous Century Tandem, capitalised
on its popularity.

Die Dreirad-Alternative

Dreiradgefährte hatten ihre überzeugten Anhänger. 1898 fuhr
der britische Motorpionier Charles Jarrott (oben) mit diesem
französischen Léon-Bollée-Tandem gut 50 km/h schnell.
Der Léon Bollée war mit seinen 650 ccm und 2,5 PS eines der
erfolgreichsten Dreiräder; andere schlugen aus seiner
Popularität Kapital, wie der seit 1901 in Altrincham (Cheshire)
gebaute Eagle (rechts), eine weitgehende Kopie des zeit-
gleichen Century Tandem.

Le tricycle pour alternative

Les tricycles ont toujours eu des partisans enthousiastes. En
1898, le pionnier de la motorisation britannique Charles Jarrott
(ci-dessus) conduit un tandem français Léon-Bollée, équipé
d'un moteur de 650 cm³ délivrant 2,5 hp et atteignant une vitesse
supérieure à 50 km/h, qui eut beaucoup de succès. D'autres
tricars, comme cet Eagle (à droite), une copie du tandem Century
construite à Altrincham (Cheshire) à partir de 1901, s'appuyait
sur cette popularité.

The red flag – and emancipation
In Britain before 1896 the law technically required any
motor car to be preceded by a man on foot carrying
a red flag – as here (above) with CS Rolls in his 3.75hp
Peugeot. When the law was repealed, motorists celeb-
rated with an 'Emancipation' run from London to
Brighton, still commemorated annually, in November.
In 1896 (right) two racing Panhards arrive at the Hotel
Metropole, Brighton.

Die rote Flagge – und ihr Ende
In Großbritannien war bis 1896 gesetzlich vorgeschrieben,
dass jedem Motorfahrzeug ein Mann mit einer roten
Flagge voranging – wie bei C. S. Rolls mit seinem 3,75-PS-
Peugeot (oben). Als das Gesetz abgeschafft wurde,
feierten die Automobilisten mit einer Rallye von London
nach Brighton. 1896 treffen (rechts) zwei Teilnehmer,
beides Panhards, am Hotel Metropole in Brighton ein.

Le drapeau rouge – et l'émancipation
Avant 1896, la loi britannique exigeait qu'une automobile
soit toujours précédée par un homme à pied portant un
drapeau rouge comme le montre la photo où C. S. Rolls
conduit une Peugeot de 3,75 ch (ci-dessus). Pour célébrer
l'abrogation de cette loi, les automobilistes organisèrent
en 1896 une course « d'émancipation » (qui se déroule
encore chaque année en novembre) entre Londres et
Brighton, où deux Panhard de course arrivent à l'hôtel
Metropole (à droite).

Reliability trials and royalty

In 1900 the Automobile Club of Great Britain and Ireland organised a 1,000-mile trial to prove the reliability and advance the popularity of the motor car in Britain. Most of the cars, like Frank Hedges Butler's Panhard (left) were imported. Early royal motorists included Prince Henry of Prussia, younger brother of Kaiser Wilhelm II, seen (above) in the 1906 Herkomer Trial , and the Prince of Wales (later King Edward VII) (below), who made his first long run in 1899, in Mr John Scott Montagu's new 12hp Daimler.

Schaufahrten und königliche Gäste

Im Jahr 1900 veranstaltete der Automobile Club of Great Britain and Ireland eine 1000-Meilen-Fahrt, um die Zuverlässigkeit des Motorwagens unter Beweis zu stellen und ihm in Großbritannien mehr Anhänger zu verschaffen. Die meisten Fahrzeuge, wie der Panhard (links) von Frank Hedges Butler, waren ausländische Produkte. Frühe blaublütige Automobilisten waren Prinz Heinrich von Preußen, der Bruder Kaiser Wilhelms II., hier (oben) bei der Herkomer-Zuverlässigkeitsfahrt 1906, und der Prince of Wales (der spätere König Edward VII.) (unten), der seine erste größere Ausfahrt im Jahr 1899 in Mr. John Scott Mantagus neuem 12-PS-Daimler unternahm.

Endurance et royauté

L'Automobile Club of Great Britain and Ireland organisa en 1900 une épreuve de 1 000 miles pour prouver la fiabilité de l'automobile et augmenter sa popularité en Grande-Bretagne. La plupart des voitures, comme cette Panhard pilotée par Frank Hedges Butler (à gauche), étaient encore importées. Les premiers conducteurs de sang royal furent le frère cadet de l'empereur Guillaume II, le prince Henry de Prusse, que l'on voit ici au cours du Herkomer Trial de 1906 (en haut), et le prince de Galles (futur roi Édouard VII) (en bas), qui participa à sa première grande course en 1899 dans la nouvelle Daimler 12 hp de John Scott Montagu.

2

Out with the Horse?
1900 to World War I

The period between 1900 and the beginning of World War I was one that saw the automobile change from being an inventor's dream, a troublesome and very expensive toy, into a real, everyday working tool, available to the masses. When the twentieth century dawned, the automobile, in spite of the early resistance of the predominantly horse-owning establishment, and in spite of the fact that it was still only to be seen in minuscule numbers, was already an inescapable fact of life. Since it wasn't going to go away, the alternative was to live with it and grow to love it. But this would be a gradual awakening.

A moment symbolic of its growing acceptance had occurred before the end of the last century, with the repeal in Britain of the 'Red Flag' Act of 1865, the notorious law under which 'road locomotives' had been restricted to a maximum speed of 4mph and requiring them to be preceded by a man carrying during the daytime a red flag, or at night time a red lantern. That law was still in force when the automobile was born, and authority frequently used it (or abused it) to show its resistance to the new horseless carriages. The red flag element had, admittedly, been repealed in 1878, but not the part about the accompanying attendant, or the walking-pace speed limit. By diligently enforcing the archaic law, the British establishment, clearly far less enlightened than most of its European and American counterparts, held the automobile back, metaphorically as well as literally, by taking away its key advantages of speed and range.

In 1896, however, a new Locomotives on Highways Act came into force, which raised the speed limit on Britain's open roads to 12mph for vehicles of up to 1.5 tons, and completely dispensed with the requirement for the vehicle to be accompanied by a pedestrian. It was Britain's biggest concession yet to the motoring movement, and on the day on which the old Act was repealed, 14 November 1896, the newly formed Motor Car Club held an 'Emancipation' run, from London to Brighton, in celebration.

Some 35 cars took part, and although many broke down or struggled with the hills on the 53-mile route from the capital to the coast, most eventually arrived, under their own power or otherwise. A measure of the significance of the moment is that the participants included Gottlieb Daimler himself in a Daimler car, French pioneer Léon Bollée in one of his own Tricars (with Camille Bollée in another), and a number of cars and drivers from overseas, including several French Panhards and Roger Benzs, plus two Duryeas and a Pennington Tricycle from America. Léon Bollée was reportedly the first to reach Brighton, clearly having taken full advantage of the new law by averaging almost 15mph, and the event is still commemorated annually in November in England as the London–Brighton Run.

Britain's emancipation didn't stretch as far as allowing motor racing on the public roads, although the Isle of Man, with its own legislature, was more accommodating. The famous series of Tourist Trophy races began there in 1905, adding to the list of classic races that were now regular fixtures around Europe. Great road racing events such as the Gordon Bennett Cup races moved around Europe and America to the home country of the previous year's winner (or in Britain's case to Ireland) and in Italy races like the Targa Florio and the Coppa della Velocità were born. Nowhere, however, was racing more important than in France, home to many of the early town-to-town races, and starting or finishing point for such events as the Paris–Berlin of 1901, the ill-fated Paris–Madrid of 1903, and the incredible Peking–Paris and New York–Paris marathons of 1907 and 1908. In 1906 France also held the first 'Grand Prix', and in time the Automobile Club of France effectively took over the running of motor sport as its own preserve.

This was a time when the sport and the industry had important mutual interests, so the great road races were proving grounds. Soon there would be another kind of proving ground, with permanent closed courses, designed both for racing and for the industry to use in testing. In 1907 the world's first purpose-built race-track opened at Brooklands in Surrey. It quickly became established as part of the broader motoring scene, a venue for record breaking and aviation as well as racing and testing, and a place which for its whole history managed to maintain something of a party atmosphere for the crowds and a gentleman's club atmosphere for the drivers (ladies included).

In America, too (where the Indianapolis Speedway opened in 1909), racing was filling the same roles of entertainment, proving ground and publicity machine. Amongst the sport's most enthusiastic supporters at the time was one Henry Ford. The son of a farmworker, Ford was formerly chief engineer at the Edison Illuminating Company, forming a lifelong friendship with Thomas Alva Edison, who himself pioneered the electric car and became Ford's neighbour in Detroit. In 1896

Ford had built a prototype car; in 1899 he formed the short-lived Detroit Automobile Company and in 1901 he created the Henry Ford Company, which by 1903 had evolved into the Ford Motor Company.

That would become one of the cornerstones of the automobile industry worldwide. Ford's methods and philosophy would totally revolutionise that industry, and in a way the whole future of the automobile – changing it from a rich man's toy into something that every class could aspire to and which could be everything from family runabout or doctor's coupé, to salesman's showcase, delivery van or farmyard workhorse.

Ford wasn't the first to build cars in volume in America. Ransom Eli Olds beat him to that at about the turn of the century with his Curved Dash Oldsmobile, and there were other important American pioneers, but none so important as Ford. Ford used racing for publicity and for development. In 1904 he even briefly held the world's land speed record himself, at 91.4mph, with the huge bodyless four-cylinder Ford Arrow '999' racer on the frozen Lake St Clair in Michigan. But Ford's real contribution, his holy grail, was to make motoring available to every man – a dream brought close to reality by his creation of the legendary Model T in 1908. With huge volumes and low prices made possible by Ford's development first of series production then the moving production line, the Model T became, during three decades, the biggest selling car in the world. By the time production ended in 1927 it had sold more than 15 million cars.

It was the most extreme example of a general trend – more cars from more car makers for an ever wider motoring population. By the turn of the century there were already more than 200 makes of car around the world and up to the war many of the greatest names of the industry appeared. In America they included Cadillac, the great conglomerate General Motors, Buick, Studebaker, Chevrolet and hundreds more. In Europe they included Mercedes, Bugatti, Vauxhall, Rolls-Royce, Rover, Austin, Lancia and, just as in America, many others that proved to be considerably less enduring.

All the time, mechanical improvements were evolving and production was growing. Four-wheel drive and front-wheel brakes both appeared for the first time on the 1903 Spyker, from Holland; front-wheel drive debuted on the American Christie racer in 1904; supercharging was used for the first time on a road car rather than a pure racer on the American Chadwick in 1908; De Dion introduced the first production V8

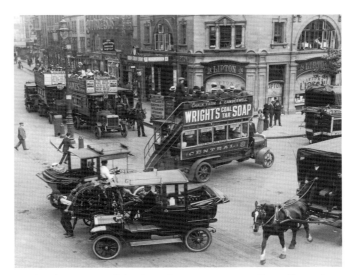

engine in 1910; and in America, newcomers Cornelian pioneered all-independent suspension in 1914.

America now clearly led the way in production volume, overtaking France as the world's biggest car builder in the early years of the century, and pulling away rapidly. In 1900 America built 4,192 automobiles; in 1903 it built 11,235; in 1908 around 63,500; in 1909, following the launch of the Model T, 123,900; and in 1914, in spite of war looming in Europe, a record 548,139 cars and 24,900 trucks.

The world was also learning to live with the automobile. Even Britain was relaxing a little, as the overall speed limit was raised to 20mph in 1903, but on the downside that would stay in force until 1930. When the Automobile Association was founded in Britain in 1905, one of its main purposes had been to provide 'scouts' to warn motorists of hidden speed traps ahead. America, oddly enough, was very slow in developing a decent road network, and for many years after Europe was already reasonably served by well surfaced major roads, American motorists fought their way through mud and dust to go anywhere. In fact the first coast-to-coast crossing of the continent by car wasn't until 1903. And that journey, by a Winton, took 65 days, of which twenty were spent on repairs, largely made necessary by the conditions. It wasn't until 1913 that the Lincoln Highway Association was formed to lobby for an adequate transcontinental road.

By that time, however, the motor vehicle had a much sterner task to face, as for the very first time it was being prepared a new role, with World War I fast approaching.

2
Ist das Pferd passé?
Von 1900 bis zum
Ersten Weltkrieg

In den Jahren zwischen 1900 und dem Beginn des Ersten Weltkriegs entwickelte sich das Automobil vom Traum der Konstrukteure, vom teuren und anfälligen Spielzeug zu einem ernst zu nehmenden Arbeitsmittel für alle Tage, das sich nun auch breitere Bevölkerungsschichten leisten konnten. Am Anfang des 20. Jahrhunderts waren die Motorfahrzeuge bei allem Widerstand der etablierteren Klassen, die an ihren Pferden festhalten wollten, bereits eine Realität, der sich niemand mehr verschließen konnte, auch wenn sie bisher nur in sehr geringen Stückzahlen zu sehen waren. Da die Autos nicht mehr fortzubekommen waren, blieb nichts anderes übrig, als sich mit ihnen anzufreunden. Und das sollte einige Zeit dauern.

Einen symbolischen Akt der Anerkennung hatte es noch zu Ende des vorangegangenen Jahrhunderts gegeben, als in Großbritannien der »Red Flag Act« von 1865 aufgehoben wurde, der das Tempo für »Straßenlokomotiven« auf maximal 4 Meilen pro Stunde begrenzt hatte und vorschrieb, dass ein Mann mit einer roten Flagge vorausgehen musste, im Dunkeln mit einer roten Laterne. Das Gesetz blieb unverändert, als die ersten Automobile auf die Straße kamen, und die Behörden gebrauchten (oder missbrauchten) es häufig, um ihre Abneigung gegen die neuen pferdelosen Kutschen zu zeigen. Seit 1878 wurde zwar auf die rote Fahne verzichtet, doch Schritttempo und ein Begleiter zu Fuß waren nach wie vor gefordert. Das britische Establishment, weniger fortschrittlich gesonnen als sein Widerpart in Amerika und auf dem Kontinent, bestand auf der Einhaltung dieses altertümlichen Gesetzes und hielt damit das Automobil im wörtlichen wie im übertragenen Sinne auf, denn die beiden Hauptvorteile, Geschwindigkeit und Reichweite, kamen nicht zum Tragen.

1896 trat jedoch ein neues Gesetz in Kraft, das die zulässige Geschwindigkeit für Fahrzeuge bis 1,5 Tonnen außerhalb von Ortschaften auf 12 Meilen pro Stunde erhöhte, und die Ankündigung zu Fuß war nicht mehr verlangt. Es war das bis dahin größte Zugeständnis Großbritanniens an die Automobilbewegung, und am 14. November 1896, dem Tag, an dem das alte Gesetz außer Kraft trat, veranstaltete der neu gegründete Motor Car Club zur Feier eine »Emanzipationsfahrt« von London nach Brighton.

Etwa 35 Wagen nahmen teil, und auch wenn einige unterwegs liegen blieben oder mit den Hügeln auf der 53 Meilen langen Strecke von der Hauptstadt zur Kanalküste schwer zu kämpfen hatten, kamen die meisten schließlich doch an, wenn auch nicht alle mit eigener Kraft. Dass der Fahrt einige Bedeu-

tung beigemessen wurde, kann man daran sehen, dass Gottlieb Daimler in einem Daimler-Wagen persönlich teilnahm, ebenso der französische Pionier Léon Bollée in einem seiner Dreiräder (und Camille Bollée in einem zweiten) und noch etliche weitere Fahrer und Fahrzeuge aus dem Ausland, darunter mehrere Panhards und Roger-Benz und sogar zwei Duryeas und ein Pennington-Dreirad aus den Vereinigten Staaten. Léon Bollée kam als Erster ins Ziel und schöpfte mit einem Durchschnitt von fast 15 Meilen die Stunde offenbar das neue Gesetz mehr als aus, und der Tag wird noch heute in England jedes Jahr mit der London-Brighton-Rallye begangen.

So weit, dass Rennen auf öffentlichen Straßen erlaubt wurden, ging die britische Emanzipation jedoch nicht – mit Ausnahme der Insel Man, die ihre eigene Legislative hat. Dort fand 1905 das erste der berühmten Tourist-Trophy-Rennen statt, der britische Beitrag zur Liste der klassischen Rennen, die nun überall in Europa veranstaltet wurden. Manche, wie der Gordon Bennett Cup, fanden in verschiedenen Ländern statt, jeweils im Land des Vorjahressiegers (wenn es ein Brite war, wich man nach Irland aus), und in Italien kamen die klassischen Rennen wie Targa Florio und Coppa della Velocità auf. Doch nirgends fanden mehr Rennen statt als in Frankreich, meist zwischen zwei großen Städten, und Paris war Ziel- oder Startpunkt internationaler Fahrten wie der Rallye Paris–Berlin von 1901, der von Unglücken überschatteten Fahrt Paris–Madrid von 1903 und der unglaublichen Marathonfahrten Peking–Paris und New York–Paris von 1907 und 1908. Im Jahr 1906 fand in Frankreich auch der erste »Grand Prix« statt, und bald war der französische Automobilclub der Hauptveranstalter von Motorsportereignissen.

Es war eine Zeit, in der Sport und Industrie wichtige Interessen gemeinsam hatten, und die großen Straßenrennen waren zugleich Testfahrten. Bald sollte es dazu eine andere Art von Teststrecke geben, die permanente, geschlossene Rennstrecke, für Sportereignisse und Versuchsfahrten gleichermaßen gedacht. 1907 eröffnete die erste eigens dafür gebaute Rennstrecke in Brooklands im englischen Surrey. Schon bald war sie eine feste Größe im Motorsport, und Rekordfahrten und Flugversuche fanden dort ebenso statt wie Tests und Rundrennen. Über Jahrzehnte erhielt sich diese Strecke für die Besucher das Flair einer Landpartie und für die Fahrer die Stimmung eines Gentlemen-Clubs (Damen zugelassen).

Auch in Amerika (wo der Indianapolis Speedway 1909 eröffnete) verband der Rennplatz Entertainment, Testfahrt und

With the launch of his rugged, mass-produced low-cost Model T in America in 1908, Henry Ford opened up the prospect of car ownership for the masses.

Henry Ford ließ mit dem robusten, preisgünstigen, in Serie produzierten Model T, das 1908 in Amerika auf den Markt kam, den Traum vom Automobil für die Massen wahr werden.

Avec le lancement de son robuste Model T à prix modéré, produit en série aux États-Unis à partir de 1908, Henry Ford offre aux masses la perspective de devenir propriétaire d'une automobile.

Reklame. Kaum einer unterstützte den Sport damals enthusiastischer als ein Mann namens Henry Ford. Der Sohn eines Landarbeiters war Chefingenieur der Edison-Lampenwerke gewesen, und eine lebenslange Freundschaft verband ihn mit Thomas Alva Edison, einem der Pioniere des Elektrowagens; Edison und Ford wurden Nachbarn in Detroit. 1896 hatte Ford seinen ersten Prototypen gebaut, 1899 gründete er die Detroit Automobile Company, der nur ein kurzes Leben beschieden war, 1901 die Henry Ford Company, aus der 1903 die Ford Motor Company hervorging.

Fords Firma sollte zum Fundament einer neuen weltweiten Automobilindustrie werden. Sein Ansatz und seine Produktionsmethoden revolutionierten die Industrie von Grund auf, ja sie gaben der Entwicklung des Motorfahrzeugs eine vollkommen neue Richtung – aus dem Spielzeug für die Reichen wurde ein demokratisches Massengut in allen erdenklichen Gestalten, als Familienkutsche, offener Zweisitzer, fahrender Verkaufsstand, Lieferwagen oder Arbeitspferd auf einer Farm.

Ford war nicht der Erste, der in Amerika Autos in größeren Stückzahlen baute. Darin war ihm Ransom Eli Olds um die Jahrhundertwende mit seinem Curved Dash-Oldsmobile zuvorgekommen, und es gab noch andere amerikanische Pioniere, doch keiner davon war einflussreicher als Ford. Ford machte mit Rennen Werbung und testete die Wagen dabei. Für kurze Zeit hielt er im Jahr 1904 sogar mit 147,1 km/h selbst den Geschwindigkeits-Weltrekord, erreicht mit einem gewaltigen Ford Arrow »999«-Rennwagenchassis auf dem zugefrorenen Lake St. Clair in Michigan. Doch Fords eigentlicher Beitrag zur Entwicklung des Automobils, sein großes Ziel, war die Motorisierung für jedermann – ein Traum, den er mit dem legendären, 1908 vorgestellten Model T fast verwirklichen konnte. Hohe Stückzahlen und ein niedriger Preis machten zunächst die Serien-, später die Fließbandproduktion möglich, und in den drei Jahrzehnten, in denen es gebaut wurde, wurde das T-Modell zum meistverkauften Automobil der Welt. Als die Produktion 1927 eingestellt wurde, waren über 15 Millionen Wagen verkauft worden.

Es war das extremste Beispiel für einen Trend, der überall zu spüren war – mehr Wagen von mehr Herstellern für ein immer größer werdendes Auto fahrendes Volk. Zur Jahrhundertwende gab es weltweit bereits über zweihundert Automarken, und als der Krieg kam, hatten sich viele der großen Namen längst etabliert. In Amerika gehörten dazu Cadillac, Buick, Studebaker, Chevrolet und Hunderte weiterer Hersteller.

In Europa waren es Mercedes, Bugatti, Vauxhall, Rolls-Royce, Rover, Austin, Lancia, und dazu kamen wie in Amerika viele andere, die oft schon nach kurzer Zeit wieder verschwanden.

Während all der Zeit entwickelten sich die Autos technisch fort, und die Produktionszahlen stiegen. Vierradantrieb und Bremsen an den Vorderrädern tauchten erstmals beim holländischen Spyker von 1903 auf, Vorderradantrieb beim amerikanischen Christie-Rennwagen von 1904, und ebenfalls in Amerika war der Chadwick von 1908 der erste Serienwagen mit Kompressor (bei Rennwagen gab es ihn schon früher); De Dion präsentierte den ersten serienmäßigen V8-Motor 1910, und die frisch gegründete Firma Cornelian konnte 1914 in den USA schon mit Einzelradaufhängung aufwarten.

Bei den Stückzahlen lag Amerika nun eindeutig vorn; schon Anfang des Jahrhunderts hatte es Frankreich als größter Autoproduzent abgelöst, und der Abstand wurde zusehends größer. Im Jahr 1900 entstanden in den Vereinigten Staaten 4192 Automobile; 1903 waren es 11 235, 1908 etwa 65 500, 1909 nach der Einführung des Model T schon 123 900 und 1914 trotz des drohenden Krieges in Europa sagenhafte 548 139 Personen- und 24 900 Lastwagen.

Und die Welt gewöhnte sich allmählich an das Auto. Selbst Großbritannien zeigte sich großzügiger und erhöhte 1903 die zulässige Höchstgeschwindigkeit auf 20 Meilen die Stunde – was dann allerdings auch bis 1930 so bleiben sollte. Als 1905 die britische Automobile Association gegründet wurde, war eins ihrer Hauptziele, »Pfadfinder« zu rekrutieren, die Autofahrer vor Geschwindigkeitskontrollen warnten. In Amerika ließ, so seltsam das war, die Entwicklung eines brauchbaren Straßensystems lange auf sich warten, und noch Jahre nachdem Europa über ein gut ausgebautes Hauptstraßennetz verfügte, mussten amerikanische Automobilisten sich auch auf den wichtigsten Strecken durch Schlamm und Staub arbeiten. Die erste Durchquerung des Kontinents mit dem Auto fand erst 1903 statt. Die Fahrt mit einem Winton-Wagen dauerte 65 Tage, von denen 20 für Reparaturen gebraucht wurden, die zumeist auf das Konto der Straßenverhältnisse gingen. Erst 1913 formierte sich die Lincoln Highway Association mit dem Ziel, den Bau einer angemessenen Transkontinentalstraße durchzusetzen.

Doch bald sollte das Automobil eine weitaus schwierigere Aufgabe zu bewältigen haben, denn der Erste Weltkrieg näherte sich mit Riesenschritten.

The Indianapolis oval opened in 1909 and before the first running of its most famous annual race, the Indy 500, in 1911, it held races of many other distances, including this 100-miler of around 1910.

Der Rundkurs von Indianapolis eröffnete 1909, und 1911 fand erstmals das berühmteste seiner jährlichen Rennen statt. Zuvor gab es Wettbewerbe über andere Distanzen, etwa dieses: die Indy 500 100-Meilen-Rennen, aufgenommen um 1910.

Avant que ne s'y déroule, en 1911, la première édition de sa plus célèbre course annuelle – l'Indy 500 – le circuit ovale d'Indianapolis, construit en 1909, accueillait plusieurs compétitions sur des distances très variées, comme celle des 100 Miles, ici vers 1910.

— 2 —

La disparition du cheval ?
De 1900 à la Première
Guerre mondiale

Entre 1900 et le début de la Première Guerre mondiale, l'automobile se métamorphose. Du rêve d'inventeurs, du jouet incommodant et cher qu'elle était à ses débuts, elle devient une machine utile quotidiennement et accessible aux masses. À l'aube du XXe siècle, l'automobile est déjà une réalité inéluctable malgré la résistance de l'establishment, dont les membres tiennent à leurs chevaux, et en dépit du fait qu'elle reste une machine relativement confidentielle qui ne circule qu'à de rares exemplaires. Puisqu'il ne semble pas envisageable qu'elle disparaisse, la seule alternative est de vivre avec et de s'en accommoder au mieux ! Mais l'éveil de cette passion demeure très lent.

L'événement qui va marquer symboliquement l'acceptation de l'automobile dans la société se produit peu avant la fin du siècle avec l'abrogation de la célèbre loi britannique de 1865 dite du « Drapeau rouge », qui prévoyait que les « locomotives routières » devaient être limitées à la vitesse de 6,5 km/h et précédées d'un homme à pied brandissant un fanion rouge le jour et une lanterne rouge la nuit. Les autorités utilisèrent (ou abusèrent) fréquemment de cette réglementation, toujours en vigueur à la naissance de l'automobile, pour témoigner leur opposition passive à ces nouvelles voitures sans chevaux. Si l'obligation de porter un drapeau rouge aurait été annulée en 1878, ce n'est pas le cas en ce qui concerne la présence de l'accompagnateur ni de la limitation de vitesse. Renforçant avec constance cette loi archaïque qui prive de facto l'automobile de ses atouts essentiels – vitesse et autonomie –, le pouvoir britannique se révèle alors bien moins progressiste que la plupart des gouvernements d'Europe continentale et des États-Unis et freine évidemment – au propre comme au figuré – l'expansion de l'automobile en Grande-Bretagne.

Le 14 novembre 1896 entre en vigueur une nouvelle loi – le Locomotives on Highways Act – qui relève à 19 km/h la limite de vitesse sur les routes de Grande-Bretagne pour les véhicules jusqu'à 1,5 tonnes, et dispense totalement les automobilistes de la nécessité d'être précédés par un piéton. Le Motor Car Club organise aussitôt une course entre Londres et Brighton (« Emancipation Run ») pour célébrer ce qui est sans doute alors l'une des plus grandes concessions accordées par la Grande-Bretagne au mouvement automobile.

La plupart des 35 voitures environ qui participent à ce rallye de 85 km entre la capitale et la côte parviennent, malgré les incidents mécaniques ou les difficultés du terrain montueux, au terme de l'étape par leurs propres moyens ou aidés. L'importance de ce mouvement peut se mesurer à la personnalité de quelques-uns des participants : Gottlieb Daimler en personne à bord d'une de ses voitures, les Français Léon et Camille Bollée chacun dans un Tricar de leur conception, auxquels s'ajoute un grand nombre de voitures étrangères comme des Panhard et des Roger-Benz, deux Duryea et un Tricycle Pennington originaire des États-Unis. Léon Bollée fut le premier à atteindre Brighton, ayant roulé à la moyenne de près de 24 km/h. Cette course événement – la « London–Brighton Run » – est commémorée chaque année en novembre en Angleterre.

L'émancipation de la Grande-Bretagne ne va pas jusqu'à autoriser les courses automobiles sur la voie publique, à l'exception du territoire de l'île de Man, qui dispose d'une législation particulière plus accommodante et permet l'organisation du Tourist Trophy. Cette course, dont la première édition a lieu en 1905, vient s'ajouter à la liste des compétitions classiques qui se déroulent désormais régulièrement. Tandis que naissent en Italie la Targa Florio et la Coppa della Velocità, d'autres grandes courses sur route ont lieu en Europe et aux États-Unis, comme la Gordon Bennett Cup, organisée chaque année dans le pays du vainqueur de l'édition précédente (en Irlande dans le cas de la Grande Bretagne). La France reste toutefois le principal lieu des compétitions automobiles ; il s'y déroule plusieurs des premières courses de ville à ville et elle est le point de départ ou d'arrivée de courses comme la Paris–Berlin de 1901, la tragique Paris–Madrid de 1903 ou encore les incroyables marathons que furent Pékin–Paris et New York–Paris en 1907 et 1908. C'est en 1906 qu'y est également organisé le premier « Grand Prix », à une époque où l'Automobile Club de France considère le sport automobile comme sa chasse gardée.

Le sport et l'industrie automobiles se découvrent alors des intérêts communs. Les grandes courses sur route sont peu à peu remplacées par les compétitions sur circuit permanent. Le premier circuit de ce genre ouvre en 1907 à Brooklands, dans le Surrey (Angleterre). Intégrant aussitôt la grande scène des sports mécaniques, il offre non seulement un décor idéal pour toutes sortes de tentatives de record, en automobile comme en aviation, ainsi que pour des courses et des essais, mais est aussi un lieu de fête pour le public et un club de gentlemen pour les conducteurs (femmes comprises).

Les compétitions automobiles jouent également ce rôle de lieu de distraction, de terrain d'essai et de tremplin publicitaire aux États-Unis, où le circuit d'Indianapolis est inauguré en 1909. Henry Ford fait partie des plus ardents supporters de ce nouveau sport. Ce fils de fermier avait été ingénieur en chef à la Edison Illuminating Company, où il s'était lié d'une profonde amitié avec Thomas Alva Edison, l'un des pionniers de la voiture électrique et son voisin à Detroit.

Ford, qui avait construit un premier prototype d'automobile en 1896, crée en 1899 l'éphémère Detroit Automobile Company puis, en 1901, la Henry Ford Company, rebaptisée deux ans plus tard Ford Motor Company. Ce sera l'une des pierres angulaires de l'industrie automobile. Les méthodes et la philosophie de Ford allaient en effet révolutionner totalement cette industrie et, d'une certaine manière, modifier l'avenir de l'automobile : la voiture ne sera plus un jouet réservé aux riches mais une machine accessible aux individus de toutes les classes sociales, du runabout familial au coupé du médecin, de la vitrine du représentant au camion de livraison ou au véhicule utilitaire du fermier.

S'il est le plus important constructeur des États-Unis, Ford n'est toutefois ni le premier ni le seul à fabriquer des automobiles en grande quantité ; Ransom Eli Olds l'a devancé dans ce domaine au tout début du siècle pour la production de son Oldsmobile Curved Dash. Ford se sert également de la compétition comme moyen de publicité et outil de développement. En 1904, il détient même le record du monde de vitesse, à 147,1 km/h, obtenu sur la glace du Lake St Clair, dans le Michigan, avec l'Arrow « 999 » à moteur Ford quatre cylindres non carrossée. Mais la véritable contribution de Ford à la nouvelle société moderne est de rendre l'automobile accessible à tous – un rêve qu'il réalise presque entièrement avec la sortie en 1908 du légendaire Model T. L'introduction par Ford de la production en série puis du montage à la chaîne dans son usine lui permet de fabriquer en grande quantité et de vendre à un prix assez bas ce modèle, qui sera, pendant près de trente ans, la voiture la plus vendue au monde. Lors de l'arrêt de la production en 1927, Ford en a vendu plus de 15 millions d'exemplaires.

Il s'agit de l'exemple le plus extrême d'une tendance générale à une époque où il y a un nombre croissant de voitures mises sur le marché par des constructeurs toujours plus nombreux pour satisfaire une population automobile de plus en plus étendue. Au tournant du siècle, il existe plus de 200 marques d'automobile dans le monde parmi lesquelles on retrouve les grands noms de l'industrie automobile : Cadillac, le vaste conglomérat de la General Motors, Buick, Studebaker, Chevrolet et des centaines d'autres aux États-Unis ; en Europe, Mercedes, Bugatti, Vauxhall, Rolls-Royce, Rover, Austin, Lancia

et, tout comme en Amérique, bien d'autres qui ne subsisteront pas.

Pendant tout ce temps, la mécanique automobile n'a cessé de s'améliorer et la production d'augmenter. Le système à quatre roues motrices ou le freinage sur les roues avant apparaissent ainsi pour la première fois sur une Spyker de 1903, construite en Hollande ; la traction avant est installée sur une Christie (voiture de course américaine) en 1904 ; le moteur à compresseur, jusque là utilisé sur des voitures de course, est adapté pour la première fois à une voiture de tourisme, une Chadwick (États-Unis) de 1908 ; De Dion introduit le premier moteur V8 de série en 1910 ; et, aux États-Unis encore, les Cornelian mettent au point la suspension indépendante en 1914.

En ce début de siècle, l'Amérique montre la voie de la production en volume et devient alors le plus gros pays de construction automobile : 4 192 unités sont construites aux États-Unis en 1900 ; en 1903 : 11 235 ; 1908 : 63 500 environ ; 1909 : à la suite du lancement du Model T, 123 900 unités ; et, en 1914, malgré les menaces de guerre sur l'Europe, les chiffres de production atteignent un record de 548 139 voitures et de 24 900 camions.

Le monde apprend également à vivre avec l'automobile. En 1903, la Grande-Bretagne assouplit un peu sa réglementation en relevant à nouveau la limite de vitesse à 32 km/h, mesure qui restera toutefois en vigueur jusqu'en 1930. C'est pourquoi l'une des principales activités de l'Automobile Association de Grande-Bretagne, fondée en 1905, est de fournir des éclaireurs (« scout ») aux automobilistes pour les prévenir à l'avance des contrôles de vitesse. Les États-Unis se révèlent étrangement assez lents à développer un réseau routier décent et les automobilistes américains circulent encore sur des routes (pour ne pas dire chemins) exécrables plusieurs années après que l'Europe se fut pourvue d'un réseau routier bien revêtu. La première traversée en automobile du continent nord-américain n'est réalisée qu'en 1903 par une Winton et dure 65 jours, dont une vingtaine perdus pour effectuer les réparations nécessitées par les conditions de circulation. Et ce n'est qu'en 1913 qu'est fondée la Lincoln Highway Association, un groupe de pression qui demande instamment la création d'une route transcontinentale convenable.

Mais l'automobile va devoir affronter une tache beaucoup plus importante et se voit attribuer pour la première fois un rôle essentiel en prévision du déclenchement imminent de la Première Guerre mondiale.

On a dusty backroad in turn of the century America, a motorcycle patrol man talks with a car driver dressed in typical motoring attire of the automobile's early days.

Auf einer staubigen Nebenstraße im Amerika der Jahrhundertwende unterhält sich ein Motorradpolizist mit einem Autofahrer, der die typische Kluft der ersten Automobilistenjahre trägt.

Discussion sur le bas-côté d'une route des États-Unis au début du siècle entre un policier motocycliste et le conducteur d'une automobile, vêtu du costume typique de chauffeur des premiers temps de l'automobile.

Trailblazing USA

Good roads came late to the USA. In 1903 the first coast-to-coast crossing, by a Winton, took 65 days. Dirt roads were normal around 1910, when this Chalmers 30 (above) encountered a chain-gang in Arkansas. In 1908, when the Thomas Flyer 60 hp (right and overleaf) set out on the New York–Paris race, there were still vast areas with no roads at all, only railways and pioneer towns.

Eine Trasse für Amerika

Spät bekam Amerika brauchbare Straßen. Die erste Durchquerung des Kontinents 1903 in einem Winton dauerte 65 Tage. Unbefestigte Straßen waren auch 1910 noch die Regel, als dieser Chalmers 30 (oben) einer Arbeitskolonne von Strafgefangenen in Arkansas begegnet. 1908, als sich der Thomas Flyer 60 hp (rechts und folgende Seite) auf den Weg zur Rallye New York–Paris machte, gab es noch weite Landstriche ohne Straßen, nur mit Eisenbahnen und den Pioniersiedlungen.

À la découverte des États-Unis

Le système routier américain ne fut amélioré qu'assez tardivement. La première traversée du continent d'est en ouest en 1903 avec une Winton, dura 65 jours. Les mauvaises routes étaient assez fréquentes dans les années 1910 lorsque cette Chalmers 30 (ci-dessus) croise des forçats dans l'Arkansas. En 1908, quand une Thomas-Flyer 60 hp (à droite et pages suivantes) s'engage dans la course New York-Paris, il subsiste de vastes régions dont les villages de pionniers ne sont desservis que par le chemin de fer.

Pioneering spirit

The Thomas Flyer won the 1908 race to Paris, having survived the mud in Colorado (left), and snow so deep in Alaska it had to turn back to Seattle to find a boat to Vladivostok. But the cars (and drivers) were tough; by the time this picture (above) was taken, the 1913 Chandler had clocked 269,000 miles, while the Chalmers crew (below) included some hunting in their 'Pathfinder' trip.

Pioniergeist

Der Thomas Flyer gewann 1908 das Rennen nach Paris. Bis er dort ankam, hatte er den Schlamm von Colorado (links) und den Schnee in Alaska zu überstehen, der so tief war, dass die Mannschaft nach Seattle zurückkehren und von dort ein Boot nach Wladiwostok nehmen musste. Aber Autos und Fahrer waren zäh. Als das Bild des Chandler von 1913 (oben) entstand, hatte der Wagen 269 000 Meilen auf dem Tacho; die Belegschaft des Chalmers (unten) nutzt ihre Erkundungsfahrt gleich zur Jagd.

L'esprit pionnier

La Thomas Flyer remporta la course New York-Paris de 1908 après avoir franchi les routes boueuses du Colorado (à gauche) et rencontré en Alaska une telle épaisseur de neige qu'il lui fallut revenir à Seattle et prendre un bateau pour se rendre à Vladivostok. Voitures et chauffeurs étaient résistants ; à l'époque où cette photo fut prise (en haut), cette Chandler de 1913 avait déjà parcouru 492 000 km pendant que l'équipage de la Chalmers (en bas) se détendait en chassant pendant le parcours de reconnaissance.

Promoting the image
The Brush Company of Detroit loved publicity. It pitted its 1910 model against a horse, and even used children (above) to promote it. The more upmarket Pope-Toledo (right) preferred images of the White House for 'The Quiet Mile-a-Minute Car'.

Auf die Reklame kommt es an
Die Brush Company aus Detroit zeigte frühes Marketing-Geschick. Das Modell von 1910 ließ sie gegen ein Pferd antreten, und auch Kinder machten Werbung dafür (oben). Der vornehmere Pope-Toledo, »jede lautlose Minute eine Meile«, ließ sich lieber vor dem Weißen Haus ablichten (rechts).

Promotion publicitaire
La Brush Company, de Detroit, aimait se faire de la publicité : elle fit courir son modèle de 1910 contre un cheval et utilisa même des enfants (ci-dessus) pour sa promotion. La firme Pope-Toledo, plus haut de gamme (à droite), préférait afficher des images de la Maison Blanche pour valoriser sa « Quiet Mile-a-Minute Car » (la « Voiture du Mile par minute »).

Cowboys and Indians

In 1908, a year before his death, Apache warrior Geronimo (above) poses at the wheel of the automobile he used during his final days as a farmer in Oklahoma, the same state in which a car named after him was built between 1917 and 1921. Also in 1908, early on in its 169-day, 13,340-mile trip to Paris, the Thomas Flyer had stopped in cowboy settlements (right) and in Utah hired an Indian guide to show them the route.

Cowboys und Indianer

Der Apachenkrieger Geronimo posiert 1908, ein Jahr vor seinem Tod, am Steuer des Wagens, den er in seinen letzten Lebensjahren in Oklahoma fuhr (oben), wo es zwischen 1917 und 1921 eine Automarke mit seinem Namen gab. Ebenfalls 1908 entstand die Aufnahme des Thomas Flyer (rechts), der zu Anfang seiner 169 Tage und 13 340 Meilen langen Fahrt nach Paris bei den Cowboys im Wilden Westen Station macht. In Utah heuerte man einen Indianerführer an, der ihnen den Weg wies.

Cow-boys et indiens

En 1908, un an avant sa mort, le chef Apache Geronimo (ci-dessus) pose au volant de l'automobile qu'il a utilisé pendant les derniers jours de sa vie de fermier dans l'Oklahoma (une voiture portant son nom sera construite dans cet État entre 1917 et 1921). La même année, au début du périple de 24 400 km qui la conduira en 169 jours jusqu'à Paris, la Thomas Flyer (à droite) s'est arrêtée dans un campement de cow-boys ; son équipage engagera plus tard comme guide un Indien de l'Utah.

The tragic race

The 1903 Paris–Madrid race was a nightmare. Marcel Renault drove one of three 'lightweight' 6.3-litre 30hp Renault racers (left). At Couhé-Vérac, in the dust cloud of another racer, he failed to see a hairpin bend, crashed at speed into the ditch (above) and was killed. Louis Renault was informed of his brother's death in Bordeaux (below), where he was leading on the road. There had already been several other deaths, and the race was abandoned.

Das tragische Rennen

Die Rallye Paris–Madrid im Jahr 1903 war ein Albtraum. Marcel Renault startete in einem von drei »leichten« 6,3-Liter-30-PS-Renault-Rennwagen (links). In Couhé-Vérac sah er in der Staubwolke eines voranfahrenden Wagens eine Haarnadelkurve nicht, fuhr mit vollem Tempo in den Straßengraben (oben) und war auf der Stelle tot. Der in Führung liegende Louis Renault erfuhr in Bordeaux vom Tod seines Bruders (unten). Es hatte bereits mehrere tödliche Unfälle gegeben, und das Rennen wurde abgebrochen.

La course tragique

La course Paris-Madrid de 1903 fut dramatique. À Couhé-Vérac, Marcel Renault, qui pilotait une des trois Renault « légères » de 6,3 l et 30 ch engagées (à gauche), ne vit pas un virage en épingle que dissimulait le nuage de poussière d'un autre concurrent et s'écrasa à pleine vitesse dans un fossé (en haut). C'est à Bordeaux, alors qu'il était en tête, que Louis Renault apprit la mort de son frère (en bas). La course fut annulée à la suite de ce tragique événement qui survenait après plusieurs autres accidents mortels.

Road racing

Mainland Britain banned motor racing on public roads, the Isle of Man welcomed it. The 1908 'Four-Inch' Race was named for the maximum permitted diameter of each of four cylinders, and won by Watson, in the Hutton, seen (above) at Ramsey Hairpin. Italy also welcomed road racing: this is Demogeot (right) at Brescia with his Darracq, in the 1907 Coppa della Velocità.

Straßenrennen

Auf der britischen Hauptinsel waren Straßenrennen verboten, doch die Insel Man hieß die Rennfahrer willkommen. Das 1908 veranstaltete »Four-Inch«-Rennen erhielt seinen Namen nach dem maximalen Durchmesser von vier Zoll pro Zylinder. Der Gewinner war Watson in einem Hutton, hier (oben) in der Haarnadelkurve von Ramsey. Auch in Italien waren die Rennfahrer gern gesehen; das Bild (rechts) zeigt Demogeot mit seinem Darracq in Brescia beim Coppa della Velocità von 1907.

Course sur route

Les courses sur route étaient interdites en Grande-Bretagne à l'exception de l'île de Man. En 1908, la course dite « Four-Inch Race », c'est-à-dire le diamètre maximum autorisé pour les cylindres des voitures participantes, fut remportée par Watson sur une Hutton, que l'on voit ci-dessus en pleine action dans l'épingle à cheveux de Ramsey. L'Italie appréciait également les courses automobiles : on voit ici à Brescia (à droite), Demogeot avec sa Darracq au cours de la Coppa della Velocità de 1907.

Horsepower

It took time for the horseless carriage to displace the horse, even in great cities like London. In July 1907 a single motor cab (right) is surrounded by horse vans and hansom cabs. By May 1910, Piccadilly Circus (above) had a growing number of automobiles among the horse omnibuses. In the heat of the summer the 'exhaust' of the horse was as big a problem as that of the car is today.

Pferdestärken

Es dauerte eine Weile, bis der pferdelose Wagen das Pferd ganz verdrängt hatte, selbst in Großstädten wie London. Im Juli 1907 ist ein einzelnes Motortaxi (rechts) umgeben von pferdegezogenen Lieferwagen und Droschken. Im Mai 1910 findet sich am Piccadilly Circus (oben) schon eine größere Zahl von Automobilen zwischen den Pferdeomnibussen. In der Sommerhitze waren die »Abgase« der Pferde ein nicht minder großes Problem als die Autoabgase heute.

Cheval-vapeur

Il était temps que les voitures sans chevaux remplacent le cheval, moyen de transport encore fréquent même dans des grandes villes comme Londres, comme ici en juillet 1907 (à droite). Il faut dire aussi qu'en été les « rejets » des chevaux représentaient un problème aussi préoccupant que les gaz d'échappement des voitures actuelles. En mai 1910, il circule déjà un plus grand nombre d'automobiles que d'omnibus à chevaux à Piccadilly Circus (ci-dessus).

Looking after the motorist

Lady mechanics (above) learning the secrets of a Horstmann light car, at Gabrielle Borthwick's School of Motoring and Engineering. In August 1912, a Napier and a Metallurgique taking part in the Challenge Tyre Company tests stopped at Wilkinson's Garage in Uxbridge, Middlesex (right) watched by officials and a young man in a pedal car. The road surface is of cobbled stones, with tramlines, both slippery when wet.

Ausbildung für Automobilisten

An der Gabrielle Borthwick's School of Motoring and Engineering erforschen Mechanikerinnen die Geheimnisse eines leichten Horstmann-Wagens (oben). Im August 1912 machen ein Napier und ein Metallurgique auf einer Testfahrt der Challenge-Reifenwerke Zwischenstopp bei Wilkinsons Garage im englischen Uxbridge, Middlesex; Angestellte und ein junger Mann im Tretauto begutachten die Fahrzeuge (rechts). Die Straßenoberfläche aus Pflastersteinen mit Straßenbahnschienen wurde bei Nässe rutschig.

À la recherche d'un mécano

Ces apprenties mécaniciennes (ci-dessus) de la School of Motoring and Engineering créée par Gabrielle Borthwick apprennent tous les secrets de la Horstmann, une voiture légère. En août 1912, une Napier et une Metallurgique (à droite), qui effectuent des essais pour la Challenge Tyre Company, se sont arrêtées au garage Wilkinson d'Uxbridge (Middlesex). La chaussée de pavés, sillonnée par les rails du tramway, représentait un risque important de dérapage par temps pluvieux.

Posing for the camera

Motorists in suburban Britain (above), including an adventurous lady driver in the runabout in the centre, ahead of the very early Panhard, show the variety of vehicles and motoring fashions in the early years of the century. The American party (right) in about 1907 enjoy the sunshine in their Matheson tourer; this, like many early American cars, had the steering wheel on the right-hand side, although Americans already drove on the right-hand side of the road.

Parade für den Fotografen

Diese Autofahrer in einer britischen Vorstadt (oben), darunter eine mutige Pilotin am Steuer des offenen Zweisitzers in der Mitte, gefolgt von einem sehr frühen Panhard-Modell, zeigen die Vielfalt von Mode, die es Anfang des Jahrhunderts für die Autofahrt gab. Die amerikanische Gruppe (rechts) genießt um 1907 die Sonne in ihrem Matheson-Tourer; der Wagen hatte, wie viele frühe Modelle der Vereinigten Staaten, das Steuerrad rechts, obwohl die Amerikaner schon damals auf der rechten Straßenseite fuhren.

Une pose pour la photo

Ces automobilistes de la banlieue britannique (ci-dessus) montrent la diversité de la mode des promenades en voiture du début du siècle. Courageuse pilote au volant d'un runabout (petite voiture) au centre devant une des premières Panhard. En 1907, comme c'est encore le cas de la plupart des premières voitures américaines, cette Matheson torpédo a le volant à droite bien que les Américains aient déjà choisi de conduire sur le côté droit de la route.

Hillclimbs, records and trials

(Previous pages) The cars of the Talbot team prepare for the Yorkshire Automobile Club's hillclimb at Pately Bridge in September 1913; third from left is a streamlined Talbot racer driven by Percy Lambert, who at Brooklands in February 1913 became the first driver ever to cover more than 100 miles in an hour. A Coventry-built Ranger Cyclecar ahead of a 100hp Isotta-Fraschini (right) in the 1914 Essex Motor Club One-Day Motor Trials.

Bergfahrten, Versuchsfahrten, Rekordfahrten

(Vorherige Seiten) Die Wagen des Talbot-Teams sind im September 1913 in Pately Bridge für die Bergfahrt des Yorkshire Automobile Club angetreten; Dritter von links ist ein stromlinienförmiger Talbot-Rennwagen, am Steuer Percy Lambert, der im Februar 1913 in Brooklands als Erster mehr als 100 Meilen binnen einer Stunde zurücklegte. Bei den One-Day Motor Trials des Essex Motor Club, 1914, fährt ein in Coventry gebauter Ranger Cyclecar einem 100 PS starken Isotta-Fraschini voraus (rechts).

Courses de côte, records et épreuves

(Pages précédentes) Les voitures de l'équipe Talbot se préparent à participer à la course de côte du Yorkshire Automobile Club à Pately Bridge, en septembre 1913 ; la troisième voiture à partir de la gauche est la fameuse Talbot de course carénée conduite par Percy Lambert, qui fut, en février à Brooklands, le premier pilote à parcourir plus de 161 km/h. Un cycle-car Ranger, construit à Coventry, précède une Isotta-Fraschini de 100 ch lors de la course du One-Day Motor Trials organisée en 1914 par l'Essex Motor-Club (à droite).

Laying the dust
In Europe and Africa as well as America, the motor car arrived onto roads more suitable for horse-drawn vehicles than the faster cars with their vulnerable pneumatic tyres. On a hairpin in Wales in 1909 (above), during reliability trials between Nottingham and Newcastle in 1908 (right), and for the official Daimler in hillclimbing trials in North Africa (overleaf), the problem of dust and stones is clear.

Eine staubige Sache
Nicht nur in Amerika, sondern auch in Europa und Afrika mussten die ersten Automobile auf Straßen fahren, die eher für Pferdehufe als für die empfindlichen Luftreifen der schnelleren Motorfahrzeuge gemacht waren. Auf der Haarnadel-kurve in Wales, 1909 (oben) und bei einer Zuverlässigkeitsfahrt zwischen Nottingham und Newcastle 1908 (rechts) ist nicht zu übersehen, wie viel Mühe Staub und Steine den Fahrern machen, und dem offiziellen Daimler-Team bei Berg-fahrten in Nordafrika (folgende Seiten) ergeht es nicht besser.

Aménager les routes
En Europe, en Afrique comme aux États-Unis, les routes sont plus adaptées aux voitures à cheval qu'à des automobiles rapides mais dont les pneumatiques sont encore fragiles. La poussière, les pierres et les obstacles divers sont évidem-ment un problème et un défi pour les conducteurs, qu'il s'agisse de négocier cette épingle à cheveux au pays de Galles, 1909 (ci-dessus), de participer à une compétition d'endurance entre Nottingham et Newcastle, 1908 (à droite), ou de conduire la Daimler officielle à l'occasion d'une course de côte en Afrique du Nord (pages suivantes).

Peking to Paris
Early in 1907 a headline in the French newspaper, *Le Matin*, asked 'Will anyone agree to go, this summer, from Peking to Paris by motor car?' Several adventurers soon said yes, and one of the great early transcontinental motor races was born. Prince Scipio Borghese, with an Itala (above) was among the first to enter, and he started alongside rivals as diverse as the fully-laden 6hp Contal tricycle (below) and the Spyker (right) from Holland.

Von Peking nach Paris
Anfang 1907 fragte eine Schlagzeile in der französischen Zeitung *Le Matin*: »Wer wäre bereit, im Sommer mit dem Motorwagen von Peking nach Paris zu fahren?« Bald hatten sich etliche Abenteurer gemeldet, und eines der spektakulärsten frühen Transkontinentalrennen war geboren. Fürst Scipio Borghese (oben) zählte mit seinem Itala zu den ersten Anmeldern, und er trat gegen so unterschiedliche Rivalen wie dieses schwer beladene Contal-6-PS-Dreirad (unten) und den holländischen Spyker (rechts) an.

De Pékin à Paris
Au début de l'année 1907, le journal français *Le Matin* demande en gros titre : « Qui veut aller cet été de Pékin à Paris en voiture ? ». La candidature immédiate de plusieurs aventuriers marque ainsi la naissance de l'une des premières grandes courses transcontinentales. L'Itala du prince italien Scipio Borghese (en haut), parmi les premiers concurrents à s'inscrire, se trouve alors opposé à des rivaux aussi divers que le tricycle français Contal de 6 ch (en bas) ou la Spyker hollandaise (à droite).

Winner's reception

Borghese and the 40hp Itala arrive in Paris on 10 August 1907 as winners of the Peking–Paris race. The trip had taken them two months and they arrived three and a half weeks ahead of the Spyker and two De Dions-Bouton, the Contal tricycle crew having given up in the Gobi Desert. The cars had been hauled through mud and dried river beds by teams of coolies, and the Itala had survived a crashing fall through an old wooden bridge. Behind the victorious Itala here are three similar cars, brought out by the Paris agent.

Empfang für den Sieger

Am 10. August 1907 traf Borghese mit dem 40-PS-Itala in Paris ein. Der Sieger der Peking-Paris-Rallye hatte zwei Monate für die Fahrt gebraucht und langte dreieinhalb Wochen vor dem Spyker und zwei De Dions-Bouton an – die Contal-Mannschaft hatte in der Wüste Gobi aufgegeben. Die Wagen mussten von Kulis durch Schlamm und ausgetrocknete Flussbette gezerrt werden, und der Itala hatte sogar den Sturz durch den Boden einer morschen Holzbrücke überstanden. Hinter dem Siegerwagen fahren drei ähnliche Modelle, vom Pariser Händler als Eskorte gestellt.

La réception du vainqueur

Remportant la course Pékin–Paris le 10 août 1907, le prince Borghese arrive à Paris à bord de son Itala 40 ch, suivi par trois autres voitures du même modèle, amenées par l'agent parisien de la marque. Il a mis deux mois et devance de trois semaines et demie la Spyker et deux De Dion-Bouton, l'équipage du tricycle Contal ayant abandonné dans le désert de Gobi. L'aventure fut rude : les voitures ont souvent dû être sorties de la boue et du lit des rivières à sec par des équipes de coolies locaux, et l'Itala elle-même faillit s'écraser en franchissant un vieux pont de bois.

Motoring for the masses

Nobody helped make the automobile accessible more than Henry Ford. The son of a farmer, Ford built his first car, the two-cylinder Quadricycle, in 1896, in a small workshop (below) behind his lodgings in Bagley Avenue, Detroit. In 1903 he founded the Ford Motor Company and some years later posed patriotically (right) in that first car. He launched his second production car, the two-cylinder 10hp Model C (above) in 1904.

Motoren für die Massen

Niemand tat mehr für die Verbreitung des Automobils als Henry Ford. Der Sohn eines Landarbeiters baute seinen ersten Wagen, den Zweizylinder-Quadricycle, im Jahr 1896 in einer kleinen Werkstatt (unten) hinter seiner Wohnung in der Bagley Avenue in Detroit. 1903 gründete er die Ford Motor Company, und einige Jahre später entstand dieses patriotische Bild (rechts) in jenem ersten Wagen. 1904 stellte er sein zweites Serienmodell vor, das Model C mit zwei Zylindern und 10 PS (oben).

L'automobile pour les masses

Personne n'a fait plus que Henry Ford pour rendre l'automobile accessible au plus grand nombre. Fils d'un fermier, Ford construit en 1896 sa première voiture, un quadricycle bi-cylindre, dans un petit atelier (en bas) situé derrière son appartement de Bagley Avenue, à Detroit. En 1903, il fonde la Ford Motor Company et, quelques années plus tard, pose fièrement (à droite) dans son véhicule. C'est en 1904 qu'il lance sa deuxième voiture de production, le Model C à moteur bi-cylindre de 10 ch (en haut).

GENTLEMEM
OUR
COUNTRY

HENRY FORD AND HIS FIRST CAR.

Wheels for the world

'I will build a motor car for the great multitude. It will be large enough for the family but small enough for the individual to run and care for. It will be constructed of the best materials ... But it will be so low in price that no man making a good salary will be unable to own one – and enjoy with his family the blessing of hours of pleasure in God's great open spaces.' In 1908 Henry Ford launched the Model T which spread around the world – including here, to Egypt.

Räder für die Welt

»Ich will einen Motorwagen für die großen Massen bauen. Er soll groß genug für die Familie sein, aber klein genug, dass ein Einzelner ihn fahren und instand halten kann. Er soll aus den besten Materialien gebaut sein ... Aber er soll so preisgünstig sein, dass kein Mann, der eine ordentliche Arbeit hat, ihn sich nicht leisten und mit seiner Familie den Segen einer Ausfahrt in Gottes weitem offenem Land genießen kann.« 1908 brachte Henry Ford das Model T auf den Markt, das seinen Siegeszug um die ganze Welt antrat – selbst in Ägypten sah man es.

Des roues pour le monde entier

« Je veux construire une voiture à moteur pour la multitude. Je la veux suffisamment grande pour toute la famille mais assez petite pour qu'un seul individu puisse la conduire et s'en occuper. Elle sera construite dans les meilleurs matériaux... Mais elle sera si peu chère que tout homme ayant un bon salaire pourra en posséder une – et jouir avec sa famille de la bénédiction que sont les heures heureuses passées dans les grands espaces créés par Dieu. » En 1908, Henry Ford lance le Model T, rapidement apprécié et exporté dans le monde entier, comme ici en Égypte.

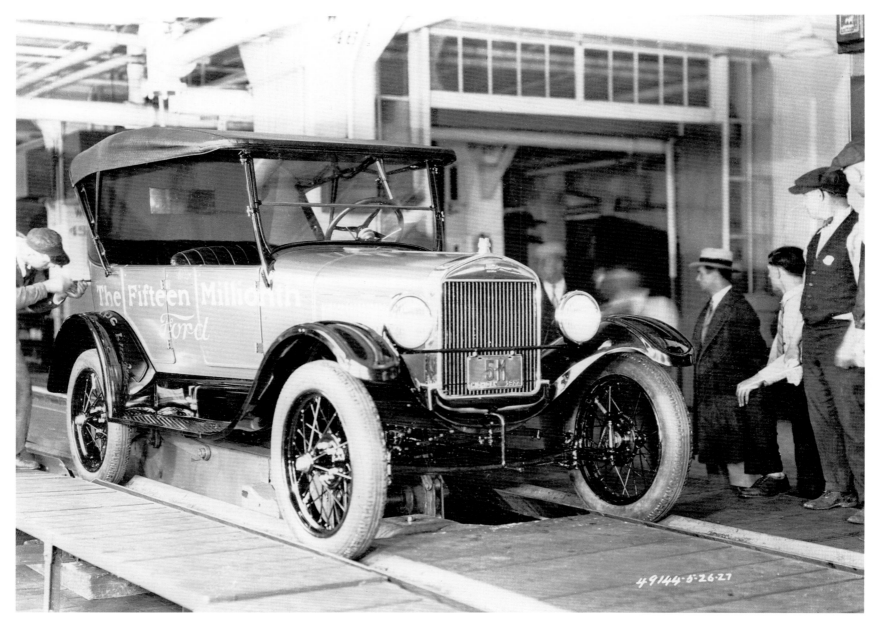

A car for all purposes

Henry Ford didn't invent mass production but with the Model T and other cars he adapted it to motor manufacture and raised it to new heights, making Ford the biggest car maker in the world. On 26 May 1927 the 15 millionth Ford rolled off the line in Detroit (above) – a Model T, of course. The T could also be anything from doctor's runabout to delivery truck (right).

Ein Auto für jede Gelegenheit

Henry Ford ist zwar nicht der Erfinder der Massenproduktion, aber mit dem Model T und anderen Modellen führte er sie in den Automobilbau ein und entwickelte ihre Verfahren zu bis dahin ungekannten Dimensionen, und bald war Ford der größte Automobilproduzent weltweit. Am 26. Mai 1927 lief der 15millionste Ford in Detroit vom Fließband (oben) – natürlich ein Model T. Den T gab es in verschiedenen Ausführungen, vom offenen Zweisitzer des Arztes bis zum Lieferwagen (rechts).

Une voiture à tout faire

Si Henry Ford n'a pas inventé le travail à la chaîne, il l'a développé et adapté à la production automobile, pour le Model T et les suivants, pour devenir grâce à cela le plus grand constructeur du monde à l'époque. Le 26 mai 1927, la 15 millionième Ford – un Model T évidemment – sortait de l'usine de Detroit (ci-dessus). Cette voiture pouvait s'adapter à presque n'importe quel usage, depuis le runabout du médecin au véhicule de livraison (à droite).

The low-cost alternative

To compete on price with cars like the Model T, Europe invented the light-car or cyclecar, usually distinguished, as in the Carden (above), built in England from 1913 to 1925, by tiny dimensions, low power and simple design. They had a following of their own, promoting demonstrations, like this one in London (right) in November 1910 with a GWK leading a Humberette and an AC Sociable, and competitions, as at South Harting hillclimb (below) in June 1913 – with the very popular GN in the foreground.

Die preiswerte Alternative

Als Antwort auf Fords Model T kamen in Europa Leicht- oder Kleinwagen auf, die schwach motorisiert und von simpler Konstruktion waren, oft winzig wie etwa der Carden (oben), der zwischen 1913 und 1925 in England gebaut wurde. Es gab eine eingeschworene Kleinwagengemeinde, die Schaufahrten veranstaltete, zum Beispiel im November 1910 in London (rechts), wo wir einen GWK gefolgt von einer Humberette und einem AC Sociable sehen, oder auch Wettbewerbe wie diese Bergfahrt in South Harting (unten) im Juni 1913 – im Vordergrund der sehr beliebte GN.

L'alternative bon marché

Pour rester compétitif en matière de prix face à des voitures comme le Model T, l'industrie automobile européenne invente la « voiture légère » – ou cycle-car – généralement reconnaissable à ses dimensions réduites, sa faible puissance et la simplicité de sa conception. Ces véhicules, représentés notamment par la Carden (en haut), construite en Angleterre de 1913 à 1925, ont des partisans actifs organisent des démonstrations – comme ici à Londres (à droite) en novembre 1910, où une GWK précède une Humberette et une AC Sociable – et des compétitions, par exemple la course de côte de South Harting en juin 1913 (en bas), à laquelle participe la très populaire GN (au premier plan).

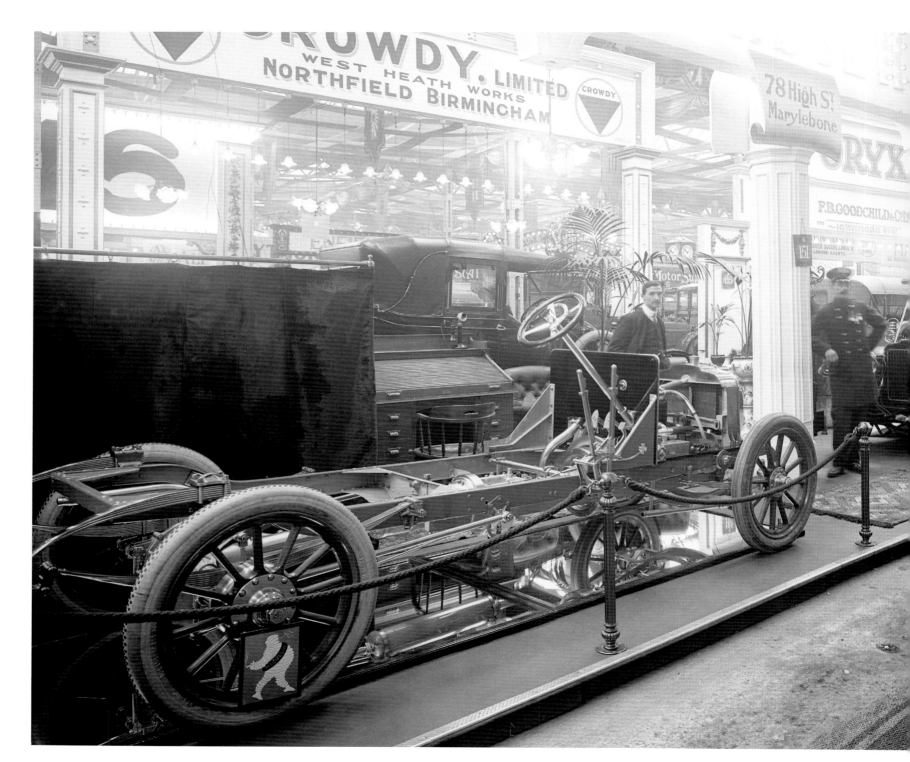

Feeding the market

Long before World War I, the choice of cars available, from manufacturers large and small, was vast and motor shows were already well established. In the days of separate chassis, as at the London Olympia Motor Show in 1911, you could take your chassis bare, as in the 15hp Brasier, or ready clothed, as in its 18hp sister (left). The Mercedes at the 1911 and 1913 Shows (above and middle right) and the 35hp Vauxhall Limousine (below right) at the 1913 Show, with a Prince Henry model in the background, also came fully bodied.

Das Angebot ist groß

Schon lange vor dem Ersten Weltkrieg bot eine Vielfalt großer und kleiner Hersteller eine breite Palette von Wagen an, und Automobilsalons waren bereits zur festen Einrichtung geworden, wie hier die Londoner Olympia Motor Show im Jahre 1911. Da die Karosserie auf einem selbstständigen Chassis saß, hatte man die Wahl, nur einen Unterbau zu kaufen, den man selbst einkleiden ließ, etwa das 15-PS-Brasier-Chassis (links), oder das komplette 18-PS-Schwestermodell daneben. Die Mercedes-Wagen von 1911 und 1913 (oben und Mitte rechts) und die 35-PS-Vauxhall-Limousine von 1913 (unten rechts, im Hintergrund das Prince-Henry-Modell) wurden mit Karosserie verkauft.

Alimenter le marché

Bien avant la Première Guerre mondiale, il existe déjà un vaste choix de modèles et de marques d'automobile, grandes ou petites, qu'il est possible de comparer à l'occasion des différents salons. À cette époque où les châssis étaient dissociés de la carrosserie, il était possible d'acheter à l'Olympia Motor Show de Londres en 1911 un châssis nu – par exemple celui de la Brasier 15 ch – ou déjà carrossé – son pendant avec moteur 18 ch (à gauche). Les Mercedes présentées aux salons de 1911 et 1913 (en haut et au milieu) ou la limousine Vauxhall 35 ch (en bas) de l'exposition de 1913 (on reconnaît un modèle Prince Henry à l'arrière-plan) étaient en revanche vendues carrossées.

Spreading the word

In June 1908, on the tenth day of the Royal Automobile Club and Scottish Automobile Club's rally (right), the cars, which included a 30hp White steamer (H-76-G), a 35hp Deasy Golden Eagle (K-65-F), and a 38hp Daimler (H-75) (contesting the RAC event only), stopped for lunch in the main street in Kirby. Fewer people saw the German Opel leaving Welbeck Abbey (above) during the Prince Henry Cup Tour in July 1911.

Gute Publicity

Im Juni 1908, am zehnten Tag der Rallye von Royal Automobile Club und Scottish Automobile Club, hielten die Teilnehmer zum Mittagessen in der Hauptstraße von Kirby (rechts). Zu sehen sind ein 30-PS-White-Dampfwagen (Kennzeichen H-76-G), ein Deasy Golden Eagle mit 35 PS (K-65-F) und ein 38-PS-Daimler (H-75), Letzterer nur für den englischen Teil gemeldet. Wenig Publikum hatte der deutsche Opel (oben), der hier beim Prince-Henry-Pokal im Juli 1911 das Herrenhaus Welbeck Abbey verlässt.

Envahir le monde

Les concurrents du rallye organisé en juin 1908 par le Royal Automobile Club et le Scottish Automobile Club – parmi lesquels on distingue une White à vapeur de 30 ch (H-76-G), une Deasy Golden Eagle (K-65-F) et une Daimler 38 ch (H-75 ; qui ne concourt que pour le rallye de la RAC) – se sont arrêtées pour déjeuner (à droite). Rares sont ceux, en revanche, qui ont vu l'Opel allemande quitter Welbeck Abbey (ci-dessus) lors du Prince Henry Cup Tour de juillet 1911.

Uphill all the way

Hillclimbing was always a popular branch of motor sport in Britain. In the Scottish Trials in June 1906 (right), hillclimbing was one of many tests in a long-distance touring event. By 1911, speed was the object, and none was quicker than Vauxhall driver AJ Hancock, record breaker at Brooklands, and master of the famous hill (above) at Shelsley Walsh, Worcestershire.

Und immer bergauf

Bergfahrten waren von Anfang an im britischen Motorsport populär. Bei den Scottish Trials im Juni 1906 (rechts) war die Bergfahrt eine von vielen Prüfungen in einer Langstrecken-Zuverlässigkeitsfahrt. 1911 ging es mehr ums Tempo, und da war niemand schneller als A. J. Hancock mit seinem Vauxhall, der nach seinen Rekordfahrten in Brooklands auch den berühmten Hügel von Shelsley Walsh in Worcestershire bezwingt (oben).

Tout en montée

La course de côte est une forme de course automobile toujours très populaire en Grande-Bretagne. Dans les Scottish Trials de juin 1906 (à droite), elle constituait une des nombreuses épreuves d'endurance pour les voitures de tourisme. En 1911, c'est toutefois la vitesse qui prime ; le pilote A. J. Hancock, sur Vauxhall, brise le record de l'ascension de Brooklands et se rend maître de la célèbre colline de Shelsley Walsh (Worcestershire) (ci-dessus).

From racer to record breaker

Arthur MacDonald at the wheel of a 1903 Napier racer. Early in 1905 at the Florida Speed Week, MacDonald's 90hp Napier covered a flying mile on Daytona Beach at 105.2mph, to take the land speed record. Only minutes later, Herbert Bowden in a twin-Mercedes-engined car nicknamed the 'Flying Dutchman' set a speed of 110.4mph, but it was disallowed as his car was overweight for the Speed Week rules, so MacDonald's record stood.

Rennfahrer und Rekordhalter

Arthur MacDonald am Steuer eines Napier-Rennwagens von 1903. Auf der Florida Speed Week Anfang 1905 legte MacDonald mit seinem 90-PS-Napier in Daytona Beach die Meile mit fliegendem Start mit 169,3 km/h zurück, ein neuer Geschwindigkeitsrekord für Landfahrzeuge. Nur Minuten später erhöhte Herbert Bowden am Steuer seines mit zwei Mercedes-Motoren bestückten »Fliegenden Holländers« den Rekord auf 177,6 km/h, doch der Wagen war nach den Regeln der Speed Week zu schwer, und MacDonald behielt den Titel.

De pilote de course à briseur de records

Arthur MacDonald au volant d'une Napier de course de 1903. Au début de l'année 1905, lors de la Florida Speed Week, la Napier 90 ch de MacDonald remporte le record du mile lancé (1,6 km) de Daytona Beach à la vitesse de 169,3 km/h. Quelques minutes plus tard, Herbert Bowden, dans une Mercedes bimoteur – baptisée « Flying Dutchman » – atteint la vitesse de 177,6 km/h mais est disqualifié car le poids de sa voiture excède le maximum autorisé par le règlement de la Speed Week.

Proving grounds
Sporting exploits were good for both technical development and publicity. Beaches provided space for maximum speeds. In July 1912, LG Hornsted's Benz (left) ran at Saltburn Sands in Yorkshire. Two years later he broke the land speed record in another Benz at Brooklands, where the Prince Henry Cup runners (above) had paraded in 1911. The Devil's Elbow (overleaf) on the 1906 Scottish Trial provided a challenge to drivers and a grandstand for spectators, here watching Reid's 30/40hp six-cylinder Beeston-Humber.

Teststrecke
Sporterfolge nützten dem technischen Fortschritt ebenso wie der Reklame. Strände boten den Platz für Rekordfahrten, wie hier im Juli 1912, wo L. G. Hornsted mit seinem Benz in Saltburn Sands, Yorkshire, Anlauf nimmt (links). Zwei Jahre später stellte er mit einem anderen Benz in Brooklands einen neuen Rekord für Landfahrzeuge auf; ebenfalls in Brooklands paradieren 1911 die Teilnehmer der Fahrt um den Prinz-Heinrich-Pokal (oben). Der Devil's Elbow (folgende Seiten) war bei den Scottish Trials von 1906 nicht nur eine Herausforderung für die Fahrer, sondern auch Tribüne für die Zuschauer, die hier Reids 30/40-PS-Beeston-Humber-Sechszylinder bewundern.

Champs d'expérimentation
La compétition et les exploits sportifs ont le double intérêt de faire avancer la technique automobile et d'offrir aux constructeurs une publicité bienvenue. Les plages sont aussi un terrain excellent pour atteindre les vitesses maximum. En juillet 1912, L. G. Hornsted (à gauche) s'élance avec sa Benz à Saltburn Sands (Yorkshire) et, deux ans plus tard, sur une autre Benz, brise le record de vitesse de Brooklands, à l'endroit même où les concurrents de la Prince Henry Cup (ci-dessus) avaient paradé en 1911. Le Devil's Elbow (pages suivantes), un virage en épingle du Scottish Trial, était un défi pour les pilotes et une tribune de choix pour ces spectateurs de 1906, qui regardent passer la Beeston-Humber six-cylindres 30/40 ch de Reid.

On the right tracks

On both sides of the Atlantic, great tracks were built for racing and as proving grounds for the industry. The first purpose-built track in the world was Brooklands, Surrey, which held its first race in July 1907. This (above) is June 1908. In the USA, Indianapolis (right) opened in August 1909 and held the first of its famous 500-mile races in 1911, won by Ray Harroun's Marmon Wasp.

Immer rundherum

Beiderseits des Atlantiks entstanden Rundkurse für Autorennen und als Teststrecken für die Industrie. Die erste speziell dafür gebaute Strecke war Brooklands im englischen Surrey, wo das erste Rennen im Juli 1907 stattfand. Die Aufnahme (oben) entstand im Juni 1908. In den USA eröffnete Indianapolis (rechts) im August 1909, und das berühmte 500-Meilen-Rennen fand erstmals 1911 statt; Sieger war damals Ray Harroun mit seinem Marmon Wasp.

Sur les bonnes pistes

Des deux côtés de l'Atlantique, on aménage de grands circuits pouvant servir à la fois de circuit de compétition et de piste d'essais pour l'industrie automobile. Le premier de ce genre fut celui de Brooklands (Surrey), inauguré en juillet 1907 (la course que l'on voit ci-dessus date de juin 1908). Aux États-Unis, le circuit d'Indianapolis (à droite), ouvert en août 1909, accueille la première épreuve des 500 Miles en 1911 ; elle sera remportée par Ray Harroun sur une Marmon Wasp.

Packing the grandstands

As well as providing the spectacle itself, the automobile increasingly also provided the mobility which took crowds in their thousands to other events, such as Goodwood for the horse racing. It is interesting to see how the Goodwood car park had grown between July 1910 (right) and July 1912 (above).

Voll besetzte Tribünen

Automobile waren nicht nur selbst eine Attraktion, sondern in immer größerem Maße auch das Verkehrsmittel, mit dem die Besucher zu Tausenden zu anderen Ereignissen kamen, etwa hier zum Pferderennen in Goodwood. Es ist interessant zu sehen, wie der Parkplatz von Goodwood zwischen Juli 1910 (rechts) und Juli 1912 (oben) gewachsen war.

Remplir les tribunes

Spectacle en soi, l'automobile est aussi un moyen de transport de plus en plus répandu qui permet à des milliers de gens d'assister à d'autres manifestations sportives, par exemple les courses de chevaux à Goodwood. Il est d'ailleurs intéressant de comparer l'étendue de l'aire de stationnement de Goodwood en juillet 1910 (à droite) et en juillet 1912 (ci-dessus).

Day-trippers

While the upper classes who could afford it had their own motor cars to go on the Grand Tour, the working classes, too, enjoyed new motorised mobility – thanks mainly to the motor bus, or 'charabanc'. These are motor-trippers in open coaches in the English seaside town of Scarborough in 1912.

Tagesausflüge

Wer nicht reich genug war, um sich einen eigenen Wagen zu leisten, brauchte deswegen auf Ausflüge nicht zu verzichten: Schon bald gab es Autobusse, mit denen auch die ärmeren Schichten in den Genuss von motorisierten Ausfahrten kamen. Hier brechen Ausflügler in offenen Charabancs vom englischen Seebadeort Scarborough auf, 1912.

Les excursionnistes

Si les aristocrates qui peuvent se le permettre possèdent leur propre voiture pour accomplir leur « Grand Tour » en Europe, les classes laborieuses profitent également de la nouvelle mobilité que leur offre l'automobile – c'est-à-dire essentiellement les autobus, dits encore « char à bancs ». On voit ici des excursionnistes en autocar découvert dans la ville balnéaire anglaise de Scarborough, en 1912.

Making life easier

The taxi-cab provided flexible point-to-point transport for all purposes. A newspaper boy passes a rank of taxis (right) waiting for customers in London's Knightsbridge in March 1907. In August 1910, holidaymakers (below) arrive at Paddington Station, London, for trains to the coast. And at events like the Epsom Derby (above) the taxi could double as private grandstand and bookmaker's stall.

Das Leben wird leichter

Taxis boten flexible Transportmöglichkeiten für jeden erdenklichen Zweck. Ein Zeitungsjunge passiert im Londoner Stadtteil Knightsbridge im März 1907 die Reihe der wartenden Taxis (rechts). Im August 1910 treffen Reisende am Londoner Bahnhof Paddington ein (unten), von wo die Züge an die Küste gehen. Bei Sportereignissen wie dem Derby in Epsom (oben) diente ein Taxi auch schon einmal als private Tribüne oder fahrbarer Buchmacherstand.

Se faciliter la vie

Les services de taxi se sont rapidement développés, comme en témoigne cette file de taxis garés le long de Knightsbridge, à Londres, en mars 1907. Ils permettent de se rendre facilement d'un point à un autre, à l'exemple de ces vacanciers (en bas) d'août 1910 qui débarquent à la gare de Paddington de Londres. Lors de manifestations comme le Derby d'Epsom (en haut), le taxi sert alors à la fois de tribune et d'échoppe de bookmaker.

Flower power

1910 must have been a good summer for flowers. Mrs Aldrich's Chalmers 30 (above), with white roses and elk's head, won a prize at the Grand Lodge Reunion in Detroit; the 'Sunflower' (opposite, below left) bloomed at Philadelphia Gymkhana and Carnival; and in Bournemouth (opposite, above and below right) they celebrated the Centenary Battle of the Flowers – all on wheels.

Flower-Power

Im Sommer 1910 muss es reichlich Blumen gegeben haben. Mrs. Aldrichs Chalmers 30 (oben) mit weißen Rosen und Hirschkopf gewann einen Preis auf der Grand Lodge Reunion in Detroit; die »Sonnenblume« (gegenüber, unten links) blühte auf einer Parade in Philadelphia, und in Bournemouth (gegenüber, oben und unten rechts) fand die Centenary Battle of the Flowers statt – alles auf Rädern.

Pouvoir des fleurs

L'été 1910 est particulièrement fleuri aux États-Unis : la Chalmers 30 de Mrs Aldrich (ci-dessus), couverte de roses blanches et ornée d'une tête de cerf, remporte ainsi un prix à la Grand Lodge Reunion de Detroit tandis qu'une « Sunflower » (ci-contre, en bas à gauche) s'épanouit au Philadelphia Gymkhana and Carnival. À Bournemouth, en Grande-Bretagne (ci-contre, en haut et en bas à droite), quelques automobilistes célèbrent la Centenary Battle of the Flowers.

Size isn't everything

In April 1912 Queen Alexandra gave a miniature Cadillac (above) based on the Model 30 and powered by Cadillac's new Electrical Starter motor, to her nephew, Crown Prince Olaf of Norway. The young King of Siam also had a miniature Cadillac, driven here (right) by the Bennett children in October 1913. The tiny Girling First Aid Motor Fire Engine (below) of 1912 wasn't a miniature toy, however, but a real working vehicle.

Größe ist nicht alles

Im April 1912 schenkte Königin Alexandra ihrem Neffen, Kronprinz Olaf von Norwegen, einen Miniatur-Cadillac (oben); Vorbild war das Model 30, und als Antrieb diente Cadillacs neuartiger elektrischer Anlasser. Auch der junge König von Siam hatte einen Miniatur-Cadillac, hier (rechts) gefahren von den Kindern der Familie Bennett im Oktober 1913. Der winzige Girling-Feuerwehrwagen von 1912 (unten) war hingegen kein Spielzeug, sondern für den Ernstfall gedacht.

La taille n'est pas tout

En avril 1912, la reine Alexandra offrit à son neveu, le prince royal Olaf de Norvège, une Cadillac miniature Model 30 (en haut), mue par le nouveau moteur Electrical Starter de Cadillac. Le jeune roi de Siam possédait également une Cadillac miniature, que les enfants Bennett ont conduite (à droite) en octobre 1913. Contrairement à ce que l'on pourrait penser, la minuscule Girling (en bas) de 1912 n'est pas un jouet mais bien un véritable véhicule de pompiers.

Stranger moments

In the interests of filming, a French actor in 1908 (top left) 'loses' his legs in an automobile accident. Aftermath of a real accident (top right) in Wales in 1909. In 1908 (opposite) a De Dion Bouton is rescued during the Irish Automobile Club's Reliabilty Trials. America's first car, the 1903 Haynes-Apperson, was built in 1894, and here in 1903 (above left) attracts the attention of the law. In 1910 (above right) French motorists in Neuilly ridicule new speed limits.

Kuriositäten am Rande

Für Filmaufnahmen (oben links) »verliert« ein französischer Schauspieler 1908 seine Beine bei einem Autounfall. Der Unfall in Wales (oben rechts) von 1909 ist hingegen echt. Bei der Zuverlässigkeitsfahrt des Irish Automobile Club, 1908, wird ein De Dion-Bouton gerettet (gegenüber). Der Haynes-Apperson (unten links) erregt hier 1903 die Aufmerksamkeit des Gesetzes, und französische Automobilisten (unten rechts) protestieren 1910 in Neuilly gegen neue Geschwindigkeitsbegrenzungen.

Des moments étranges

Si c'est pour un film que ce cascadeur français (en haut à gauche) « perd » en 1908 les jambes dans un accident de voiture, l'accident au Pays de Galles en 1909 est bien réel (en haut à droite). Lors de la course d'endurance organisée en 1908 par l'Irish Automobile Club, cette De Dion-Bouton est sortie de l'ornière (ci-contre). Une Haynes-Apperson de 1903 (ci-dessus, à gauche), est escortée par la police. En 1910 (ci-dessus, à droite), des automobilistes de Neuilly tournent en ridicule les nouvelles règles de limitation de vitesse.

3

Building up the War Machine

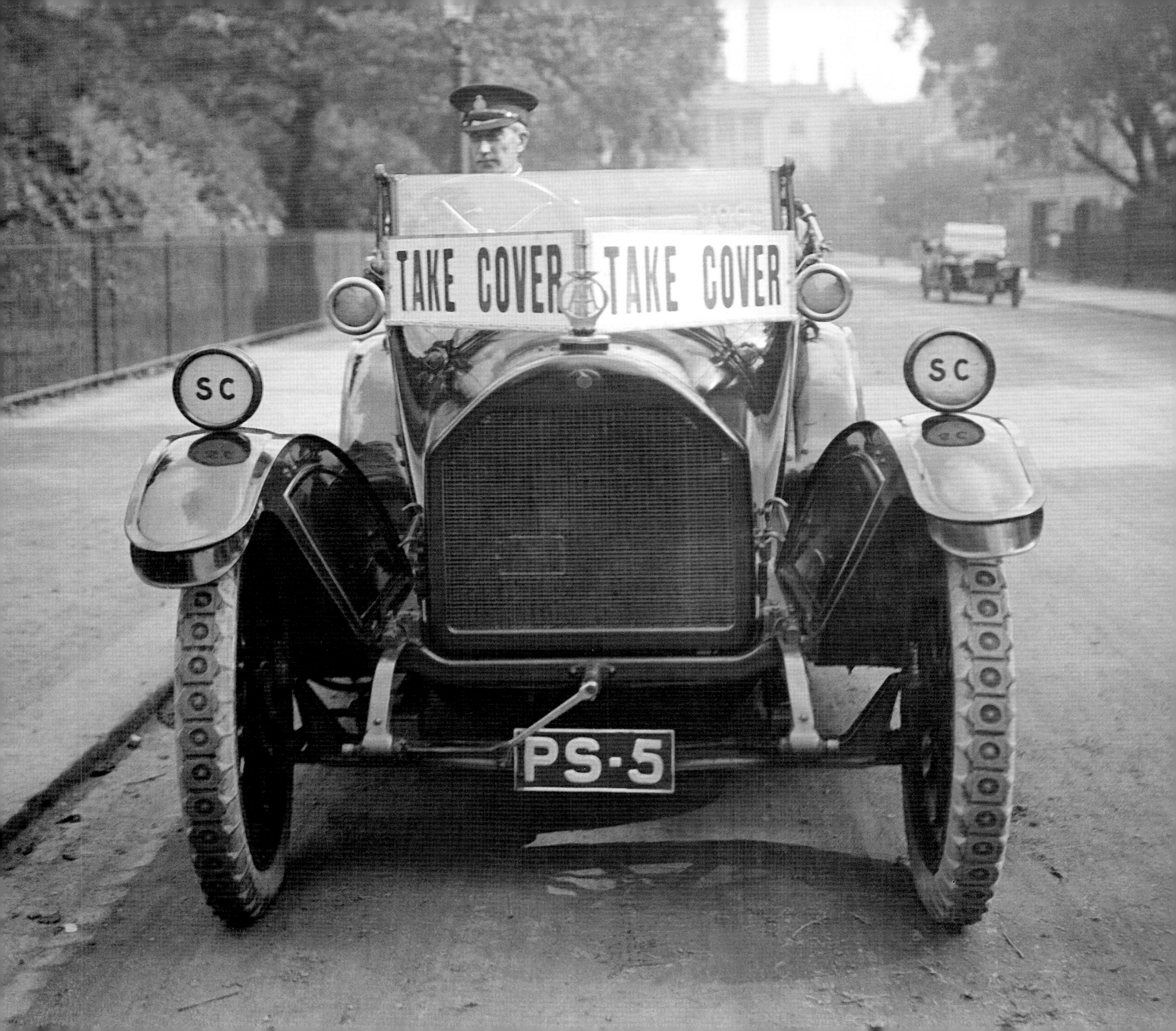
TAKE COVER
TAKE COVER
SC
SC
PS-5

3

Building up the War Machine

Previous page: by October 1917, war had taken to the air as well as to wheels, with regular bombing raids on British cities by Germany's Zeppelin airships. The automobile played its part not only by carrying guns and searchlights but, as here, in more mundane ways too, such as patrolling the streets to give early warning of impending attacks.

Vorherige Seite: Im Oktober 1917 war zum Land- längst der Luftkrieg hinzugekommen, und die deutschen Zeppeline flogen häufige Bombenangriffe auf englische Städte. Automobile taten ihren Dienst nicht nur als fahrbare Plattformen für Geschütze und Suchscheinwerfer, sondern auch vergleichsweise zivil zur Warnung der Bevölkerung, wenn ein Angriff bevorstand.

Page précédente : en octobre 1917, la guerre menace dans les airs comme sur les routes, les villes britanniques étant régulièrement bombardées au cours des raids des Zeppelin allemands. L'automobile est alors utilisée non seulement pour le transport des canons et des projecteurs de défense anti-aérienne mais, comme ici de manière plus pragmatique, pour effectuer des patrouilles dans les rues et prévenir les habitants de l'imminence des attaques.

In November 1916, the British magazine *The Autocar*, the world's first magazine dedicated to 'the interests of the mechanically propelled road carriage', celebrated its 21st anniversary. Its editorial recalled the progress made by 'the movement' to date, by looking at the motor vehicle's (and the motorist's) role in the Great War, which had already been raging in Europe for more than two years.

It summed up the automobile's coming of age in what had become dark times: 'there is no movement or industry of a primarily peaceful nature which has been of greater service to our country in this terrible world war than the automobile movement. The enthusiasm, the interest and the capital which were devoted to it up to the outbreak of war were indeed well spent, as leaving out the invaluable work which is being done by the motor industry in manufacturing motor vehicles of all kinds, shells, guns and all sorts of munitions, we must bear in mind that but for the motor car there would have been no output of British aero engines in this country sufficiently large to help us very much'.

Under the heading 'The Nation's Debt to Automobilism', it went on to promote the cause and to criticise the enemy within: 'The policy of the Government prior to the war had starved the aero engine and aeroplane industry in a notably shortsighted manner. On the other hand, the powerful automobile industry, which had depended on public and not Government patronage, was able to make good the shortsightedness of our rulers, as it is no secret that a very large proportion of the aero engines and aeroplanes which are being used in the war have been built by motor car manufacturers'.

'Then again', *The Autocar*'s 1916 birthday notes continued, 'without these same motor engineers there would have been no engines for the "tanks", no adequate supply of mechanical transport, no gun tractors, no motor ambulances, and no motor bicycles for the despatch riders. In short, despite almost every discouragement from the Government and the magistracy, from the railways and other vested interests, the motor machine in one way and another has done its country splendid service, and we only hope that the authorities who have been compelled to control and so cripple the industry, and who without compulsion tried for some time to cripple private motoring altogether, will bear these things in mind when brighter days dawn'.

In that heartfelt editorial is enshrined the position the motor car movement had reached by the time the war inter-

vened – the continuing resistance of some areas of the establishment, the strength in spite of it of the industry, and its vital new role. It was not a position confined to Britain: the basics were similar almost everywhere.

The mechanisation of war had begun long before the automobile was invented, with siege engines and catapults, traction engines and railway guns. Cugnot's steam-powered 1769 gun carriage, commissioned by the French Minister for War and financed by the state, has already been mentioned. Later steam wagons, too, with their possibilities of heavy transportation and for towing artillery, had been of considerable interest to various armies, so from the day the lighter, more compact petrol-engined motor car was invented its adaptation to military purposes was inevitable.

Its first role in war, long before it became a front-line fighting machine, was in transporting officers behind the lines, later for scouting and communications duties, roles that may look relatively undemanding now but which a century ago were at the outer limits of the motor vehicle's abilities and of the military authorities' envelope of faith. In spite of all the doubts, motor vehicles were used in the Boer War, at the dawn of the century, when officers of the British army in South Africa employed an American-built Locomobile steam car and British-made MMC tricycles from the Motor Manufacturing Company. Modest as their contribution was, the military automobile had arrived.

As in civilian life, and as alluded to by *The Autocar*'s writer, there was resistance to its coming, not surprisingly centred in the still prestigious cavalry regiments and championed by military leaders who, like their civilian counterparts, still believed fervently in the horse as the most versatile and faithful servant of their needs.

To a degree they were right. On the home front the motor car could serve handsomely as a gun or searchlight carrier, a fire tender or ambulance; in the field it was a different story. The horse, initially, would go where a motor vehicle couldn't hope to go, and carry loads the motor vehicle was quite unfitted to carry. Nevertheless, in Germany at the turn of the century the Kaiser had offered a valuable prize for the design of an effective military vehicle, and in Britain the War Office had held motorised transport trials more than ten years before the war began. When it did begin, however, in 1914, the British army still had fewer than a hundred vehicles of its own, and only the ability to call on privately owned commercial vehicles, under a subsidy scheme, allowed them to muster some 1,200 vehicles for the early campaigns of the British Expeditionary Force.

It is true, too, that the early motor car was ill-suited to front-line warfare. It was developing fast, growing more powerful, more complex and more capable, but the ordinary motor car was still fragile and temperamental, still challenged by hills and difficult terrain, by punctures and mechanical break-downs. It needed constant attention and, like the horse, it needed feeding, but its diet was far harder to find in the field than the horse's. Yet these were challenges which had to be overcome, and increasingly horsedrawn and mechanised war-fare would begin to work in parallel.

In the early days, the use of hastily requisitioned transport brought some darkly humorous moments. Trucks went to the front still bearing advertisements for everyday products including Golden Shred marmalade and several brands of tobacco. Double-decker buses carried troops while still bear-ing London street destination boards and the poor camouflage of their bright red colour scheme. Most famously, when Paris was threatened by the advance of the enemy during the Battle of the Marne, hundreds of the city's taxis were commandeered to rush troops to the front – and their drivers paid the full fare, plus a generous tip ...

Few military ventures had such a lighter side. Soon the transport was given armour to resist attacks; inevitably the next move was to give it an armoury. The first armoured cars were exactly that – mobile gun platforms based on large, powerful, fast and robust tourers that took famous names like Rolls-Royce and Mercedes to the front line alongside the more humble Vauxhalls, Renaults and Opels. For all of them, one of the weakest areas was the tyres, which were prone to punc-tures and limited the vehicle's mobility in the worst conditions and toughest terrain. In 1915, Winston Churchill suggested the idea of a heavily armoured, heavily armed vehicle running on caterpillar tracks, which would enable it to cross mud, trenches and barbed wire. In December 1915 the prototype British 'tank' was completed, and by the middle of 1916 tanks were being sent to the Somme in substantial numbers, changing the course of a war which latterly had become bogged down, literally and metaphorically, in the muddy trenches.

Through it all, production of private vehicles in Europe vir-tually stopped, as motor manufacturers turned their attentions to military vehicles, munitions, aero engines, boats and all the

Motor-mounted volunteers of the Ulster Unionist paramilitary force during training in 1914. Their vehicle, almost inevitably, is a Model T Ford.

Freiwillige der paramilitärischen Ulster Unionists bei der Ausbildung, 1914. Das Fahrzeug, auf das ihr Maschinengewehr montiert ist, ist – wie könnte es anders sein – ein Ford Model T.

Les volontaires motorisés de la force paramilitaire des Unionistes de l'Ulster pendant leur entraîne-ment en 1914. Leur véhicule est, bien évidemment, une Ford Model T.

other components of the war machine. America, meanwhile, not coming into the war directly until 1917, continued to build private vehicles more or less through the duration of the war (and also to build the strength of its industry). At the same time, it played a huge role in supplying vehicles and materials to the European Allies, including vast numbers of trucks and the Liberty aero engine. Even pacifist Henry Ford contributed, with the Ford Motor Company building everything from ambulances to aero engines.

And there was another element in all this. *The Autocar* had gone on to point out that not only had the motor industry played its part in supplying the hardware of war but the move-ment had played its part in supplying the people. Practised in civilian life in living with the automobile, they became the ones to maintain, to drive the armoured cars and tanks, to fly the aeroplanes and crew the motor vessels. 'The nation as a whole owes a great debt to automobilism ...', it said, but added a further note of cynicism: 'petrol has become so far a part of the life of the nation that it is difficult to find any branch of either navy or army which does not depend in one way or another upon the services of those who, prior to the war, burnt petrol on the altar of speed, and because of that were hated by all those reactionaries who abominated anything that was newer or faster than they were accustomed to in their own youth. The war has not enlightened all these anti-motorists even now, as we have had many evidences of their prejudice during its progress, and they will be quite as active when it is over'. They were, but by then the industry would be more active and stronger than even its opponents.

Im November 1916 feierte die britische Zeitschrift *The Autocar*, die weltweit erste Publikation, die sich die »Interessen der mechanisch betriebenen pferdelosen Kutsche« auf die Fahnen geschrieben hatte, ihren 21. Geburtstag. Der Leitartikel schrieb von dem Fortschritt, den »die Bewegung« binnen dieser Jahre gemacht hatte, und führte als Beispiel die Rolle an, die Automobile (und Autofahrer) im Weltkrieg spielten, der seit über zwei Jahren in Europa tobte.

Es waren dunkle Zeiten, in denen das Auto ins Erwachsenenalter eintrat. »Keine andere Entwicklung, keine andere Friedensindustrie hat in diesem entsetzlichen Weltkrieg unserem Land einen größeren Dienst erwiesen als die Automobilbewegung. Der Enthusiasmus, das Interesse und das Kapital, die bis Kriegsausbruch in sie investiert wurden, waren wahrlich gut investiert, denn nicht nur die Motorindustrie leistet mit der Fabrikation von Motorfahrzeugen aller Art, von Granaten, Waffen und Munition wertvolle Arbeit in so vielen Bereichen, sondern dazu kommt noch, dass es ohne das Automobil keine britischen Flugzeugmotoren in der Menge gegeben hätte, die wir brauchen, um uns wirklich wirksam verteidigen zu können.«

Unter der Überschrift »Was die Nation dem Automobil verdankt« setzt sich der Artikel vehement für die Sache des Motorfahrzeugs ein und kritisiert die Gegner im eigenen Land. »Die Regierungspolitik der Vorkriegszeit hat in ihrer Kurzsichtigkeit die Entwicklung von Flugzeug- und Flugmotorenindustrie schwer behindert. Doch aus eigener Kraft konnte die Automobilindustrie, die durch private Investitionen gedieh und nicht auf Staatsaufträge angewiesen war, den Mangel an Vorsorge, den unsere Regierung walten ließ, wettmachen – denn es ist kein Geheimnis, dass ein Großteil der Flugmotoren und Flugzeuge im Kriegseinsatz aus Automobilwerken stammt.«

»Und«, fährt der Leitartikel zum 21. Geburtstag des *Autocar* im Jahre 1916 fort, »ohne die Ingenieure dieser Motoren gäbe es auch keinen Antrieb für die Panzer, keine brauchbaren Truppentransporter, keine Traktoren für die Geschütze, keine motorisierten Ambulanzen und keine Motorräder für die Meldefahrer. Kurz, obwohl Regierung und Verwaltung, Eisenbahnen und andere Interessengruppen alles getan haben, seine Ausbreitung zu verhindern, hat der Motorwagen auf die unterschiedlichsten Arten und Weisen seinem Land hervorragende Dienste geleistet, und wir können nur hoffen, dass die Behörden, die bisher angehalten waren, die Industrie zu gängeln und zu behindern, und die für einige Zeit sogar den privaten Motorverkehr ganz unterbinden wollten, dies nicht vergessen werden, wenn wieder glücklichere Tage kommen.«

Dieser flammende Artikel hält fest, welchen Stand die Automobilbewegung erreicht hatte, als der Krieg in die Entwicklung eingriff; er erinnert an den Widerstand, den Teile des Establishments nach wie vor leisteten, aber auch an die Stärke, die trotz allem die Industrie inzwischen erreicht hatte, und an ihre wichtige neue Rolle. Das galt nicht nur für Großbritannien: Die Ausgangslage war in den meisten Ländern ähnlich.

Die Mechanisierung des Krieges hatte schon begonnen, lange bevor das Automobil erfunden war, mit Belagerungsmaschinen und Katapulten, Traktoren und Geschützen auf Eisenbahnwagen. Von Cugnots dampfbetriebener Zugmaschine, 1769 für das französische Kriegsministerium gebaut und von diesem finanziert, war schon die Rede. Auch später interessierten sich die Armeen vieler Länder für die Dampfmaschinen, die schwere Lasten und Geschütze ziehen konnten, und als leichtere, kompaktere Wagen mit Verbrennungsmotor aufkamen, verstand sich ihre Verwendung für militärische Zwecke von selbst.

Die erste Aufgabe der Automobile, lange bevor sie an der Front zum Kampf eingesetzt wurden, war der Transport von Offizieren hinter den Linien; später kamen Aufklärung und Kommunikation hinzu – durchweg Aufgaben, die uns heute einfach scheinen, die jedoch vor einem Jahrhundert die Motorfahrzeuge an die Grenzen ihrer Möglichkeiten brachten, ebenso wie das Vertrauen der Militärs in ihre Gebrauchstüchtigkeit. Trotz aller Zweifel zogen zu Anfang des Jahrhunderts Automobile in den Burenkrieg: Die britischen Offiziere in Südafrika hatten einen amerikanischen Locomobile-Dampfwagen und Dreiräder der britischen Motor Manufacturing Company zur Verfügung. Der Beitrag dieser Militärfahrzeuge war bescheiden, doch mit ihnen begann die Zeit des motorisierten Kriegs.

Wie im zivilen Leben und wie vom Leitartikler des *Autocar* angedeutet, regte sich Widerstand gegen die Neuerung, vor allem – verständlicherweise – in den damals noch sehr angesehenen Kavallerieregimentern, angeführt von hohen Militärs, die genau wie viele zivile Würdenträger felsenfest davon überzeugt waren, dass das Pferd der vielseitigste und verlässlichste Diener für ihre Zwecke war.

Bis zu einem gewissen Grade hatten sie damit auch Recht. An der Heimatfront konnte das Auto als Unterbau für Geschütze oder Suchscheinwerfer, als Ambulanz oder Feuerwehr zeigen, was es konnte; doch auf dem Felde sah es anders aus. Ein Pferd kam durch Gelände, bei dem zumindest in den ersten Jahren ein Motorfahrzeug keine Chance hatte, und es konnte weitaus schwerere Lasten tragen als ein Automobil. Trotzdem hatte in

The automobile was a tool of social and political uprising as well as war. In December 1918 a Red Flag is carried through the streets during the revolution in Berlin.

Nicht nur im Krieg, auch bei sozialen und politischen Umwälzungen war das Automobil dabei. Während der Novemberrevolution von 1918 trägt dieser Wagen die rote Fahne durch die Straßen von Berlin.

L'automobile était un moyen de manifestation sociale et politique mais aussi guerrier. Le drapeau rouge parcourt ainsi les rues de Berlin pendant les révoltes de décembre 1918.

Deutschland der Kaiser schon zur Jahrhundertwende einen stattlichen Preis für den Entwurf eines brauchbaren Militärfahrzeugs ausgesetzt, und in Großbritannien hatte das Kriegsministerium schon zehn Jahre vor Kriegsbeginn Versuchsfahrten mit Motorwagen unternommen. Doch als der Krieg dann 1914 ausbrach, hatte das britische Militär nicht einmal hundert Fahrzeuge zur Verfügung, und nur ein Gesetz, das die Requisition privater Lastkraftwagen gegen Entschädigung erlaubte, sorgte dafür, dass das britische Expeditionskorps zu seinen frühen Feldzügen mit immerhin 1200 Fahrzeugen ausrücken konnte.

In der Tat, die frühen Automobile waren nur schlecht für den Einsatz an der Front geeignet. Zwar ging die Entwicklung mit Riesenschritten voran, die Konstruktionen wurden ausgereifter, die Wagen kräftiger und fahrtüchtiger, aber es waren noch immer zerbrechliche, unzuverlässige Gefährte, die vor hohen Steigungen und schwierigem Gelände, bei Reifenpannen und mechanischen Schäden rasch kapitulieren mussten. Die Wagen brauchten ständige Wartung, und wie ein Pferd mussten sie gefüttert werden, nur dass ihre Nahrung auf einem Feldzug weniger leicht zu finden war als die der Pferde. Doch das waren Herausforderungen, die sich meistern ließen, und in immer größerem Maße standen Pferd und Motorfahrzeug im Kriegseinsatz Seite an Seite.

In den frühen Kriegstagen sorgten die in aller Eile beschafften Transportmittel oft für unerwarteten Humor. Lastwagen fuhren mit ihrer Werbung für alltägliche Produkte, darunter »Golden Shred«-Marmelade und mehrere Tabakmarken. Doppeldeckerbusse transportierten Truppen noch mit den Tafeln ihrer Londoner Zielorte angesteckt, und die leuchtendrote Farbe war auch nicht die beste Tarnung. Die berühmteste Episode dieser Art kam, als während der Marneschlacht der Feind auf Paris marschierte und Soldaten mit Hunderten von Pariser Taxis an die Front chauffiert wurden – die Fahrer bekamen die Fahrten zum vollen Tarif bezahlt, und ein großzügiges Trinkgeld dazu ...

Doch nur wenige militärische Einsätze hatten eine solche komische Seite. Schon bald waren die Mannschaftswagen gepanzert, und von da war es nur noch ein kleiner Schritt zur eigenen Bewaffnung. Die ersten Panzerwagen waren nichts anderes als mobile Geschützstellungen auf großen, kräftigen, schnellen und robusten Tourenwagen, und so kamen illustre Namen wie Rolls-Royce und Mercedes zusammen mit ihren bescheideneren Vettern von Vauxhall, Renault oder Opel an die Front. Alle hatten einen wunden Punkt gemeinsam, und das waren die Reifen, die leicht beschädigt wurden und gerade in schwierigem Terrain die Möglichkeiten der Wagen sehr

einschränkten. 1915 regte Winston Churchill an, ein schwer gepanzertes und schwer bewaffnetes Fahrzeug auf Raupenketten zu bauen, das auch Schlamm, Gräben und Stacheldraht nicht aufhalten könnte. Im Dezember 1915 war der erste britische »tank« fertig gestellt, und im Sommer 1916 kamen Panzer schon in größeren Mengen an die Somme und brachten Bewegung in den Krieg, der in den schlammigen Schützengräben im wahrsten Sinne des Wortes stecken geblieben war.

Während all dieser Zeit kam die Produktion von Automobilen für den privaten Markt in Europa fast ganz zum Erliegen, denn die Hersteller hatten mit Militärfahrzeugen, Munition, Flugzeugmotoren, Booten und all den anderen Materialien, die sie für die Kriegsmaschinerie lieferten, alle Hände voll zu tun. Amerika hingegen, das erst 1917 direkt in den Krieg eingriff, erhielt die Zivilproduktion fast uneingeschränkt aufrecht, und stärkte entsprechend die dortige Industrie. Doch leisteten die Vereinigten Staaten mit der Lieferung von Fahrzeugen und Kriegsmaterial, darunter Lastwagen in großer Zahl und Liberty-Flugzeugmotoren, einen unschätzbaren Beitrag zur Unterstützung der europäischen Alliierten. Auch der Pazifist Henry Ford half mit, und die Ford Motor Company baute Kriegsmaterial vom Krankenwagen bis zum Flugzeugmotor.

Und noch etwas kam hinzu. *The Autocar* wies in jenem Artikel auch darauf hin, dass die Automobilindustrie für den Krieg nicht nur Maschinen lieferte, sondern auch für Fachkräfte gesorgt hatte, die diese Maschinen bedienen konnten. Nur wer im Zivilleben den Umgang mit Automobilen erlernt hatte, konnte sie im Krieg warten, konnte die Panzer und Panzerwagen fahren, die Flugzeuge fliegen und die Motorschiffe bedienen. »Das ganze Land hat der Automobilbewegung viel zu verdanken«, fuhr die Zeitschrift fort, doch fügte sie mit einer gewissen Verbitterung hinzu: »Das Leben der Nation ist inzwischen so sehr vom Benzin durchdrungen, dass man kaum noch einen Zweig von Armee oder Marine findet, der nicht auf die eine oder andere Weise auf die Dienste derer angewiesen ist, die vor dem Krieg das Benzin auf dem Altar der Geschwindigkeit opferten und sich damit den Hass all jener Reaktionäre zuzogen, die alles verabscheuten, was neuer oder schneller war als das, was die sie in ihrer Jugend gekannt hatten. Nicht einmal der Krieg hat bisher all diese Autogegner zur Einsicht gebracht; ihre Vorurteile haben wir in dessen Verlauf oft genug zu spüren bekommen, und sie werden auch nicht schweigen, wenn er vorüber ist.« Das sollte sich bewahrheiten, doch inzwischen war die Industrie längst stärker und aktiver geworden als selbst ihre stärksten Gegner.

The prelude to the shot which rang around the world. Archduke Franz Ferdinand of Austria and his wife drove into Sarajevo on 28 June 1914, shortly before the assassination by Serb nationalist Gavrilo Princip.

Das Vorspiel zum Schuss, der um die Welt ging. Erzherzog Franz Ferdinand und seine Gemahlin treffen am 28. Juni 1914 in Sarajevo ein, kurz vor ihrer Erschießung durch den serbischen Nationalisten Gavrilo Princip.

Prélude au coup de revolver qui ébranlera le monde. Accompagné de son épouse, l'archiduc François Ferdinand d'Autriche entre dans Sarajevo le 28 juin 1914, peu avant d'être assassiné par le nationaliste serbe Gavrilo Princip.

En novembre 1916, l'éditorialiste de la revue britannique *The Autocar*, premier magazine au monde consacré « aux intérêts des véhicules terrestres à propulsion mécanique », profite du 21ᵉ anniversaire de sa fondation pour résumer les progrès réalisés jusqu'alors par « le mouvement » et souligner le rôle du véhicule automobile (et de l'automobiliste) dans la Grande Guerre, qui fait rage en Europe depuis plus de deux ans.

Évoquant l'entrée en majorité de l'automobile en cette période sombre, le journaliste explique : « Il n'y a aucune activité ni aucune industrie de nature aussi fondamentalement pacifique à avoir rendu autant de services importants à notre pays dans cette terrible guerre mondiale que le mouvement automobile. L'enthousiasme, l'intérêt et les capitaux qui lui ont été consacrés jusqu'au déclenchement de la guerre ont en effet été bien employés. Si l'on excepte l'œuvre inappréciable accomplie par l'industrie dans la construction de véhicules automobiles de tous genres, la fabrication de canons, d'obus et de toutes sortes de munitions, nous devons garder présent à l'esprit que la production d'aéromoteurs britanniques dans ce pays n'aurait pas été suffisante pour nous être d'une aide quelconque. »

Sous le titre « La dette de la Nation envers l'Automobile », l'article se poursuit en plaidant la cause de l'automobile et en critiquant l'ennemi de l'intérieur : « La politique gouvernementale, menée sans grande prévoyance avant-guerre, a épuisé l'industrie des aéromoteurs et des aéroplanes. La puissante industrie automobile, qui dépendait de l'appui du public et non du gouvernement, a su en revanche compenser la myopie de nos dirigeants car ce n'est un secret pour personne qu'une très grande proportion des aéromoteurs et des aéroplanes utilisés pendant la guerre ont été fabriqués par des constructeurs d'automobiles. »

The Autocar de 1916 poursuit : « Sans ces ingénieurs, il n'y aurait pas eu de moteurs pour les engins blindés, pas de transports mécanisés, pas de tracteurs pour tirer les canons, pas d'ambulances motorisées et pas de motocyclettes pour les estafettes. Bref, malgré la quasi désapprobation du gouvernement et de la magistrature, des compagnies et autres investisseurs du chemin de fer, l'engin mécanisé a rendu, d'une manière comme d'une autre, un magnifique service au pays. Nous voulons espérer que les autorités qui, en imposant ces contrôles, ont paralysé l'industrie et, sans obligation aucune, tentèrent un moment de freiner entièrement l'automobile de tourisme, garderont ces choses à l'esprit lorsque viendront des jours meilleurs. »

Ce vibrant éditorial ne fait qu'exprimer la situation de l'automobile lors de la déclaration de guerre : la résistance de certains membres de l'establishment à laquelle s'oppose la puissance de l'industrie automobile et son nouveau rôle essentiel. Cette situation n'est pas particulière à la Grande-Bretagne et se retrouve, dans les grandes lignes, presque partout ailleurs.

Cela fait bien longtemps, avant l'invention de l'automobile que la guerre est mécanisée et utilise des machines de siège et des catapultes, des engins de traction ou des canons sur rail ; on a déjà également mentionné le fardier à vapeur de Cugnot, commandé vers 1769 par le ministre français de la Guerre et financé par l'État. Plusieurs armées se sont aussi rendues compte du formidable intérêt que représentaient les machines à vapeur, capables de transporter de lourdes charges et de déplacer l'artillerie ; aussi était-il inévitable que le moteur à essence, plus léger et plus compact, ait été adapté à son tour à des fins militaires.

Le principal rôle attribué aux véhicules automobiles pendant la guerre, bien avant qu'ils ne participent aux combats en première ligne, fut de transporter les officiers de l'arrière, de servir aux déplacements des patrouilles de reconnaissance et d'assurer les liaisons ; ces missions étaient, il y a près d'un siècle, l'extrême limite de ce que pouvait exécuter un véhicule à moteur – et de la confiance que plaçaient en lui les autorités militaires. Des véhicules automobiles – une locomobile à vapeur, construite aux États-Unis, et des tricycles britanniques MMC (Motor Manufacturing Company) – furent employés au début du siècle pendant la guerre des Boer par l'armée britannique en Afrique du Sud. L'automobile militaire faisait ses premières armes, pour modeste qu'ait été sa contribution.

Comme l'indique le journaliste de *The Autocar*, l'introduction de l'automobile dans l'armée britannique rencontre également une forte résistance dans certains milieux militaires, qui se concentre notamment dans les prestigieux régiments de cavalerie et qu'appuient des chefs militaires qui, à l'instar des dirigeants de la société civile, croient encore avec ferveur en l'avenir du cheval pour satisfaire leurs besoins de la manière la plus polyvalente et la plus fidèle.

Ils n'avaient pas tout à fait tort. En effet, alors que l'automobile tient parfaitement son rôle en dehors du champ de bataille, servant sans problème de véhicule d'incendie et d'ambulance, voire au transport d'un canon ou d'un projecteur anti-aérien, il en est tout autrement au front. Le cheval peut en revanche aller là où un véhicule à moteur ne peut espérer passer et transporter des charges pour lesquelles celui-ci n'est pas adapté. Malgré tout,

Military motoring in World War I saw these Belgian troops using a Mors command car and a heavily armoured 1911 Rolls-Royce Silver Ghost, here in 1917.

Zur automobilen Ausstattung des Ersten Weltkriegs gehörten ein Mors-Kommandowagen der belgischen Truppen und ein schwer gepanzerter Rolls-Royce Silver Ghost von 1911, hier aufgenommen im Jahr 1917.

En 1917, ces troupes belges disposent d'un « command car » Mors et d'une Rolls Royce Silver Ghost blindée de 1911.

l'empereur d'Allemagne a offert dès le début du siècle une forte récompense à celui qui concevait un véhicule militaire efficace et le War Office britannique subventionne des essais de transport motorisé. En 1914, l'armée britannique dispose tout de même de moins d'une centaine de véhicules auxquels s'ajoutent les véhicules de commerce privés qu'elle peut réquisitionner (sous réserve d'accorder des indemnités à leurs propriétaires) ; en réalité, elle parvient à peine à rassembler près de 1 200 véhicules pour les premières campagnes de sa Force expéditionnaire.

Il est vrai que ces premiers véhicules ne sont pas guère adaptés aux conditions que l'on rencontre sur le front. Si l'automobile se développe rapidement, avec des modèles plus puissants, plus complexes et plus utilisables, la voiture ordinaire reste fragile et capricieuse, a du mal à franchir les côtes et à circuler en terrain difficile, connaît des crevaisons et des casses mécaniques fréquentes, et nécessite une attention et un entretien constants ; de plus, s'il est facile de nourrir un cheval, il devient plus compliqué d'assurer le ravitaillement en carburant d'une automobile en plein champ de bataille. Toutes ces difficultés peuvent être surmontées, les partisans de la mécanique et les adeptes du cheval allaient enfin travailler ensemble.

Aux premiers jours de la guerre, l'envoi sur le front de véhicules de transport réquisitionnés à la hâte eut des conséquences assez drôles : sur les routes, des camions défilent portant encore sur les flancs des réclames pour la confiture ou des marques de tabac ; les autobus londoniens à impériale affectés au transport des troupes malgré leur couleur rouge vif continuent d'indiquer leur terminus de destination. Plus célèbres furent les taxis parisiens auxquels il fut ordonné d'amener les troupes sur le front lorsque Paris était menacé par l'avance ennemie lors de la première Bataille de la Marne – les chauffeurs reçurent le prix de la course plus un généreux pourboire ... Peu d'expéditions militaires eurent un côté aussi léger !

Les véhicules sont bientôt équipés d'un blindage pour résister aux attaques puis, tout naturellement, armés. Les premiers blindés ne sont en réalité que des plates-formes de canon mobiles installées sur de grosses et puissantes berlines, rapides et solides, qui portent des noms aussi célèbres que Rolls-Royce et Mercedes ou de plus humbles comme Vauxhall, Renault et Opel. Le point faible de tous ces véhicules demeure les pneumatiques, sujets aux crevaisons et dont la fragilité restreint la mobilité du véhicule en terrain difficile. En 1915, Winston Churchill avance l'idée de construire un véhicule lourdement blindé et armé roulant sur des chenilles afin qu'il puisse passer dans la boue et franchir tranchées et réseaux de barbelés. Le prototype du « tank » britannique est achevé en décembre 1915 et un grand nombre d'exemplaires sont expédiés sur le front de la Somme dès le milieu de l'année 1916, où ils permettent de modifier le cours d'une guerre qui s'enlise ensuite, au propre comme au figuré, dans des tranchées boueuses.

Pendant ce temps, la production de voitures particulières est pratiquement interrompue en Europe puisque les constructeurs de moteurs s'occupent alors de fabriquer des véhicules militaires, des munitions, des aéroplanes et des moteurs d'avion, des navires et bien d'autres types d'engins de guerre. Les États-Unis, qui n'entrent pas directement dans le conflit avant 1917, continuent cependant de construire des automobiles tout en renforçant la puissance de leur industrie et de fournir aux Alliés du matériel et des véhicules, dont un grand nombre de camions et d'aéromoteurs Liberty. Même le pacifiste Henry Ford contribue, avec la Ford Motor Company, à l'effort de guerre en produisant tout ce qu'il peut, des ambulances aux aéromoteurs.

À tout cela s'ajoute un autre élément qu'analyse l'éditorial de *The Autocar :* non seulement l'industrie automobile a joué un rôle essentiel en fournissant le matériel de guerre mais aussi le personnel spécialisé. Ayant connu l'automobile dans la vie civile, les automobilistes sont chargés d'entretenir et de conduire les véhicules blindés et les tanks, de piloter les aéroplanes et de manœuvrer les navires à moteur. « L'ensemble de la nation a une grande dette envers l'automobiliste ... » admet l'éditorialiste en ajoutant un peu cyniquement : « Le pétrole fait désormais partie à un tel point de la vie de la nation qu'il est difficile de trouver un secteur de la marine ou de l'armée de terre qui ne dépende pas d'une manière ou d'une autre des services que peuvent leur apporter ceux qui, avant la guerre, brûlaient ce même pétrole sur l'autel de la vitesse et qui, à cause de cela, furent détestés par les réactionnaires qui abominaient tout ce qui était plus moderne ou plus rapide que ce qu'ils connaissaient depuis leur jeunesse. La guerre n'a cependant pas ouvert les yeux à tous ces ennemis de l'automobile. Nous avons encore aujourd'hui de nombreuses preuves de leurs préjugés – qui resteront au moins aussi actifs lorsque ce sera fini. » Si ce fut effectivement le cas, l'industrie automobile saura se montrer alors plus entreprenante et plus forte que ses adversaires.

Gathering clouds

Although the British army had tried motorised transport in a very limited way in the Boer War, and had held motor trials at the beginning of the century, the army establishment was still very much in favour of the horse; the motor industry would have to prove its own case. In February 1913 SF Edge's Napier Company and others presented a parade of vehicles adapted for military use, including searchlight carriers, fire pumps and field kitchens, at the Guildhall, London.

Silberstreif am Horizont

Die britische Armee hatte zwar einige erste Versuche zur Motorisierung schon im Burenkrieg unternommen und sich zu Anfang des Jahrhunderts Fahrzeuge vorführen lassen, doch die Offiziere bevorzugten eindeutig nach wie vor das Pferd; die Motorindustrie musste schon selbst zeigen, was sie konnte. Im Februar 1913 präsentierte S. F. Edges Napier Company zusammen mit weiteren Herstellern vor der Londoner Guildhall diese Parade von für den Militäreinsatz präparierten Fahrzeugen, darunter ein fahrbarer Suchscheinwerfer, eine Feuerwehr und eine Feldküche.

Les nuages s'amoncellent

Malgré les essais, très limités, de transports motorisés effectués par l'armée britannique pendant la guerre des Boers, et d'autres tentatives au début du siècle, l'état-major reste partisan du cheval et contraint l'industrie automobile à faire ses preuves. C'est pourquoi la Napier Company de S. F. Edge (et d'autres) organisent au Guildhall de Londres, en février 1913, un défilé de véhicules adaptés à l'usage militaire, parmi lesquels des porte-projecteurs anti-aériens, des citernes mobiles et des cantines roulantes.

American manoeuvres

Although World War I began in Europe with doubts about motorising the military, America was more open-minded. In about 1915, Captain Jenkins at the wheel of his Acme car (left and above right) with Major Brush, Captain Beekman and Lieutenants Veenvliet and Wilson, inspected the 71st New York Regiment, during exercises at Creedmoor, Long Island. Around the same time, General Woods carried foreign military attachés in his White steam car (below right) to observe manoeuvres. Before switching production to petrol cars in 1911, White had been one of America's greatest steam car exponents.

Amerikanische Manöver

In Europa war die Motorisierung des Militärs zu Anfang des Ersten Weltkriegs noch umstritten, doch die Amerikaner zeigten sich aufgeschlossener. Um 1915 inspiziert Captain Jenkins am Steuer seines Acme (links und oben rechts) zusammen mit Major Brush, Captain Beekman und den Lieutenants Veenvliet und Wilson das 71. New Yorker Regiment beim Manöver in Creedmoor, Long Island. Etwa zur gleichen Zeit chauffierte General Woods im White-Dampfwagen (unten rechts) ausländische Militärattachés zur Beobachtung eines Manövers. White war einer der größten Vorkämpfer des Dampfantriebs in den Vereinigten Staaten gewesen, doch 1911 gingen auch sie zum Verbrennungsmotor über.

Manœuvres américaines

Alors que l'Europe émet encore des doutes quant à l'intérêt d'une armée motorisée, les États-Unis se montrent plus ouverts. En août 1915, c'est au volant de son Acme (à gauche et en haut à droite) que le capitaine Jenkins, accompagné du major Brush, du capitaine Beekman et des lieutenants Veenvliet et Wilson, passe l'inspection du 71st New York Regiment pendant des exercices à Creedmoor (Long Island). Vers la même époque, le général Woods emmène quelques attachés militaires étrangers dans une White à vapeur (en bas à droite). La firme White fut l'un des plus grands constructeurs de voitures à vapeur avant de passer en 1911 à la production de voitures à essence.

Armoured cars

In the early days of mechanised warfare, armoured cars were more or less exactly just that – heavy cars carrying their own design of armour. The Belgian Minerva (above), built on a 38hp chassis before the factory in Antwerp was captured in October 1914, and the convoy of French troops in armoured cars (right), both show how wheels and tyres remained vulnerable.

Panzerwagen

In den Anfangstagen der motorisierten Kriegsführung war die Bezeichnung wörtlich zu verstehen – Panzerwagen waren schwere Limousinen, die mit einer zusätzlichen Panzerung versehen waren. Der belgische Minerva (oben), der auf einem 38-PS-Chassis gebaut wurde, bis die Fabrik in Antwerpen im Oktober 1914 in Feindeshand fiel, und der Konvoi von französischen Panzerwagen (rechts) zeigen, dass Räder und Reifen verwundbare Punkte blieben.

Voitures blindées

Aux débuts de la guerre mécanisée, les voitures blindées n'étaient rien de plus que des véhicules lourds équipés d'une carrosserie blindée. Cette Minerva belge (ci-dessus) a été construite sur le châssis de la 58 ch avant que les Allemands n'occupent l'usine d'Anvers en octobre 1914. Le manque de protection des roues et des pneumatiques des camions blindés, comme ceux de ce convoi français (à droite), les rend encore très vulnérables.

Supplying the front

Far more than its involvement in the actual fighting,
motor transport became important for its role in
carrying personnel and supplies. The German soldiers
with their gasmasks (left) were en route to the Western
Front around 1916, in what appears to be a tourer made
by Brennabor, which immediately before the war was
Germany's second largest manufacturer, after Opel. On
another front, the French Berliet trucks (right) were
part of a French military convoy in June 1915.

Nachschub für die Front

Eine wichtigere Rolle als im Gefechtseinsatz spielten
die Motorfahrzeuge hinter den Linien als Transportmittel
für Truppen und Nachschub. Die deutschen Soldaten
mit ihren Gasmasken (links) sind um 1916 unterwegs
zur Westfront; der Tourenwagen scheint ein Brennabor
zu sein, vor dem Krieg in Deutschland der zweitgrößte
Hersteller nach Opel. Im Juni 1915 rollt der französische
Konvoi mit Berliet-Lastwagen (rechts) an die Front.

L'approvisionnement du front

À défaut d'être impliqués véritablement dans les combats,
les véhicules automobiles jouent un rôle de plus en
plus important dans le transport du personnel et du
ravitaillement. Vers 1916, ces soldats allemands avec leurs
masques à gaz (à gauche) sont en route pour le Front
Ouest dans ce qui semble être une Brennabor, le deuxième
plus grand constructeur, en Allemagne d'avant-guerre
après Opel. En juin 1915, un convoi militaire français
composé de camions Berliet (à droite) fait une halte avant
de gagner le front.

... and keep the meter running!

Having belatedly accepted the need for motor vehicles, the authorities responded by requisitioning private ones for all purposes. The most famous were the 'Taxis of the Marne', including this 1910 Charron (left), nicknamed 'Eloise' and with graffiti intact. The Paris taxis were commandeered to rush reinforcements to the Battle of the Marne – and the drivers received the full fare on their meters, plus a 27 per cent tip. In August 1914 private vehicles had also been commandeered in Paris (above), and some British army transport at La Ferté-sous-Jouarre (below) was still in civilian livery.

... aber die Uhr läuft!

Da die Militärs nicht rechtzeitig Vorsorge getroffen hatten, mussten für alle erdenklichen Zwecke Privatwagen requiriert werden. Die berühmtesten waren die »Taxis von der Marne«, darunter der Charron von 1910 (links) mit Spitznamen »Eloise« und noch mit originalen Graffiti versehen. Die Pariser Taxis wurden beschlagnahmt, um in aller Eile Verstärkung an die Marnefront zu bringen – die Fahrer erhielten den vollen Fahrpreis, den der Taxameter anzeigte, und 27 Prozent Trinkgeld dazu. Schon im August 1914 waren in Paris Privatwagen eingefordert worden (oben), und mancher britische Truppentransporter, wie der in La-Ferté-sous-Jouarre aufgenommene (unten), trug noch seine zivile Beschriftung.

... et laissez tourner le compteur !

Ayant finalement reconnu l'utilité des véhicules à moteur, les autorités s'empressent de réquisitionner des automobiles privées pour remplir tous types de missions. L'épisode le plus célèbre est évidemment celui des « Taxis de la Marne », parmi lesquels figurait ce Charron de 1910 (à gauche), surnommé Eloïse ; plusieurs centaines de taxis parisiens furent ainsi retenus pour transporter les troupes de renfort lors de la première bataille de la Marne – les chauffeurs reçurent le prix indiqué au compteur plus 27% de pourboire. En août 1914, nombre de véhicules privés sont réquisitionnés à Paris (en haut) tandis qu'on peut rencontrer à La Ferté-sous-Jouarre (en bas) des véhicules de transport britanniques restés en livrée civile.

Home fronts

Around Europe, individuals and organisations provided
motorised support for the official services on the
home fronts. In January 1916 members of the Southend
Motor Volunteers drive Red Cross ambulances, led by
a transport officer in a Lorraine-Dietrich of around 1912,
with sporty wheel discs and the fuel filler cap prominent
on the scuttle. De Dietrich had started car production
in France before the turn of the century and Lorraine-
Dietrich was created in 1904 – the company also being
an important supplier of light trucks and aero engines
during the war.

An der Heimatfront

Überall in Europa sorgten Privatleute und Organisationen
für die motorisierte Unterstützung der Heimatfront ihres
Landes. Hier sitzen im Januar 1916 Vertreter der Southend Motor Volunteers am Steuer von Rotkreuzwagen,
angeführt von einem Transportoffizier in einem Lorraine-
Dietrich von etwa 1912 mit seinen sportlichen Rad-
abdeckungen und dem auffälligen Tankverschluss oben
auf der Motorhaube. De Dietrich hatte in Frankreich die
Autoproduktion schon vor der Jahrhundertwende aufgenommen, und die Firma Lorraine-Dietrich, im Krieg
auch ein wichtiger Hersteller von leichten Lastwagen
und Flugzeugmotoren, entstand 1904.

À l'intérieur

Dans toute l'Europe, des particuliers et des organisations
ont assuré la logistique en fournissant des véhicules aux
services officiels. En janvier 1916, les ambulances de la
Croix-Rouge, conduites par des membres du Southend
Motor Volunteers, sont précédées par un officier du train
installé à bord d'une Lorraine-Dietrich de 1912 environ,
reconnaissable à ses roues lenticulaires de sport et son
bouchon de réservoir d'essence au-dessus du radiateur.
Si les premières voitures françaises De Dietrich datent du
tournant du siècle, la firme Lorraine-Dietrich, créée
fin 1904, fut un important fournisseur de camions légers
et de moteurs d'avion pendant la guerre.

Helping the war effort

In October 1916 Mr Weeke's 40/50hp Rolls-Royce Silver Ghost (above) was decorated with slogans promoting 'Our Day', and was helping to collect funds to help soldiers at the front, through the Red Cross. In January 1917, support for the 34th Essex Voluntary Aid Detachment's Red Cross ambulance, which appears to be built on a 20hp Vauxhall chassis (right), included boy scouts as well as volunteer nurses.

Alle helfen mit

Im Oktober 1916 hat Mr. Weeke seinen 40/50-PS-Rolls-Royce Silver Ghost (oben) mit Slogans dekoriert, dass »unser Tag« gekommen ist, und sammelt Geld für das Rote Kreuz zur Versorgung der Soldaten an der Front. Im Januar 1917 stellen neben freiwilligen Krankenschwestern auch Pfadfinder die Besatzung dieses Rotkreuzwagens des 34. Essex Voluntary Aid Detachment, der offenbar auf einem 20-PS-Vauxhall-Chassis gebaut ist (rechts).

L'aide à l'effort de guerre

En octobre 1916, c'est à bord de sa Rolls-Royce Silver Ghost 40/50 ch que Mr Weeke participe à la collecte des fonds destinés à aider les soldats du front qu'organise la Croix-Rouge (ci-dessus). En janvier 1917, l'équipe de l'ambulance de la Croix-Rouge du 34th Essex Voluntary Aid Detachment, apparemment construite sur la base d'un châssis Vauxhall 20 ch (à droite), comprend des boys scout et des infirmières volontaires.

Real horsepower prevails

As here for German troops in Finland, more often than not there were no roads on the battlefield. In the mud and general confusion there were many occasions when the horse could go to areas where the motor vehicle could not, where the horse could overcome conditions which would see motor transport quickly and uselessly bogged down, and where the horse's demand for fuel of its own did not outweigh its usefulness.

Vorrang für echte Pferdestärken

In der Regel führten, wie hier bei deutschen Truppen in Finnland zu sehen, keine Straßen auf die Schlachtfelder. Im Schlamm und der allgemeinen Orientierungslosigkeit drangen Pferde oft noch weiter vor, wenn die Automobile längst hoffnungslos festsaßen, und auch das Verhältnis von Nahrungsaufwand zu Gebrauchswert war bei den Pferden anfangs deutlich besser.

Rien ne vaut les chevaux

Il n'existe bien souvent pas de routes desservant les champs de bataille, comme ici en Finlande pour les troupes allemandes. Il est alors fréquent que, dans la boue et la confusion générale, seuls les chevaux puissent alors passer à des endroits où les transports motorisés se seraient immobilisés.

Grim reality

A British armoured car crippled by enemy gunfire late in the war (above), one of its crew dead alongside it, and its Vickers Maxim machine guns disabled with their cartridge belts torn away. Civilians, too, were inevitable victims. Refugees on the trailers of motor lorries (right) pass Italian troops on horse transport at the Isonzo front, north eastern Italy, October 1916.

Die trostlose Realität

Ein britischer Panzerwagen gegen Ende des Krieges, durch feindlichen Beschuss kampfunfähig gemacht (oben); ein Besatzungsmitglied liegt tot daneben, und aus den Vickers-Maxim-Maschinengewehren sind die Patronengurte gerissen. Auch Zivilisten wurden immer wieder Opfer des Krieges. Flüchtlinge auf Lastwagen und Anhängern passieren an der nordostitalienischen Isonzofront im Oktober 1916 eine italienische Nachschubkolonne mit Pferdewagen (rechts).

Une réalité grinçante

Cet engin blindé britannique, immobilisé sous le feu ennemi, ses mitrailleuses Vickers Maxim désormais inutilisables, le cadavre d'un membre de l'équipage gisant à côté (ci-dessus), témoignent des durs combats de la fin de la guerre. Les civils, inévitables victimes regroupées en convoi sur des remorques de camions (à droite), passent devant les troupes italiennes à cheval près du front d'Isonzo, au nord-est de l'Italie, en octobre 1916.

Maintaining standards
While conditions on the battlefields of 1916 (left) could be as grim and bare as the moon, there were certain standards to be observed, too – as with these French soldiers in July 1916 (above) washing a car used by the headquarters staff in a stream swollen by rainwater, of which there was often more than enough.

Ordnung muss sein
Die Kampffelder konnten 1916 (links) kahl und unwirtlich wie eine Mondlandschaft sein, doch trotzdem wurde die Form gewahrt – etwa bei den französischen Soldaten (oben), die im Juli 1916 einen Wagen des Offiziersstabs mit Wasser aus einem über die Ufer getretenen Bach waschen; Regenwasser gab es oft mehr als genug.

Conserver la discipline
Malgré les conditions difficiles et l'aspect désolé du champ de bataille en 1916 (à gauche), la discipline conserve tous ses droits et ses devoirs pour ces soldats français, photographiés en juillet (ci-dessus) en train de laver la voiture des officiers du quartier général avec l'eau du ruisseau qui a débordé.

The help of famous men

Henry Ford was a pacifist but his company contributed hugely to the Allied cause with the supply of equipment and vehicles, especially the ubiquitous Model T, in large numbers at this US supply station (left) in 1917. In 1915 Ford sent a 'peace ship', the *Oscar II*, to Europe to try to halt the war; in the same year, Sir Thomas Lipton's yacht *Erin* (above) was serving as a Red Cross hospital ship.

Die Hilfe berühmter Männer

Henry Ford war Pazifist, doch seine Werke belieferten die Alliierten mit Kriegsmaterial und Fahrzeugen in gewaltigen Mengen, vor allem dem allgegenwärtigen Model T, hier (links) auf einer amerikanischen Nachschubbasis im Jahr 1917. 1915 schickte Ford ein »Friedensschiff«, die *Oscar II*, nach Europa, um dem Krieg Einhalt zu gebieten; im selben Jahr stellte Sir Thomas Lipton seine Jacht *Erin* (oben) als Hospitalschiff dem Roten Kreuz zur Verfügung.

Le soutien des hommes célèbres

Bien qu'Henry Ford soit un pacifiste, son entreprise contribue beaucoup à la cause alliée en fournissant équipement et véhicules, notamment un grand nombre de Model T, regroupés en 1917 dans ce dépôt de ravitaillement américain (à gauche). En 1915, Ford avait déjà expédié un « navire de paix », l'*Oscar II*, en Europe pour essayer d'enrayer la guerre tandis que, la même année, sir Thomas Lipton prête à la Croix-Rouge son yacht l'*Erin* (ci-dessus) pour servir de navire-hôpital.

4

Post-War Optimism: A Time to Grow

The 1920s was a decade of optimism and a jolly kind of social revolution against the old, deeply conservative, class-ridden establishment, but tempered by the losses of the previous decade and by difficulties still to come. For the motor car it was a time to grow. World War I, for all its human tragedy, had been a proving ground for great advances in the design of the automobile, and beyond that it was the catalyst for an entirely new generation of motorists. Men and women who had had their first experience of the motor car while in uniform now naturally aspired to its freedom in civilian life.

Economies had been stretched to the limit by the four-year conflict, but at the end of it, heading for the Roaring Twenties, the strongest manufacturers had become stronger than ever, technically and financially, and the industry was taking a new, more coherent shape. By 1920 half the cars in the world were Model T Fords, but there were still literally hundreds of smaller manufacturers – the ones who, before the war, had aspired to breaking into the commercial mainstream but who for the most part had come and gone with frightening speed and regularity. Now, the would-be manufacturers still came and went, but the ones who survived were likely soon to find themselves absorbed into much larger empires, as the era of the big corporations started in earnest.

As the 1920s began, Henry Ford bought out all the other stockholders in the Ford Motor Company for $100 million, to give himself complete control. In 1922 he took over the Lincoln Company, strengthening his ability to compete with the growing General Motors Corporation, which had been formed in 1908, merged with Chevrolet in 1917, and was reorganised into a much more efficient edifice in 1920. And in 1924, engineer Walter P Chrysler launched his first car, sowing the seeds for what, alongside Ford and General Motors, became the third of America's Big Three car makers, growing ominously when Chrysler took over Dodge in 1928, at a cost of $175 million.

General Motors carried its expansion into Europe, taking over Vauxhall Motors in 1925, followed by Opel of Germany in 1929, and during 1927 Chevrolet had overtaken Ford as the biggest seller in the American market, as the Model T finally went out of production, making way for the new generation Model A. In Europe, Ford-style mass production was spreading to other manufacturers. In France, André Citroën took over the old Mors factory in 1919 and began building his first car, the Citroën Model A, which became one of the biggest-selling

European cars of the era. In 1922 Sir Herbert Austin's British rival for the Model T, the tiny Austin Seven, arrived. This was the year in which Ford themselves built more than a million Ts, on the way to a peak production in 1923 of more than two million of the industry's most famous car to date.

Ford's old adage for the Model T, 'you can have any colour you like so long as it's black', was based on a real situation: in 1924 DuPont introduced quick drying enamel paints, but in the early days the only quick drying colour, and therefore the only one able to keep pace with Henry's production processes, had been black …

At times, world economic outlooks were also black. The 1920s started with a slump in America which destroyed the car market and many smaller companies with it. In the mid-1920s there would be serious economic depression in Europe, with the same effect as in America. Yet for every company that disappeared, it seemed another sprang up. In Britain the first MG and the first Triumph were both built in 1923; and the decade in America, beyond the coming of Chrysler, saw the births of Duesenberg in 1920, Checker Cab in 1921, Pontiac in 1926, and Chrysler twins Plymouth and De Soto in 1928. The mergers and takeovers continued in Europe, too. Sunbeam, Talbot and Darracq got together in 1920; Daimler and Benz became Daimler-Benz in 1926; William Morris took over the ailing Wolseley Company in 1927; and the Rootes brothers swallowed Humber and Hillman in 1928 as a prelude to what became the Rootes Group.

The war had seen big advances in technology, especially (thanks largely to aero-engine development) engine technology and metallurgy, benefiting even the most ordinary makes. Cars were recognisably more modern, with all steel bodies becoming the norm after Dodge introduced them in 1917, and closed cars eventually becoming more common than open ones. Through the 1920s the developments continued, some of them about improved engineering, many of them reflecting higher expectations of comfort and convenience. 1920 brought the first hydraulic brakes, developed by Lockheed in America and fitted by newcomer Duesenberg; 1921 saw twin overhead camshafts from Ballot in France and supercharging for a production car from Mercedes in Germany; factory-fitted radios began to appear on various American makes in 1922; Chrysler adopted Firestone's more comfortable 'Balloon' tyres in 1924; Pierce-Arrow pioneered vacuum-assisted brakes in 1926, while Cadillac and La Salle offered syncromesh gearboxes in 1929, all of which made the motorist's life that bit more pleasant.

surtout lorsque la carrosserie en acier, introduite par Dodge en 1917, devient la norme – et les voitures fermées deviennent progressivement plus nombreuses que les voitures ouvertes. Les perfectionnements techniques qui sont apportées à l'automobile au cours des années 1920 concernent la mécanique mais portent surtout sur l'amélioration du confort et de l'utilisation de la voiture. C'est en 1920 qu'apparaît le premier système de freins hydrauliques, développé par Lockheed aux États-Unis et aussi adoptés par la nouvelle firme Duesenberg ; en 1921, le français Ballot invente le double arbre à cames en tête tandis que Mercedes installe un compresseur sur les moteurs de ses voitures de production ; en 1922, la radio est montée en série sur plusieurs modèles américains ; en 1924, Chrysler équipe ses voitures de pneus « ballon », plus confortables, fabriqués par Firestone ; en 1926, Pierce-Arrow inaugure un système de freinage avec servo à dépression tandis que Cadillac et La Salle installent une boîte de vitesses synchronisées sur leurs modèles en 1929. Tout est fait en réalité pour rendre plus agréable la vie de l'automobiliste.

Les sports mécaniques continuent évidemment de jouer un rôle important dans le développement des nouvelles technologies et leur mise au point. Aux États-Unis, où la guerre n'a pas interrompu la compétition, les courses se déroulent essentiellement sur des pistes ovales en terre et des circuits à plancher de bois et virages relevés, particulièrement rapides et dangereux. Si, au début des années 1920, la vitesse moyenne approche les 190 km/h sur ce dernier type de circuit, ce n'est qu'en 1925 (avec la victoire de Pete de Paolo sur Duesenberg dans la classique course du Memorial Day) que seront dépassés les 160 km/h de moyenne aux 500 Miles d'Indianapolis, la course la plus célèbre des États-Unis.

Le grand circuit relevé de Brooklands en Grande-Bretagne, équivalent au plus ancien d'Indianapolis, profite de cet âge d'or de la compétition. Les courses s'y déroulent presque toujours au milieu d'une foule immense qui, comme réunie à l'occasion d'une gigantesque garden-party, en profite pour s'adonner aux joies de la convivialité et de l'automobile. Outre la compétition, Brooklands sert également de circuit d'essais pour les constructeurs et de haut-lieu de rendez-vous pour tous les briseurs de records. C'est là que Kennelm Lee Guinness établit à 215,2 km/h avec une Sunbeam le dernier record de vitesse en circuit fermé. En effet, les mesures seront ensuite effectuées en ligne droite, et de préférence sur de vastes plages de sable. Les principaux circuits de l'époque sont Montlhéry en France, Pendine au Pays de Galles, Southport en Angleterre et la légendaire plage de Daytona Beach en Floride.

Au début des années 1920, le record de vitesse est toujours celui de 1914, c'est-à-dire 199,68 km/h, obtenu à Brooklands par L. G. Hornsted sur Benz ; d'autres pilotes sont toutefois déjà allés plus vite, mais sans que leur record soit enregistré officiellement, comme l'Américain Tommy Milton, qui atteint 251,05 km/h à Daytona Beach à bord d'une Duesenberg. Cette course au record, qui se prolonge dans les années 1920 et 1930, connaît alors son heure de gloire : les vitesses atteintes par les machines, des monstres de technologie presque tous propulsées par des moteurs d'avion, emportent l'imagination du public et la moindre tentative d'un pilote bénéficie d'une extraordinaire publicité.

L'époque se découvre de nouveaux héros, plus pacifiques que ceux de la Grande Guerre, comme le célèbre trio britannique que forment le « Welsh Wizard » (le sorcier gallois) Parry Thomas, les légendaires pilotes de course sir Henry Segrave et Malcolm Campbell (qui sera également fait chevalier en 1931 par le roi George V). À eux seuls ces trois pilotes – Thomas et sa Leyland-Thomas « Babs » qu'il a lui-même conçue, Segrave et ses Sunbeam, et enfin Campbell sur Sunbeam puis sur ses Napier-Campbell « Bluebird » (du nom d'une pièce de théâtre de Maeterlinck) – battent neuf fois successivement le record de vitesse entre 1924 à 1929, leur écrasante domination n'étant remise en cause que par l'Américain Ray Keech qui, à bord de la redoutable White-Triplex Special, équipée de trois moteurs d'avion Liberty, atteint les 333,95 km/h à Daytona Beach en 1928.

Thomas paiera le prix de ses folles tentatives sur le circuit de Pendine en mars 1926, après avoir relevé le record du circuit à 275,17 km/h. Segrave sera le premier à franchir la barrière des 200 mph (321,8 km/h) en atteignant 327,9 km/h à Daytona en 1927 avec sa Sunbeam « 1000 ch », et c'est encore lui qui, après une lutte acharnée contre Campbell et Keech, sera finalement le plus rapide des trois en portant en 1929 le record de vitesse à 372,39 km/h avec son Irving-Napier.

Toute cette période des années 1920 est marquée à un tel point par l'esprit de Brooklands, cette quête absolue du danger et des plaisirs de la vitesse, de piloter aussi bien sur des circuits à piste de bois que dans les grandes courses que sont les Grands Prix, le Mans ou la Targa-Florio, qu'on pourrait presque oublier le formidable essor de l'industrie automobile et la popularité croissante de la voiture. En fait, pour l'Automobile aussi ce furent des Années Folles !

Cities on the move

In the 1920s, as the world recovered from the war, the motor car became firmly established everywhere. In 1922, outside the Bank of England in London (right) you have to look hard to find horses among the Daimlers, Rolls-Royces and motor omnibuses. By 1929, even Bombay (above) had many cars among the horses.

In die Städte kommt Bewegung

Je mehr die Welt sich in den zwanziger Jahren vom Krieg erholte, desto selbstverständlicher wurden Automobile im Straßenbild. Bei der Aufnahme, die 1922 vor der Bank of England entstand (rechts), muss man schon genau hinsehen, um noch die Pferde zwischen den Daimler- und Rolls-Royce-Wagen und den Motoromnibussen zu erkennen. 1929 gab es sogar in Bombay (oben) neben den Pferdefuhrwerken schon viele Autos.

Les villes en mouvement

L'automobile commence à envahir le monde dans les années 1920. En 1922, il faut bien chercher pour distinguer encore quelques chevaux au milieu des Daimler, des Rolls-Royce et des omnibus qui circulent à Londres devant la Banque d'Angleterre (à droite). En 1929, même à Bombay (ci-dessus), les voitures sont déjà presque plus nombreuses que les attelages.

Worlds apart

In America and Europe the automobile had different faces.
Both these pictures are from 1925: in America the Dodge tourer
(above) at a meeting of the National Manufacturers Association
in California, is a workhorse, loaded with produce; in England
the Morris tourer (right) is following a meet of the West Kent
Hounds, its occupants greeted by a hunt official.

Dazwischen liegen Welten

Autofahren in Europa und in Amerika waren zwei grundverschie-
dene Dinge. Beide Bilder entstanden 1925: Der amerikanische
offene Dodge (oben), aufgenommen in Kalifornien bei einer
Versammlung der National Manufacturers Association, ist ein
Arbeitspferd, mit landwirtschaftlichen Produkten beladen; in
England hingegen folgt der offene Morris (rechts) einer Fuchs-
jagd der West Kent Hounds, und ein Jagdgehilfe begrüßt die
Insassen.

Un monde à part

Comme le révèlent ces deux photographies, prises en 1925,
l'automobile prend des visages différents en Amérique et en
Europe. Aux États-Unis, lors d'un meeting de la National
Manufacturers Association en Californie, cette torpédo Dodge
(ci-dessus) est un outil de travail, bon à tout faire ; en Angleterre, en revanche, cette Morris (à droite) sert les aristocrates
qui suivent une meute de la West Kent Hounds, salués par
une chasseresse.

Mass production, individual style

The starting-point of low cost mass manufacture is thousands of identical steel body pressings (above), the key to production speed was the moving assembly line, like the ones these Model A Fords (below) passed along in 1928. But there was always room for added style, as in the interior of the Standard Swallow (right), or SS, forerunner of the Jaguar marque.

Massenproduktion und Exklusivität

Das Ausgangsmaterial für eine preisgünstige Massenproduktion sind Tausende von identischen Karosserieteilen aus Pressstahl (oben), und der Schlüssel zur hohen Geschwindigkeit der Produktion war das Fließband, wie hier bei den A-Modellen von Ford im Jahr 1928 (unten). Aber daneben ließen sich auch Stilwünsche einbringen, etwa beim Interieur des Standard-Swallow (rechts), einer Vorläufermarke des Jaguar.

Production en série personnalisée

Si ces milliers de morceaux de carrosserie emboutis (en haut) sont le point de départ d'une production en série à faible coût de revient, la clé de la vitesse de fabrication est la chaîne d'assemblage mobile, comme celle de ces Ford Model A (en bas) en 1928. Il reste toutefois possible de personnaliser sa voiture, notamment pour l'intérieur de cette S.S. (à droite), c'est-à-dire une Standard à carrosserie Swallow, précurseur de la marque Jaguar.

Something for the ladies

Summer dresses and parasols for lady racegoers with an AC sporting tourer (above) at Brooklands for the sunny Whitsuntide meeting in June 1922. A gloomier day for the ladies in London (right) being handed a ticket by the traffic policeman. Their car is an MG M-Type, first of the famous Midgets, launched in 1928.

Etwas für die Damen

Sommerkleider und Sonnenschirm für die Damen, die mit einem AC-Sportviersitzer (oben) im Juni 1922 zum sonnigen Pfingsttreffen nach Brooklands gekommen sind. Eher finster ist den beiden zumute, denen ein Londoner Polizist eben einen Strafzettel verpasst (rechts). Sie sitzen in einem MG M-Type, dem Ersten der berühmten Midgets, 1928 auf den Markt gekommen.

Une voiture pour les dames

Vêtements d'été et parasols pour ces turfistes venus à Brooklands dans leur torpédo de sport AC (ci-dessus) pour assister au meeting de Whitsuntide en juin 1922. La journée s'annonce plus mal pour ces deux femmes (à droite), auxquelles un policier londonien dresse une contravention. Leur voiture est une MG Midget Type M, la première de cette célèbre série lancée en 1928.

Life, death and the automobile

The dark side of the spread of motoring was the
destruction it sometimes wrought. The safety warnings
in St Louis in 1923 (above left) and on a snowy city street
in 1925 (below left) underline the dangers. This Los
Angeles garage owner (above right) created a 'barometer'
to show the price of his gasoline. During Prohibition
(below right) the automobile became a way to run
illegal alcohol past the law, and in this case to campaign
against the law.

Leben und Sterben mit dem Automobil

Die Schattenseite der Autokultur waren die oft schweren
Unfälle. Die Warnschilder in St. Louis, 1923 (oben links),
und auf einer verschneiten Stadtstraße im Jahr 1925
(unten links) ermahnen zum vorsichtigen Fahren. Ein
Tankstellenbesitzer in Los Angeles (oben rechts)
präsentiert ein »Barometer«, auf dem er den Benzinpreis
anzeigt. Während der Prohibitionszeit (unten rechts)
waren Automobile nicht nur Mittel, um Alkohol
zu schmuggeln, sondern auch gute Träger für Protest-
slogans gegen die Gesetze.

La vie, la mort et l'automobile

L'expansion de l'automobile a aussi son côté noir.
Ces panneaux à St Louis en 1923 (en haut à gauche) et,
en 1925, dans cette rue enneigée (en bas à gauche)
soulignent déjà les dangers de la vitesse. Le propriétaire
de ce garage de Los Angeles (en haut à droite) a conçu
un « baromètre » des prix de l'essence. Pendant la
période de la prohibition (en bas à droite), que combat
cette conductrice, l'automobile est devenue un moyen
efficace de transport illégal de l'alcool.

Quite an impact
Today, crash testing is a precise science which every manufacturer has to submit to in order to comply with stringent international regulations. In 1928 when this American inventor demonstrated a new 'anti-shock' bumper, it was rather more informal – and dangerous.

Ein schwerer Schlag
Heute sind Crashtests eine exakte Wissenschaft, und jeder Hersteller muss internationale Bestimmungen erfüllen. 1928, als dieser amerikanische Erfinder seine neuartigen »absorbierenden« Stoßstangen vorführte, war der Test noch improvisiert – und gefährlich.

Un choc
Les « crash test » répondent aujourd'hui à des normes précises que tout fabricant doit satisfaire afin que ses voitures soient en conformité avec les règlements internationaux. En 1928, lorsque cet inventeur américain fait la démonstration de son nouveau pare-chocs, l'opération est moins officielle et beaucoup plus dangereuse.

From floor to ceiling – and roof
New and used cars, including several B14 type saloons, stacked from floor to ceiling (left) in a multi-level Citroën showroom in the late 1920s. At the Fiat factory Lingotto in Turin, completed in 1923 and seen here in 1929, the rooftop (right) included a test track, with banked curves at each end, where chassis were tested. The rooftop track was later made famous in the cult film *The Italian Job*, and the building is now a Fiat museum.

Vom Boden bis zur Decke – und auf dem Dach
Neu- und Gebrauchtwagen, darunter eine Reihe von B14-Limousinen, stehen im großen Schauraum eines Citroën-Händlers der späten zwanziger Jahre mehrere Etagen hoch. In der Turiner Fiat-Fabrik Lingotto, fertig gestellt 1923 und hier (rechts) in einer Aufnahme von 1929 zu sehen, befand sich auf dem Dach eine Teststrecke mit Hochkurven an beiden Enden, wo die Chassis einer Probefahrt unterzogen wurden. Später wurde die Rennstrecke auf dem Dach durch den Kultfilm *Charlie staubt Millionen ab* berühmt; heute ist das Gebäude ein Fiat-Museum.

Du sol au plafond – et au toit !
La salle d'exposition à plusieurs niveaux de Citroën, à la fin des années 1920, propose de nombreuses voitures neuves et d'occasion, dont plusieurs berlines B14, empilées du sol au plafond (à gauche). La toiture de l'usine Lingotto de Fiat, à Turin, achevée en 1923 et que l'on voit ici (à droite) photographiée en 1929, servait aussi de piste d'essais, avec des virages relevés à chaque extrémité, pour tester les châssis des voitures en fabrication. Cette piste fut rendue célèbre par le film *L'Or se barre*. L'ensemble du bâtiment abrite aujourd'hui le musée Fiat.

Social climbing

A Riley Redwing sports car, named for its polished aluminium body and red-painted wings, tackles Beggar's Roost hill (above) during the annual London–Land's End Trial in around 1925. Not going quite so well, PC Wheeler's Alfa Romeo (right), around the same year, requires some assistance to get to the top of Crowell during the Inter-Varsity Trials.

Alle wollen nach oben

Ein Riley-Redwing-Sportwagen (der seinen Namen, »Rotdrossel« nach den roten Kotflügeln zum Aufbau aus gebürstetem Aluminium trug) versucht sich während der jährlichen Zuverlässigkeitsfahrt London–Land's End am Beggar's Roost Hill, um 1925 (oben). P. C. Wheelers Alfa Romeo (rechts), etwa im selben Jahr während der Inter-Varsity Trials beim Aufstieg auf den Crowell aufgenommen, braucht hingegen ein wenig Nachhilfe.

Une ascension sociale

Vers 1925, la Riley Redwing, une voiture de sport qui doit son nom à sa carrosserie en aluminium poli et à ses ailes rouges, s'attaque à la colline de Beggar's Roost (ci-dessus) lors de la compétition annuelle London–Land's End. Un peu moins performante, l'Alfa Romeo de P. C. Wheeler (à droite), vers la même année, a besoin d'aide pour atteindre le sommet du Crowell lors des Inter-Varsity Trials.

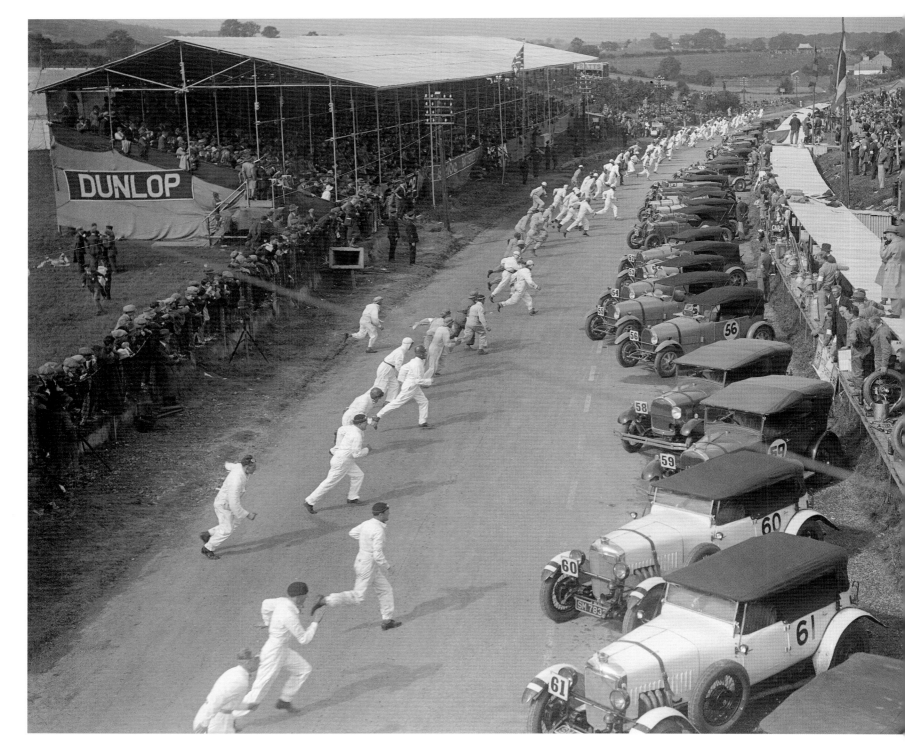

Speed kings

The start of the 1929 Tourist Trophy (left) on the Ards circuit, near Belfast, considered to be the greatest TT of them all. From the front, the cars include two super-charged Arrol-Asters, two Fords and four Bugattis. The race was won by Rudi Caracciola in the supercharged 7.1-litre Mercedes-Benz. The huge, aero-engined 1,000hp Sunbeam (above) with which, in 1927, Major Henry Segrave took the land speed record past 200mph, is wheeled out in February 1926. Segrave's great record-breaking rival, with his Bluebirds, was (Sir) Malcolm Campbell, seen (below) in his garage with a Bugatti Type 35 in 1928.

Im Rausch der Geschwindigkeit

Der Start zur 1929er Tourist Trophy auf dem Ards-Rundkurs bei Belfast (links), die vielen als größte unter allen TT-Veranstaltungen gilt. Zu den Wagen zählen, von vorn, zwei Arrol-Aster mit Kompressor, zwei Fords und vier Bugattis. Sieger wurde Rudi Caracciola auf dem Mercedes-Benz-7,1-Liter-Kompressorwagen. Der gewaltige, von einem 1000-PS-Flugzeugmotor angetriebene Sunbeam (oben), mit dem Major Henry Segrave 1927 erstmals einen Land-Geschwindigkeitsrekord von über 200 Meilen pro Stunde fuhr, wird im Februar 1926 aus den Werkshallen gerollt. Segraves größter Rivale beim Wettstreit um den Weltrekord war (Sir) Malcolm Campbell mit seinen Bluebirds; hier (unten) sehen wir ihn 1928 in seiner Garage mit einem Bugatti Typ 35.

Les rois de la vitesse

Le Tourist Trophy, qui se déroule ici à gauche sur le circuit de Ards, près de Belfast, est considéré comme la plus grande compétition de voitures de tourisme. Au moment de ce départ, en 1929, on reconnaît successive-ment deux Arrol-Aster à moteur à compresseur, deux Ford et deux Bugatti. La course fut remportée par Rudi Caracciola sur une Mercedes Benz à moteur de 7,1 l à compresseur. C'est avec cette grande Sunbeam bimoteur, développant 1000 ch (en haut), photographiée ici en février 1926, que le major Henry Segrave remportera le record de vitesse à Daytona avec 326 km/h. Le grand rival de Segrave était sir Malcolm Campbell, que l'on voit ici dans son garage en 1928 (en bas) près d'une Bugatti Type 35.

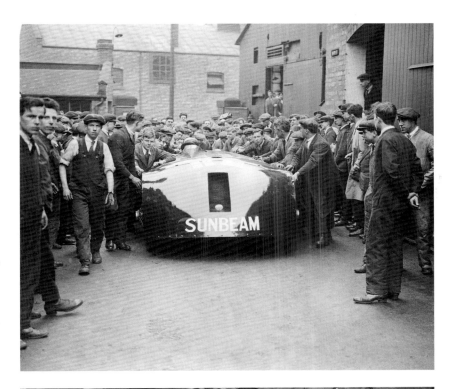

Track ...

Fashionably dressed for the conditions in leather boots, leather coat, fur collars, fur-lined helmets and flying goggles for April showers at Brooklands in 1920 – the year racing restarted after the interruption of the war. This first meeting was postponed because of the weather, but many stayed to socialise.

Auf dem Rennplatz ...

Modische Kleidung, passend zum Wetter, mit Lederstiefeln, Ledermantel, Pelzkragen, Pelzmütze und Pilotenbrille für die Aprilschauer in Brooklands, 1920 – das Jahr, in dem nach der kriegsbedingten Unterbrechung der Rennbetrieb wieder aufgenommen wurde. Dieser erste Lauf wurde wegen schlechten Wetters verschoben, doch viele Zuschauer blieben der Gesellschaft wegen.

Sur la piste ...

Ces deux jeunes femmes, vêtues de cuir pour la circonstance – bottes, veste à col de fourrure, d'un casque fourré avec lunettes d'aviateur – viennent assister à la reprise des courses automobiles à Brooklands, interrompues après la guerre. Cette première réunion, qui eut lieu en avril 1920, fut toutefois ajournée en raison des conditions météorologiques. Toutefois, beaucoup de spectateurs restèrent en quête de divertissement.

... and field

Lighter clothes for the summer sunshine in the mid-1920s for two girls near Newbury, looking for a picnic spot for their friends in the Buick. Especially after it had adopted this Packard-like radiator shape in 1925, the Buick was the 'middle-class' mainstay of the General Motors empire in America, and for some years Buicks were built in Britain as well as in the USA and Canada.

... und im Grünen

Leichter gekleidet sind die beiden jungen Frauen, die Mitte der zwanziger Jahre bei sommerlichem Sonnenschein in Newbury nach einem Picknickplatz für sich und ihre Freunde im Buick suchen. In Amerika war Buick, besonders nach Einführung des dem Packard nachempfundenen neuen Kühlergrills im Jahr 1925, die General-Motors-Marke für die Mittelschicht, und einige Jahre lang wurden die Wagen nicht nur in den USA und Kanada, sondern auch in Großbritannien gebaut.

... et aux champs

Promenade estivale près de Newbury, au milieu des années 1920, soit à pied, soit en berline Buick. C'est après avoir adopté en 1925 cette forme de radiateur de type Packard que Buick devint le pilier des classes moyennes de l'empire General Motors aux États-Unis. Les modèles de cette marque furent réalisés pendant quelques années, aux États-Unis et au Canada mais aussi en Grande-Bretagne.

Vanishing marques

Between the wars the motor industry saw amalgamation and the growth of the fittest, and the demise of many once-famous names. From the 22nd Annual International Automobile Show at London's Olympia in 1928, Fiat and Rover are survivors; but most of the rest, from Clyno to Sunbeam, are long gone.

Marken verschwinden

Die Zeit zwischen den Kriegen war gezeichnet von Fusionen und Firmenübernahmen; die gesunden Firmen wuchsen, doch viele einst berühmte Namen verschwanden. Fiat und Rover sind zwei Überlebende der 22. Internationalen Automobilausstellung im Londoner Olympia, 1928, doch die meisten anderen, von Clyno bis Sunbeam, gibt es schon lange nicht mehr.

Des marques disparues

Entre les deux guerres, l'industrie automobile connaît des regroupements et la montée en puissance des firmes sachant le mieux s'adapter au marché, mais aussi la disparition de certaines des marques jusqu'alors parmi les plus célèbres. Du 22ᵉ Annual International Automobile Show de 1928, à l'Olympia de Londres, il ne reste plus aujourd'hui que Fiat et Rover et la plupart des autres – de Clyno à Sunbeam – ont depuis longtemps disparu.

The heart of the matter

Looking at engines, from the handsome overhead-valve six-cylinder (left) of the 3-litre 21hp Lanchester, launched in 1925, to the Wolseley-based overhead-camshaft 847cc four-cylinder (right) of the Morris Minor, unveiled in 1928. The engine doctor with the stethoscope (above) is examining the rugged four-cylinder side-valve engine of a Model T, which was about to reach the end of its long life in 1927.

Hand aufs Herz

Das Herzstück eines jeden Autos, vom stattlichen kopf-gesteuerten Sechszylinder (links) des 3-Liter-21-PS-Lanchester von 1925 bis zum 1928 vorgestellten 847-ccm-Vierzylinder mit oben liegender Nockenwelle des Morris Minor (rechts), ursprünglich eine Wolseley-Konstruktion. Der Motordoktor mit dem Stethoskop (oben) untersucht den unverwüstlichen seitengesteuerten Vierzylinder des Model T, das 1927 ans Ende seiner langen Produktions-zeit gekommen war.

Le cœur des choses

Certaines femmes apprécient aussi les moteurs : qu'il s'agisse du magnifique Lanchester six cylindres à soupape en tête, développant 21 ch pour 3 l de cylindrée, (à gauche), lancé en 1925, ou du quatre cylindres 847 cm³ à arbre à cames en tête sur base Wolseley (à droite) de la Morris Minor, dévoilé en 1928. Ce médecin mécanicien examine au stéthoscope (ci-dessus) le grossier moteur quatre cylindres à soupapes latérales d'une Ford Model T, dont la longue carrière allait s'achever en 1927.

SWIFT →

LUCAS

THIS IS BRITISH

S M

The Power Unit
of the
Morris Minor

Helping hands

Mister High Test (promoting Pratt's
Motor Spirit) on his way to the 1929
Olympia Motor Show in an Austin
Seven tourer (above), gives assistance to a very young road-user on
a tricycle. The Seven, introduced
in 1922, was a success around the
world. In 1926, with public transport
stopped by the General Strike, London
motorists (right) give lifts to others,
but face the queues.

Solidarität im Straßenverkehr

»Mister Hight Test« (der für Pratt's
Motor Spirit warb), 1929 im offenen
Austin Seven auf dem Weg zum
Autosalon im Londoner Olympia,
greift einem sehr jungen Verkehrs-
teilnehmer auf dem Dreirad unter
die Arme (oben). Der 1922 vorgestellte
Seven war rund um den Erdball
erfolgreich. Beim Generalstreik von
1926 streikten auch die Londoner
Verkehrsbetriebe; Autofahrer (rechts)
nahmen andere mit, mussten aber
den Stau in Kauf nehmen.

Une main secourable

« Mister High Test » (qui fait la
réclame pour le Motor Spirit de Pratt)
se rend à Londres pour l'Olympia
Motor Show de 1929 dans une berline
Austin Seven (ci-dessus), une voiture parue en 1922 qui rencontra un
grand succès dans le monde entier.
La Grève générale de 1926 les ayant
privé de transports publics, les
automobilistes londoniens (à droite)
inaugurent le covoiturage mais
doivent subir les embouteillages de
la capitale britannique.

All part of the service

Britain's Automobile Association was founded in 1905 to help the motorist, here with 'mechanical rescue' patrols (top right), or lifts (above left) during a city transport strike. In 1927 you could have your Austin washed (top left) at a new service station, and in 1929 your Morris (opposite) filled by a uniformed attendant. The traffic cop in Florida in 1929 (above right) is helping motorists observe a 35mph limit.

Stets zu Diensten

Die britische Automobile Association wurde 1905 als Hilfsorganisation gegründet; sie baute die Motorrad-Pannenhilfe auf (oben rechts) und organisierte einen Fahrdienst (unten links), wenn die Verkehrsbetriebe streikten. 1927 konnte man seinen Austin in einer neuen Service-Station waschen lassen (oben links), 1929 den Tank seines Morris vom Tankwart füllen lassen (gegenüber). Der Verkehrspolizist in Florida (unten rechts), 1929, hilft den Autofahrern, sich an das Tempolimit von 35 Meilen zu halten.

Le service avant tout

L'Automobile Association de Grande-Bretagne fut fondée en 1905 pour aider les automobilistes en difficulté grâce à des patrouilles de « secours mécanique » (en haut à droite) ou lors d'une grève des transports (ci-dessus, à gauche). À partir de 1927, vous pouvez faire laver votre Austin dans les nouvelles stations-service (en haut à gauche) et, en 1929, le garagiste porte un uniforme (ci-contre). Une police de la route en Floride incite les automobilistes à respecter la limite de vitesse de 56 km/h (ci-dessus, à droite).

Style, power and practicality

Elegance, in LA Murdoch's coachbuilt Rolls-Royce Phantom (above) at Le Touquet, 1927; power, in FW von Meinster's Maybach (opposite, above), the first in America, in 1924, and at the time said to be the world's most powerful automobile; sporting genes in the MG Magna (opposite, below left), cousin to the sporty Midgets; and family motoring on a budget in a very early example of the Austin Seven (opposite, below right), launched in 1922 at a cost of £165, with a top speed of 40mph.

Stil, Kraft und praktischer Nutzen

L. A. Murdochs von einem Karossier eingekleideter Rolls-Royce Phantom, 1927 in Le Touquet aufgenommen (oben), ist schiere Eleganz; F. W. von Meinsters Maybach (gegenüber oben), im Jahr 1924 der Erste, der nach Amerika kam, steht für Kraft – er galt seinerzeit als leistungsstärkstes Automobil der Welt; der MG Magna (gegenüber, unten links), ein Vetter der flotten Midgets, steht für Sportlichkeit; und der Austin Seven, hier ein frühes Exemplar (gegenüber, unten rechts) war der Inbegriff des Familienautos für wenig Geld – als er 1922 auf den Markt kam, kostete er £ 165 und war immerhin 65 km/h schnell.

Style, puissance et sens pratique

Élégance pour la Rolls-Royce Phantom carrossée en coupé de ville de L. A. Murdoch (ci-dessus), au Touquet en 1927 ; puissance pour la Maybach de F. W. von Meinster (ci-contre, en haut), la première voiture de ce type aux États-Unis en 1924 et, à l'époque, l'automobile prétendument la plus puissante du monde ; une allure élancée pour la MG Magna (ci-contre, en bas à gauche), cousine des sportives Midget ; enfin, voiture familiale à petit budget incarnée par un des tout premiers exemplaires de l'Austin Seven (ci-contre, en bas à droite), lancée en 1922 au prix de 165 £ et donnée pour une vitesse maximum de 65 km/h.

Motoring in miniature

In 1929 Mr High Test (top left) towers over an Austin Seven. Child actor Davey Lee's car (top right) was a petrol-powered late-1920s replica of one of Barney Oldfield's racers. Gus Petzel's miniature racer (above left) is seen in Yosemite National Park in 1926, and in 1920 'Custer' (above right) was said to be the smallest car in the USA. A stripped Peugeot Bébé is dwarfed by the big six-cylinder Renault (opposite) in 1926.

Wie klein darf es sein?

Mr. High Test überragt turmhoch den Austin Seven, 1929 (oben links). Der Kinderschauspieler Davey Lee (oben rechts) posiert Ende der 20er Jahre am Steuer einer Miniaturausgabe von Barney Oldfields Rennwagen. Die Aufnahme zeigt Gus Petzels Miniatur-Rennwagen (unten links) 1926 im Yosemite-Nationalpark, und im Jahr 1920 galt »Custer« (unten rechts) als kleinstes Automobil der USA. Eine aufs Nötigste reduzierte Peugeot Bébé (gegenüber) steht 1926 wie ein Zwerg neben dem mächtigen Sechszylinder-Renault.

Automobiles miniatures

En 1920, la « Custer » (ci-dessus, à droite) est la plus petite voiture des États-Unis, minuscule par rapport à cette Peugeot Bébé et ridicule à côté de la grosse six cylindres Renault (ci-contre) de 1926. Même attitude narquoise du policeman près de la voiture de l'acteur enfant Davey Lee (en haut à droite), une réplique d'une voiture de course de Barney Oldfield de la fin des années 1920, du garde face à la voiture de Gus Petzel (ci-dessus, à gauche) en 1926, ou de « Mister High Test » (en haut à gauche) avec la petite Austin Seven.

Pushing back the frontiers

An Australian explorer (above) on his way to Adelaide in around 1930 in his kerosene-powered Chevrolet tourer. In September 1919 the aptly named Miss Wanderwell had set off from Atlantic City, NJ, to attempt to drive around the world; in March 1923 (below) she reached Barcelona. In 1922 the half-tracked Citroën Kegresse became the first car to cross the Sahara Desert; the drive system was invented by Russian Imperial engineer Adolphe Kegresse, and it was just as happy in the Alps (right).

An neue Grenzen

Um 1930 durchquerte ein australischer Forscher, hier auf dem Weg nach Adelaide, mit einem kerosinbetriebenen offenen Chevrolet (oben) den Kontinent. Eine junge Dame mit dem passenden Namen Miss Wanderwell startete im September 1919 von Atlantic City, N.J., zu einer Weltumrundung im Automobil; im März 1923 hatte sie Barcelona erreicht (unten). 1922 durchquerte der Citroën Kegresse mit Halbkettenantrieb als erstes Fahrzeug die Wüste Sahara; das von Adolphe Kegresse im Russland des Zaren ersonnene Antriebsverfahren bewährte sich auch in den Alpen (rechts).

Repousser les frontières

Cet explorateur australien (en haut), qui traverse l'Australie dans sa Chevrolet à kérosène, pose sur la route d'Adelaide vers 1930. La justement nommée Mlle Wanderwell, partie d'Atlantic City, N.J., en septembre 1919 pour faire le tour du monde, atteint finalement Barcelone en mars 1923 (en bas). En 1922, une Citroën à chenillettes Kégresse devient la première voiture à traverser le désert du Sahara ; ce système d'entraînement, inventé par Adolphe Kégresse, un ingénieur russe, se révèle tout aussi efficace dans la neige des Alpes (à droite).

TELL DADDY WE ARE ALL HAPPY UNDER BRITISH RULE

Politics and personalities

Waving patriotically from the British-built Sheffield-Simplex
in Aden in November 1921 (above) was Edward, Prince of Wales.
The huge Mercedes cabriolet (opposite, above) was an
imposing stage for Adolf Hitler in Nuremberg, August 1927.
In June 1927, a New York motorcade welcomed transatlantic
aviator Charles Lindbergh (opposite, below left); in 1925
outriders escort President Calvin Coolidge's Cadillac (opposite,
below right).

Politik und Persönlichkeiten

Edward, Prince of Wales, nimmt im November 1921 in einem
britischen Sheffield-Simplex eine patriotische Parade in Aden ab
(oben). Das gewaltige Mercedes-Kabriolett (gegenüber, oben)
war eine imposante Tribüne für Adolf Hitler in Nürnberg,
August 1927. Im Juni 1927 begrüßte New York den Transatlantik-
flieger Charles Lindbergh mit einem Wagenkonvoi (gegenüber,
unten links); den Cadillac von Präsident Calvin Coolidge,
aufgenommen 1925, begleitet eine Motorradeskorte (gegenüber,
unten rechts).

Hommes politiques et personnalités

Édouard, prince de Galles, salue royalement la foule depuis
sa Sheffield-Simplex britannique lors de sa visite à Aden en
novembre 1921 (ci-dessus). En 1925, le président américain
Calvin Coolidge choisit une Cadillac pour se déplacer, escorté
par des motards (ci-contre, en bas à droite). En juin 1927, si
c'est un cortège joyeux d'automobiles qui accueille l'aviateur
Charles Lindbergh après sa traversée de l'Atlantique (ci-contre,
en bas à gauche), en août de la même année, le gros cabriolet
Mercedes d'où Adolf Hitler salue ses troupes défilant dans
les rues de Nuremberg semble déjà plus menaçant (ci-contre,
en haut).

Creature comforts

Made-to-measure luggage space on a 1923 Steyr (top left).
Hanomag's small, rear-engined Kommissbrot (above left) was
named because it resembled a loaf of army bread. A patent,
lever-operated sliding roof on a Singer Sunshine saloon (above
right), in 1928. Early radio (opposite), with Super-Het receiver
on the running board of a six-cylinder 80hp HCS, around 1925.
HCS was one of two companies founded by Harry C Stutz in
1920, after he had left the original Stutz Company.

Alles für die Bequemlichkeit

Der Steyr von 1923 (oben links) kann mit einem maßgeschneiderten
Kofferabteil aufwarten. Hanomags kleiner Heckmotorwagen
(unten links) nannte man seiner Form wegen »Kommissbrot«.
Das Sonnendach des Singer Sunshine von 1928 (oben rechts)
wird vom patentierten Hebelmechanismus geöffnet. Ein frühes
Autoradio (gegenüber): Der Superhet-Empfänger steht auf
dem Trittbrett eines 80-PS-Sechszylinders von H.C.S., etwa 1925.
H.C.S. war eine von zwei Firmen, die Harry C. Stutz 1920 gründete.

Le confort avant tout

La Steyr de 1923 a un coffre à bagage fait sur mesure (en haut à
gauche). La petite Hanomag à moteur arrière (ci-dessus, à gauche)
fut appelée Kommissbrot pour sa ressemblance avec le pain noir
allemand. Un système de toit ouvrant par levier est une option qui
améliore la berline Singer Sunshine, 1928 (ci-dessus, à droite).
Vers 1925, le marchepied de cette H.C.S. 80 ch six cylindres semble
idéal pour accueillir la radio à récepteur Super-Het (ci-contre).
H.C.S. fut l'une des deux firmes fondées par Harry C. Stutz en 1920.

Daring to be different

Skaters (top left), paced by a car whose skinny, unstudded tyres must have made the driver's job hard, on Lake Onota, Massachusetts, in 1924. The Peugeot that thought it was a boat (top right) in 1926. AV Roe demonstrating the Avro Mobile (above left) in 1924. The Red Bug electric buckboard (above right), built in America in 1929. Inspecting an anti-dazzle device (opposite) on an Austin's headlamps, 1925.

Es geht auch anders

Die beiden Schlittschuhläufer (oben links), 1924 auf dem Lake Onota (Massachusetts), haben einen vierrädrigen Schrittmacher; bei den schmalen Reifen kann das Steuern nicht leicht gewesen sein. Ein Peugeot von 1926 (oben rechts) für den Käpt'n zu Lande. A.V. Roe präsentierte sein Avro Mobile (unten links) 1924. Das automobile Minimum: Ein Red-Bug-Elektrowagen (unten rechts), 1929 in Amerika gebaut. An den Scheinwerfern eines Austin (gegenüber) werden 1925 blendfreie Gläser getestet.

Oser la différence

En 1924, ces patineurs du lac Onota (Massachusetts) courent contre une voiture (en haut à gauche). La même année, A.V. Roe fait la démonstration de son Avro Mobile (ci-dessus, à gauche), presque aussi étrange que cette Peugeot transformée en bateau en 1926 (en haut à droite) mais plus pratique que la « buckboard » électrique Red Bug (ci-dessus, à droite), construite aux États-Unis en 1929. En 1925, le public teste un dispositif anti-éblouissement adapté sur les phares d'une Austin (ci-contre).

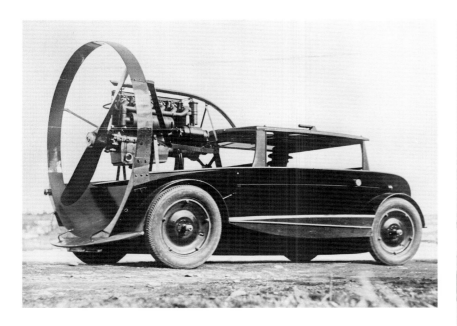

Dead-end designs

George McLaughlin's propeller-powered car (top left) of 1926
was designed to travel on ice and snow, but the propeller car
with wings (above right) certainly wasn't meant to fly. In 1926
André Mercier equipped his 5hp Peugeot (above left) with a
cage to allow him to roll it over. The Dynasphere, from 1932,
(opposite) rolled along like a wheel, with the driver suspended
inside.

Manches setzte sich nicht durch

George McLaughlins Propellerwagen von 1926 (oben links)
sollte auch bei Eis und Schnee fahren können; der fahrende
Doppeldecker hingegen (rechts) dürfte sich wohl kaum in
die Lüfte erhoben haben. André Mercier stattete seinen 5-PS-
Peugeot (unten links) mit einem Überrollbügel aus. Der
Dynasphere von 1932 (gegenüber) rollte wie ein Rad, doch
der Fahrer saß im Inneren.

Conceptions extrêmes

Si la voiture à propulsion par hélice inventée en 1926 par
George McLaughlin (en haut à gauche) a été conçue pour
voyager sur la glace et la neige, cette petite voiture à hélice
et bouts d'ailes (à droite) n'était pas destinée à voler. La même
année, André Mercier équipe sa Peugeot 5 ch d'une cage
circulaire (ci-dessus, à gauche). Autre fantaisie, la Dynasphere,
de 1932, utilisait le principe de la roue, le conducteur étant
suspendu à l'intérieur (ci-contre).

—— 5 ——
Age of Concern? Optimism, Despair, Decadence, Depression

While the 1920s had been a decade largely concerned with recovering from one world war,
the 1930s were lived under the gathering threat
of another to come, and it held a strange mixture of optimism and despair, decadence and depression.

In Europe, in fact in most of the world, the decade started
with economic and political uncertainty, a struggle between a
desire for disarmament on the one hand and mistrust between
national neighbours on the other, a time of massive unemployment contrasting with a determination to make life better.
The motor car, after 45 years, was well established as a hard
working part of everyday life. It was growing more sophisticated, more refined, and its numbers were growing rapidly.

America was still the world's leading vehicle producer and
1929 had been the most productive year to date for that country's industry; 5,337,087 cars built was a record which would
survive for 20 years. October 1929, however, also saw the Wall
Street Crash, and from 1930 to 1932 American car production
fell by 75 per cent, as incomes fell by more than 40 per cent.
The home of the big, extravagant, expensive automobile even
looked towards European-type small cars, and launched a US-
built version of the Austin Seven. The American version only
lasted for four years. The Seven did translate successfully to
Germany as the Dixi, which became the first four-wheeler
BMW, to France as the Rosengart, and to Japan (in spirit if not
in exact detail) as the Datsun, launched in 1932 by what
became the Nissan Motor Co.

Small, inexpensive cars held the industry together in
Europe, but not without drama. In 1932, André Citroën introduced his first front-drive car but its development costs almost
broke the company, until the popularity of the new model (and
what amounted to a takeover by tyre-maker Michelin) saved it.
Similarly, Ford opened a new British factory in 1931 and the
huge investment almost crippled that company, until, again in
1932, they introduced another small car. The 8hp Model Y was
a small Ford designed, as ever, in America but specifically for
European needs. It was to be built in France, Germany, Spain,
even Japan, as well as in Britain.

It wasn't quite as cheap as the sparsely trimmed, open-top
Morris Minor which had been offered for £100 in 1931, but it was
a real saloon, reasonably equipped, and undercutting both
Austin and Morris's cheapest saloons, with prices from £120. By
1934, more than half of Britain's sub-9hp sales fell to the Model
Y, rescuing Ford in Britain just as the Traction-Avant had

rescued Citroën in France. Predictably, it fuelled a price war,
and in 1935 Morris fought back with their Eight, the first Morris
to be built on moving production lines, mechanically a more
sophisticated car than the Ford, and a big success, with prices
from £118. In the meantime, however, Ford cut the price of the
Model Y to £115, then in 1935 to £100, and so the battle went on.

In Italy in 1936, Fiat introduced another clasic small car, the
'Topolino' 500, but at the other end of the scale, depression or
no depression, some of the most luxurious, powerful, complex
and expensive cars ever made were coming onto the market,
in brave defiance of the conditions. In America, right at the end
of the 1920s, Duesenberg had launched the 6.9-litre straight-
eight overhead-camshaft Model J, the most expensive car in
the world. In 1932 they supercharged it as the SJ, then offered
the short chassis SSJ, which was rarer and even more strato-
spherically expensive. Like many of the fine cars of the era it
was offered in bare chassis form, to be bodied, at great further
expense, by some of the greatest coachbuilders in motoring
history. In Europe, the same system applied to classic marques
from Bugatti to Hispano-Suiza, Rolls-Royce to Mercedes-Benz,
creating some of the most beautiful cars of all time, for the for-
tunate few who rose above the general constraints.

There were newcomers, including, from 1934, SS – which
went on to become Jaguar. On the downside, great old names
became victims of the economic conditions (including Duesenberg in 1937), while many that didn't disappear completely were
swallowed by predatory corporations. In 1931 Bentley was absorbed by Rolls-Royce, while Daimler bought Britain's oldest car
maker, Lanchester; and in 1932 the Rootes Group was formed,
based around the old Hillman and Humber companies, with others,
including Sunbeam, Talbot and Darracq, absorbed later.

While the shape of the industry was changing, so was the
shape of its products. At the start of the 1930s, nine out of ten
American cars had closed bodies, only one an open top; that
was the exact opposite of the split just ten years before. As the
novelty of motoring had worn off, practicality had become
dominant. Expectations of refinement and convenience were
filtering down from exotic models to more humble ones. That
included such features as electric starting, easy changing syn-
chromesh gears (standardised by Vauxhall on its Cadet in 1931),
independent suspension and other mechanical improvements,
which all spread through the motoring world in the 1930s.

The car became easier to live with, thanks to improved reliability but also to easily cleaned finishes including new paints

and chromium plating. The demand for comfort and convenience continued to grow, and features like radios and heaters began to be standard rather than optional. Many novelties were pioneered in America, not least because America, with its low gasoline prices, could feed bigger engines to carry more equipment in bigger, heavier, more powerful cars. At the extremes, the 1930s saw a fashion for massive multi-cylinder engines from the prestige marques, led by Cadillac's 7.4-litre V16 in 1930, followed by V16s from American rival Marmon.

There were any number of V12s, not only in America but also in Europe, including those from Rolls-Royce, Daimler, Horch, Maybach, Mercedes-Benz, and the esoteric French Voisin. In 1932, Henry Ford (who as recently as 1926 had said he saw no reason for six cylinders, let alone eight) introduced the first truly mass-produced, low-cost V8, under the slogan 'The greatest thrill in motoring'. It was one of his biggest successes, selling 300,000 cars in 1932 and half a million in 1934, comfortably outselling all America's other multi-cylinder cars. Nonetheless, by 1933 Ford was in third place in the USA, behind General Motors and Chrysler, whose most spectacular move in the 1930s was introducing the controversial Airflow in 1934, starting a trend to streamlined designs, also reflected in Europe, by Panhard in particular.

Through the 1930s we continued to learn to live with the car. In Britain the 20mph speed limit was abolished on open roads with effect from January 1931, while third-party insurance became compulsory, in a decade which also saw the first version of the Highway Code, the introduction of Belisha Beacons (named after Transport Minister Leslie Hore-Belisha), cat's-eyes, a 30mph speed limit in urban areas, and compulsory driving tests. By 1935 there were some 35 million cars in the world. In America, where sales boomed as the Depression lifted, one in six people by the late-1930s owned a car – more than ten times as many as the world average, with Europe way behind, with around one car to every 30 Britons or one to every 25 Frenchmen.

Faced with growing traffic problems, America introduced the first parking meter, in Oklahoma City in July 1935, and New York employed psychologists to study motoring offenders. Increasingly reluctant to leave their cars behind, Americans enjoyed the first drive-in movie theatre in 1934, in Camden NJ, and the first drive-in bank, in 1937, in Los Angeles.

That was the best year for the American industry since the record output of 1929, but around the world it saw the beginning of a decline, as the threat of war came closer. Ironically,

The land of the automobile. In 1936 six lanes of cars stream across the new Golden Gate Bridge in San Francisco, shortly after its opening by President Roosevelt.

Das Land des Automobils. 1936, kurz nach ihrer Eröffnung durch Präsident Roosevelt, strömen die Wagen auf sechs Spuren über die Golden-Gate-Brücke in San Francisco.

Le pays de l'automobile ! En 1936, six files de voitures traversent le nouveau pont du Golden Gate de San Francisco, peu après son inauguration par le président Roosevelt.

before it came, Adolf Hitler had sown the seeds of the future for the German car industry and a new kind of motoring in Germany and beyond. In 1934 he started a programme to build a network of autobahns, the first of which was opened between Frankfurt and Darmstadt in 1935, increased to some 800 miles by 1937. In 1936 he announced a new car, designed (by Dr Ferdinand Porsche) to be affordable by virtually every German and in 1938 the foundation stone was laid for a factory to build the Volkswagen 'People's Car'. And Hitler further promoted technical research by providing massive funds for the Mercedes and Auto Union teams which completely dominated Grand Prix motor racing at the end of the decade.

On 3 September 1939, Tazio Nuvolari's Auto Union won the Belgrade Grand Prix. It was the day on which Britain declared war on Germany. Within months, Europe's factories would again be building military vehicles and munitions, not cars.

In den zwanziger Jahren war die Welt ganz damit beschäftigt gewesen, sich vom vorherigen Krieg zu erholen, doch die Dreißiger standen schon unter dem drohenden Schatten des nächsten und waren geprägt von einer seltsamen Mischung aus Angst und Aufbruchsstimmung, aus Wirtschaftskrise und hemmungslosem Lebensgenuss.

In Europa, überhaupt in großen Teilen der Welt, begann die Dekade mit einer Zeit ökonomischer und politischer Unsicherheit; dem Wunsch nach Abrüstung stand ein tiefes Misstrauen zwischen benachbarten Nationalstaaten gegenüber, der großen Arbeitslosigkeit die Sehnsucht nach dem schöneren Leben. Das Automobil war inzwischen 45 Jahre alt und aus dem täglichen Leben nicht mehr fortzudenken; die Wagen wurden anspruchsvoller und bequemer, und ihre Zahl stieg immer weiter.

Die Vereinigten Staaten waren nach wie vor der größte Autoexporteur weltweit, und 1929 war für die dortige Industrie das bis dahin produktivste Jahr gewesen: Die Rekordzahl von 5 337 087 gebauten Fahrzeugen sollte erst zwanzig Jahre später wieder erreicht werden. Doch im Oktober 1929 kam der Börsenkrach an der Wall Street, und zwischen 1930 und 1932 ging die amerikanische Automobilproduktion um 75 Prozent zurück; Löhne sanken um über 40 Prozent. Wo bisher große, teure, extravagante Wagen gefragt waren, versuchte man es nun mit Kleinwagen nach europäischem Muster, und der Austin Seven wurde sogar in Lizenz gefertigt. Dieses amerikanische Unternehmen hielt sich zwar nur vier Jahre lang, doch anderswo waren die Lizenzbauten erfolgreicher – in Deutschland, wo der Seven als Dixi (der erste BMW) gebaut wurde, in Frankreich als Rosengart und in Japan, wo ihn, wenn auch in Details verändert, 1932 der Vorläufer der Nissan Motor Co. als Datsun auf den Markt brachte.

Kleine, billige Modelle hielten die Industrie in Europa am Leben, aber nur mit Mühe. 1932 stellte André Citroën seinen ersten Frontantriebswagen vor, doch die Entwicklungskosten trieben die Firma beinahe in den Bankrott, und nur der Erfolg des Wagens (und die De-facto-Übernahme durch den Reifenhersteller Michelin) rettete sie. Auch die britische Ford-Filiale stand durch die hohen Kosten für die Errichtung eines neuen, 1931 eröffneten Werks am Rande des Ruins, bis sich auch hier, ebenfalls 1932, der Erfolg mit einem Kleinwagen einstellte. Das Y-Modell mit 8 Steuer-PS war zwar, wie alle Fords, in Amerika entworfen worden, doch speziell für europäische Bedürfnisse, und wurde außer in England auch in Frankreich, Deutschland, Spanien und sogar in Japan gebaut.

Der Ford war mit Preisen ab £ 120 nicht ganz so billig wie der spartanische offene Morris Minor, der 1931 für £ 100 angeboten wurde, aber dafür war es eine echte Limousine mit vernünftiger Ausstattung und preiswerter als die günstigsten geschlossenen Wagen von Austin und Morris. 1934 waren schon über die Hälfte aller in Großbritannien verkauften Wagen unter 9 PS Y-Modelle, und der Y rettete die britischen Ford-Werke ebenso, wie der Traction-Avant in Frankreich Citroën gerettet hatte. Wie nicht anders zu erwarten, entbrannte ein Preiskampf, und 1935 schlug Morris mit dem Eight zurück, dem ersten Morris, der am Fließband gebaut wurde. In der Konstruktion war er anspruchsvoller als der Ford, und bei Preisen ab £ 118 ließ der Erfolg nicht lange auf sich warten. Inzwischen hatte Ford jedoch den Preis für das Y-Modell auf £ 115 reduziert, 1935 sogar auf £ 100, und so setzte sich der Kampf fort.

Ein weiterer Kleinwagen-Klassiker kam 1936 in Italien auf den Markt, der Fiat 500 »Topolino«; andererseits entstanden trotz Wirtschaftskrise und unbeirrt von allen düsteren Verkaufsaussichten in diesen Jahren auch einige der luxuriösesten, kräftigsten, aufwendigsten und teuersten Automobile aller Zeiten. In Amerika hatte Duesenberg Ende der Zwanziger das Modell J vorgestellt, mit seinem 6,9-Liter-Reihen-Achtzylinder mit oben liegender Nockenwelle das teuerste Auto der Welt. 1932 folgte der SJ mit Kompressor, dann der SSJ auf kürzerem Chassis, dessen Preis bei den geringen Stückzahlen in noch astronomischeren Höhen lag. Wie bei vielen Luxuswagen der Zeit wurde das Chassis auch einzeln verkauft, und der Kunde konnte sich bei einem der renommierten Karossiers gegen noch größere Kosten einen Aufbau nach Maß fertigen lassen. In Europa galt das für die klassischen Marken, von Bugatti bis Hispano-Suiza, vom Rolls-Royce bis zum Mercedes-Benz, und für die Auserwählten entstanden einige der schönsten Wagen, die je gebaut wurden.

Neue Hersteller kamen hinzu, darunter seit 1934 SS, der Vorläufer von Jaguar. Manche großen Namen verschwanden (darunter 1937 auch Duesenberg), manche bestanden als Marken weiter, wurden jedoch von Konkurrenten geschluckt. 1931 ging Bentley an Rolls-Royce, und die britische Daimler kaufte Lanchester, den ältesten Hersteller des Landes; 1932 entstand aus Hillman und Humber die Rootes-Gruppe, in der später Sunbeam, Talbot, Darracq und andere aufgingen.

Doch nicht nur die Industrie wandelte sich, auch ihre Produkte nahmen neue Gestalt an. Zu Beginn der dreißiger Jahre hatten von zehn Neuwagen in den USA neun einen geschlossenen Aufbau, nur einer war noch offen; zehn Jahre zuvor war das Verhältnis genau umgekehrt gewesen. Nun, da der Reiz des Neuen verflogen war, kam es bei Motorfahrzeugen vor allem auf den praktischen Nutzen an. Bequemlichkeit und raffinierte Konstruktion waren nicht mehr den exotischeren Modellen vorbehalten, sondern fanden sich auch in Alltagswagen. Dazu gehörten der elektrische Anlasser, das synchronisierte Getriebe (bei Vauxhall erstmals 1931 im Modell Cadet als Standard eingebaut), einzeln aufgehängte Vorderräder und andere mechanische Verbesserungen, die sich im Laufe der dreißiger Jahre in der gesamten Motorwelt ausbreiteten.

Das Leben mit dem Auto wurde einfacher, die Wagen waren zuverlässiger und mit ihren glatten Flächen, neuen Lacken und Chromteilen leichter zu pflegen. Komfort und leichte Bedienung spielten eine immer größere Rolle, und Dinge wie Radio und Heizung, bisher als Zubehör angesehen, wurden immer mehr zum Standard. Viele Neuerungen kamen aus Amerika, nicht zuletzt deswegen, weil die niedrigen Benzinpreise größere Motoren erschwinglich machten, die wiederum größere, schwerere, stärkere und besser ausgerüstete Wagen ermöglichten. Im Extrem führte diese Tendenz zu gewaltigen Vielzylindermotoren bei den Prestigemarken, allen voran Cadillacs 7,4-Liter-V16 von 1930 und die V16-Maschinen seines Rivalen Marmon.

V12-Motoren gab es in großer Zahl, nicht nur in den Vereinigten Staaten, sondern auch bei europäischen Herstellern, darunter Rolls-Royce, Daimler, Horch, Maybach, Mercedes-Benz und in Frankreich der unkonventionelle Voisin. Henry Ford (der 1926 noch gesagt hatte, er sehe keinen Grund für sechs Zylinder, geschweige denn acht) brachte 1932 unter dem Slogan »Der Motor, der das Herz höher schlagen lässt« den ersten in wirklich großen Stückzahlen produzierten, preisgünstigen V8 auf den Markt. Es sollte einer seiner größten Erfolge werden; 1932 verkaufte er 300 000 Wagen damit, 1934 eine halbe Million und damit deutlich mehr als alle anderen amerikanischen Hersteller von Vielzylindermotoren. Trotzdem war Ford 1933 bei den Produktionszahlen auf den dritten Platz hinter General Motors und Chrysler zurückgefallen; Chryslers spektakulärster Schritt der dreißiger Jahre war 1934 die Einführung des viel diskutierten Airflow, mit dem der Trend zu Stromlinienkarosserien begann, die bald auch in Europa zu sehen waren, allen voran bei Panhard.

Auch die dreißiger Jahre standen im Zeichen der Anpassung des Lebensstils an die neue Mobilität. In Großbritannien wurde das 20-Meilen-Tempolimit außerhalb von

geschlossenen Ortschaften zum Januar 1931 aufgehoben, die Haftpflichtversicherung wurde Vorschrift, und im Laufe des Jahrzehnts kamen die ersten Straßenverkehrsregeln (Highway Code), Fußgängerüberwege (in England mit einer Lampe gekennzeichnet, dem »Belisha Beacon«, der seinen Namen nach dem damaligen Verkehrsminister Leslie Hore-Belisha bekam), Katzenaugen als Straßenmarkierung, das Dreißigmeilentempo auf innerstädtischen Straßen und schließlich die Führerscheinprüfung. 1935 gab es etwa 35 Millionen Kraftfahrzeuge auf der Welt. In Amerika schossen die Verkaufszahlen wieder in die Höhe, als die Wirtschaftskrise vorüber war, und Ende der dreißiger Jahre besaß jeder sechste Amerikaner ein Auto – mehr als das Zehnfache des weltweiten Durchschnitts und wesentlich mehr als in Europa, wo ein Auto auf 30 Briten und eines auf 25 Franzosen kam.

Amerika spürte allmählich die Überfülle des Verkehrs; 1935 wurde in Oklahoma City die erste Parkuhr aufgestellt, und die Stadt New York ließ Verkehrssünder von Psychologen untersuchen. Die Amerikaner verließen ihre Wagen nur noch ungern, und in Camden, N.J., entstand 1934 das erste Drive-in-Kino; die erste Drive-in-Bank folgte 1937 in Los Angeles.

1937 war für die amerikanischen Hersteller das beste Jahr seit dem Rekordjahr 1929, doch in anderen Ländern gingen die Produktionszahlen im Angesicht des drohenden neuen Krieges bereits zurück. Ironischerweise war es gerade Adolf Hitler, der noch vor dem Krieg das Fundament für die spätere deutsche Autoindustrie und eine in Deutschland und weltweit gänzlich neue Art des Autofahrens legte. 1934 begann er sein großes Programm für den Autobahnbau; die erste Strecke zwischen Darmstadt und Frankfurt wurde 1935 dem Verkehr übergeben, und 1937 umfasste das Netz etwa 1300 Kilometer. Hitler war es auch, der 1936 den Bau eines neuen, von Dr. Ferdinand Porsche konstruierten Wagentyps ankündigte, der für praktisch jeden Deutschen erschwinglich sein sollte, und 1938 legte er den Grundstein für die Fabrik, die den »Volkswagen« bauen sollte. Auch die technische Entwicklung trieb die Naziregierung voran und stellte den Mercedes- und Auto-Union-Mannschaften, die die Grand-Prix-Szene am Ende des Jahrzehnts beherrschten, große Geldmittel zur Verfügung.

Am 3. September 1939 gewann Tazio Nuvolaris Auto Union den Grand Prix von Belgrad. Es war der Tag, an dem Großbritannien Deutschland den Krieg erklärte. Binnen Monaten sollten die Fabriken Europas wieder Bomben und Militärfahrzeuge statt Personenwagen bauen.

Sometimes, there was unrest. In 1937 members of the new United Auto Workers Union held a sit-down strike in the General Motors body plant in Flint, Michigan.

Manchmal gab es Unruhen. 1937 hielten die Mitglieder der frisch gegründeten Automobilarbeitergewerkschaft einen Sitzstreik im General-Motors-Karosseriewerk in Flint, Michigan, ab.

En 1937, les syndicalistes du tout nouveau United Auto Workers Union organisent une grève sur le tas dans l'usine de carrosserie de la General Motors de Flint (Michigan).

Si les années 1920 ont été particulièrement marquées par les réparations nécessitées par la guerre mondiale, les années 1930 se déroulent sous la menace d'un nouveau conflit dans une atmosphère étrange où se mélangent optimisme et désespoir, décadence et dépression.

En Europe, comme dans le monde entier, cette décennie démarre dans l'incertitude économique et politique, où s'opposent la volonté de désarmer et la méfiance entre nations voisines, et où la situation de chômage massif contraste avec une certaine détermination à vouloir rendre la vie meilleure. L'automobile qui, 45 ans après sa naissance, fait désormais partie de l'univers quotidien de tous, devient plus élégante, plus raffinée et chaque année toujours plus nombreuse.

Les États-Unis restent le principal pays producteur d'automobiles, avec 5 337 087 véhicules construits en 1929, une année record qui n'aura pas d'équivalent pendant une vingtaine d'années. Le krach de Wall Street en octobre 1929 fait toutefois chuter de 75 pour cent la production automobile américaine, accompagnée d'une baisse de 40 pour cent des salaires. Les Américains abandonnent alors quelque peu leurs grosses automobiles extravagantes et chères pour se tourner vers les petites voitures de style européen, comme par exemple l'Austin Seven, qui sera alors construite et commercialisée sous licence au États-Unis jusqu'en 1932. La Seven sera également exportée avec succès pour être assemblée en Allemagne par Dixi (bientôt réunie à BMW), en France par Rosengart et à partir de 1932 au Japon (dans l'esprit sinon dans la lettre) sous le nom de Datsun, par la future Nissan Motor Company.

L'époque est aussi difficile pour les constructeurs automobiles européens, même si les petites voitures bon marché leur permettent d'assurer leur pérennité. Ainsi, lorsqu'en 1932 André Citroën sort sa première voiture à traction avant, les coûts de développement manquent presque de ruiner l'entreprise, sauvée in extremis par la popularité du nouveau modèle (et par l'intervention de Michelin, le fabricant de pneumatiques, qui reprend l'entreprise). Une mésaventure semblable arrive à Ford à l'occasion de l'ouverture en 1931 d'une nouvelle usine d'assemblage en Grande-Bretagne ; les investissements nécessités paralysent presque l'activité de l'entreprise qui ne parvient à se redresser qu'en 1932 grâce à la sortie d'une nouvelle petite voiture : la Ford Model Y 8 hp. Celle-ci, conçue comme toujours aux États-Unis mais correspondant, cette fois au moins, aux besoins du marché européen, était destinée à être assemblée en France, en Allemagne, en Espagne, en Grande-Bretagne et même au Japon.

Si elle n'est pas aussi bon marché que la Morris Minor découverte aménagée de manière spartiate vendue 100 £ en 1931, il s'agissait en revanche d'une véritable berline, assez bien équipée et vendue 120 £, c'est-à-dire à un prix inférieur aux moins chères des berlines Austin et Morris. En 1934, le Model Y représente plus de la moitié des ventes de voitures en Grande-Bretagne d'une puissance inférieure à 9 ch, ce qui sauve Ford UK tout comme la traction avant a sauvé Citroën en France. Une guerre des prix est alors inévitable. Morris riposte en 1935 en sortant la Eight – première Morris assemblée sur une chaîne de montage mobile – une voiture mécaniquement plus sophistiquée que la Ford, vendue 118 £, et qui remporte un grand succès. Ford avait toutefois baissé entretemps le prix du Model Y à 115 £, pour arriver à 100 £ en 1935. La bataille ne faisait que commencer.

Tandis que l'Italien Fiat sort en 1936 une nouvelle petite voiture classique, la « Topolino » 500, à l'autre extrémité de la gamme sont commercialisées – dépression économique ou pas – certaines des voitures les plus luxueuses, les plus puissantes, les plus complexes et les plus chères jamais construites. Aux États-Unis, juste à la fin des années 1920, Duesenberg sort la voiture la plus chère du monde, son Model J équipé d'un moteur 6,9 l huit-cylindres en ligne à arbres à cames en tête. Ce moteur est équipé d'un compresseur en 1932 et le modèle baptisé SJ, bientôt proposé avec châssis court sous le nom de SSJ, un modèle encore plus rare et encore beaucoup plus cher. À l'instar de la plupart des voitures de luxe de cette époque, elle pouvait être achetée nue et carrossée sur mesure par certains des plus grands carrossiers de l'histoire de l'automobile à un tarif encore plus astronomique. Le même principe est également adopté en Europe et permet à des marques classiques comme Bugatti et Hispano-Suiza, Rolls-Royce ou Mercedes-Benz de proposer à une rare clientèle fortunée quelques-unes des plus belles voitures de tous les temps.

Si de nouvelles marques naissent – notamment, en 1934, Swallow Side (plus connue sous le nom de SS), futur Jaguar – d'anciens grands constructeurs disparaissent (par exemple Duesenberg en 1937) ou sont absorbées par d'autres firmes. C'est ainsi que Bentley est absorbé par Rolls-Royce en 1931 tandis que Daimler achète Lanchester, le plus ancien constructeur de Grande-Bretagne ; en 1932, le Rootes Group est créé par la réunion des anciennes entreprises Hillman et Humber, suivies plus tard par Sunbeam, Talbot et Darracq.

Divine inspiration? The three-wheeler's passenger is a sculpture of an angel, rescued from the Houses of Parliament in London during building work in 1934.

Ein Bote des Himmels? Der Beifahrer dieses Dreirads ist eine Engelsskulptur, die 1934 bei Bauarbeiten am Londoner Parlamentsgebäude in Sicherheit gebracht wird.

Inspiration divine ? Le passager de ce tricycle est la statue d'un ange sauvée du Parlement de Londres lors de travaux entrepris en 1934.

Si l'industrie automobile évolue, il en est de même des voitures. Au début des années 1930, neuf voitures américaines sur dix ont une carrosserie fermée, une seule est décapotable. L'attrait et l'envie de nouveauté ayant diminué, les automobilistes se préoccupent désormais plus de l'aspect pratique de leur véhicule. C'est ainsi que se généralise l'installation du démarreur électrique, de la boîte de vitesses synchronisées (en standard sur la Vauxhall Cadet à partir de 1931), des suspensions indépendantes et d'autres améliorations mécaniques.

L'automobile bénéficie d'une fiabilité accrue et d'un entretien plus facile, notamment des peintures et des chromes. La radio et le chauffage ne sont plus en option mais intégrés en série. De nombreuses nouveautés sont introduites sur les modèles construits aux États-Unis, ne serait-ce que parce que les Américains bénéficient d'un prix de l'essence très bas qui leur permet d'utiliser des moteurs plus puissants capables de tracter de grosses et lourdes voitures, surchargées d'équipement. Ceci explique aussi l'apparition en 1930, de gros moteurs sur les modèles des marques de prestige, comme des moteurs V16 7,4 l chez Cadillac ou Marmon, son concurrent direct.

La mode des moteurs V12 se développe non seulement aux États-Unis mais également en Europe, notamment chez Rolls-Royce, Daimler, Horch, Maybach, Mercedes-Benz et l'ésotérique français Voisin. En 1932, Henry Ford (qui avait dit en 1926 qu'il ne voyait aucune raison de passer au six-cylindres, et encore moins au huit-cylindres) sort un V8 bon marché, premier moteur véritablement construit en série, accompagné du slogan : « La plus grande émotion automobile ». Ce fut un de ses plus grands succès ! En 1932, il vend 300 000 voitures équipées de ce moteur et près d'un demi million en 1934, dépassant sans peine les chiffres de vente de toutes les autres automobiles à moteur multi-cylindres des États-Unis. Malgré cela, en 1933, Ford n'occupe aux États-Unis que la troisième place des constructeurs, derrière General Motors et Chrysler. Ce dernier, qui sort en 1934 l'Airflow, un modèle spectaculaire et controversé, lance la mode des voitures à profil aérodynamique, qui sera reprise également en Europe, notamment chez Panhard.

L'automobile s'intègre de plus en plus dans la vie quotidienne et commence à modifier le comportement de certains gouvernements. C'est en Grande-Bretagne, où la limitation de vitesse à 32 km/h est ainsi abolie sur les routes en janvier 1931 tandis que l'assurance au tiers devient obligatoire et qu'est instaurée une première version du Code de la route. C'est aussi à cette époque que sont installés les lampadaires signalant les passages cloutés (appelés « Belisha Beacons » en Grande-Bretagne du nom du ministre des Transports Leslie Hore-Belisha), qu'apparaissent les cataphotes, la limitation de vitesse à 48 km/h en agglomération et le permis de conduire obligatoire. Près de 35 millions de véhicules circulent dans le monde en 1935. Aux États-Unis, où les ventes reprennent formidablement avec la fin de la Dépression, une personne sur six possède une automobile à la fin des années 1930 – soit plus de dix fois la moyenne mondiale –, l'Europe restant loin derrière avec près d'une voiture pour 30 habitants en Grande-Bretagne et une pour 25 en France.

Face aux problèmes croissants de circulation dans les villes, Oklahoma City installe le premier parcmètre du monde en juillet 1935, tandis que New York emploie des psychologues pour examiner les contrevenants. Les Américains, qui ont de plus en plus de mal à renoncer à leur voiture, organisent leur vie autour des « drive-in » : le premier cinéma de ce genre est créé en 1934 à Camden (New Jersey) et la première banque aménagée en 1937 à Los Angeles.

Alors que l'industrie automobile américaine connaît cette année-là ses meilleurs chiffres de vente depuis le record de 1929, l'imminence de la guerre entraîne un certain déclin des constructeurs dans le reste du monde. C'est pourtant à cette époque qu'Adolf Hitler trace la voie de l'avenir pour l'industrie automobile allemande. En 1934, il lance en effet un vaste programme de construction d'un réseau d'autoroutes, dont le premier tronçon ouvre entre Francfort et Darmstadt en 1935 et qui sera de près de 1300 km en 1937. Il annonce également en 1936 la création d'une nouvelle voiture que chaque Allemand pourra acheter et pose en 1938 la première pierre de l'usine où sera assemblée la « voiture du peuple » conçue par Dr Ferdinand Porsche : la coccinelle Volkswagen. Hitler encourage également la recherche en technique automobile en attribuant d'importantes subventions aux équipes Mercedes et Auto Union qui dominent alors totalement les courses de Grand prix à la fin de la décennie.

Le 3 septembre 1939, l'Auto Union de Tazio Nuvolari remporte le Grand Prix de Belgrade, le jour même où la Grande-Bretagne déclare la guerre à l'Allemagne. En l'espace de quelques mois, les usines des constructeurs automobiles européens vont à nouveau se convertir pour assembler des véhicules militaires et fabriquer des munitions.

Henry Ford created another major success with his new V8 in 1932, and it sold around the world, including Egypt in the case of this stylish De Luxe Roadster.

Ein weiterer großer Erfolg Henry Fords war der neue V8-Motor von 1932, der weltweit Anklang fand – sogar, wie dieser elegante De Luxe Roadster zeigt, in Ägypten.

Henry Ford remporte un nouveau succès en 1932 grâce à la sortie de la Ford V8, qu'il vend dans le monde entier, y compris en Égypte avec cet élégant Roadster De Luxe.

A car is born

Completed chassis for a variety of four- and six-cylinder models waiting for bodies and trim to be fitted at the Morris factory in Cowley, Oxfordshire, in February 1930. They all have the petrol tank mounted in the front scuttle, and there is an interesting mixture of wire and steel-spoked 'artillery' wheels.

Ein Auto entsteht

Fertige Chassis verschiedener Vier- und Sechszylinder-modelle warten im Februar 1930 im Morris-Werk in Cowley, Oxfordshire, auf Karosserien und Ausstattung. Allen gemeinsam ist der Tank im Spritzblech; die Räder sind eine interessante Mischung aus Draht- und »mili-tärischen« Stahlspeichenrädern.

Une voiture est née

En février 1930, ces châssis pour modèles de quatre à six cylindres attendent que les ouvriers de l'usine Morris de Cowley (Oxfordshire) leur adaptent une carrosserie et procèdent aux aménagements intérieurs. On remarque le réservoir d'essence monté à l'avant et l'utilisation de roues à rayons ou à bâtons.

The next steps

Still in the Morris factory in February 1930 (above), the bodies to match up with the cars on the previous spread are being trimmed and upholstered by hand, on movable trolleys. The MG factory in nearby Abingdon (right), in January 1932, shows chassis (with Morris-based running gear) being assembled at fixed stations, and driven to the next stage.

Die nächsten Schritte

Ebenfalls im Morris-Werk im Februar 1930 werden (oben) die Karosserien für die Fahrgestelle der vorherigen Seiten fertig gestellt; die Arbeit der Ausstatter und Polsterer erfolgt von Hand, und die Aufbauten ruhen auf beweglichen Plattformen. Ein Blick in die MG-Fertigung im nahe gelegenen Abingdon (rechts) im Januar 1932 zeigt, wie die Chassis (mit Antriebs-einheiten auf Morris-Basis) an festen Arbeitsplätzen montiert werden und dann mit eigener Kraft zur nächsten Station fahren.

Les étapes suivantes

Toujours en février 1930 dans l'usine Morris (ci-dessus), les ouvriers s'occupent de garnir et de tapisser les carrosseries, posées sur une chaîne mobile, qui seront adaptées au châssis des voitures de la page précédente. L'organisation de l'usine MG de la ville voisine d'Abingdon (à droite), en janvier 1932, est différente : les châssis en cours d'assemblage, équipés d'une boîte de vitesse à base Morris, sont construits à poste fixe avant d'être emmenés à l'atelier suivant de la chaîne de fabrication.

Town and country

The four-cylinder Alvis tourer (left) of the early 1930s was a well-made, fairly expensive light car from a manufacturer who started with quite ordinary designs in 1920 before making a long line of elegant, sporty models. The crowds near Croydon aerodrome (above), with Austins, Morrises, Rovers and Standards all prominent, were waiting for the return of pioneer flyer Amy Johnson from France.

Stadt und Land

Der offene Vierzylinder-Alvis der dreißiger Jahre (links) war ein gut konstruierter, recht kostspieliger leichter Wagen von einem Hersteller, der im Jahr 1920 mit konventionellen Entwürfen begonnen hatte, bevor eine lange Reihe von ebenso eleganten wie sportlichen Modellen kam. Die vielen Besucher des Flugfelds von Croydon (oben) warteten auf die Rückkehr der Fliegerin Amy Johnson aus Frankreich. Im Gedränge sind Austin, Morris, Rover und Standard zu erkennen.

Ville et campagne

L'Alvis torpédo quatre-cylindres (à gauche), datant du début des années 1930, était une voiture légère et bien construite mais plutôt chère. La marque avait commencé vers 1920 par diffuser des modèles assez ordinaires avant de créer une assez vaste gamme de modèles sportifs et élégants. Rassemblées près de l'aérodrome de Croydon (ci-dessus), ces Austin, Morris, Rover et Standard, toutes de modèles imposants, attendent le retour de France d'Amy Johnson, une des pionnières de l'aviation britannique.

Sporting motorists

The dry-land swimmers (left) are
posing with a Delage D8, adorned
with a glass radiator ornament
by René Lalique. The coachbuilt
Delage has a capacious, separate
trunk, the sporting 14/45hp Talbot
six-cylinder Weymann Sunshine
Coupé (above) has room for a bag
of golf clubs, above the petrol tank
and behind the fabric covered body,
with its imitation landau irons
on the rear quarters, and opening
windscreen and rear window.

Der Hang zum Sportlichen

Die beiden Badenixen (links)
posieren auf dem Trockenen vor
einem Delage D8, komplett mit
gläsernem Kühlerschmuck von
René Lalique. Der in Handarbeit
gebaute Delage verfügte über ein
geräumiges Kofferabteil; das flotte
Weymann Sunshine-Coupé auf
Basis des 14/45-PS-Talbot-Sechs-
zylinders (oben) hat dafür über
dem Tank ein spezielles Abteil für
die Golftasche und glänzt mit stoff-
bezogener Karosserie, imitierten
Landauer-Bügeln an den Dach-
holmen und aufklappbarer Front-
und Heckscheibe.

Automobilistes sportifs

Ces nageuses (à gauche) posent
près d'une Delage D8, ornée d'une
mascotte de radiateur en verre due
à René Lalique. Si la Delage offre
une vaste malle arrière rapportée
en coffre, la Talbot Sunshine Coupé
14/45 ch six-cylindres (ci-dessus)
permet de ranger un sac de golf
au-dessus du réservoir d'essence ;
la carrosserie Weymann, en tissu
avec fers imitation landau sur les
déflecteurs arrières, dispose d'un
pare-brise et d'une vitre arrière
ouvrants.

Getting away from it all

On a sunny day in May 1933 (above) caravans are hitched behind a Hillman Minx and a slightly larger Hillman Wizard saloon for a trip to the countryside. In March 1931 racing driver Earl Howe's supercharged Mercedes SS (below) is loaded onto a platform ready to be hoisted aboard the cross-Channel 'Auto-Carrier', in the days before roll-on/roll-off ferries. A very English setting for an American tourer (right), still using 'artillery' type wooden wheels and ready to explore the countryside in around 1930.

Die Ferne lockt

An einem sonnigen Maitag des Jahres 1933 bekommen (oben) der Hillman Minx und der etwas größere Hillman Wizard zum Ausflug ins Grüne zwei Wohnwagen angehängt. Im März 1931 wird der Mercedes-SS-Kompressorwagen des Rennfahrers Earl Howe auf einer Plattform an Bord des »Auto-Carrier« zur Fahrt über den Ärmelkanal gehievt – die Zeit der Roll-on-Roll-off-Fähren war noch nicht gekommen (unten). Der amerikanische Tourenwagen mit den damals schon altmodischen Holzspeichenrädern steht um 1930 in einer sehr englischen Umgebung (rechts) bereit für eine Landpartie.

S'éloigner de tout

Ces automobilistes profitent de cette journée ensoleillée de mai 1933 (en haut) pour accrocher leur caravane à une Hillman Minx, l'autre à une Hillman Wizard berline, un peu plus spacieuse. En mars 1931, on charge la Mercedes SS à moteur à compresseur du pilote de course Earl Howe (en bas) sur une plate-forme avant de l'embarquer à bord d'un des cargos trans-Manche qui ont précédé les ferries rouliers. Un cadre très anglais pour cette berline américaine (à droite), qui dispose encore, vers 1930, de roues à bâtons en bois.

Towed and towing ...

With a sprinkling of snow but no mountains, a member of the Lake District Ski Club (above) is towed along behind a four-cylinder 1052cc Standard Nine saloon of around 1936. In May 1936 (below), it is the car that is getting the tow, with Monica the elephant from Liverpool Zoo pulling a Hillman Minx saloon, Hillman's big-selling model launched at the 1931 Olympia Motor Show and regarded as a more up-market alternative to the rival 10hp Austins and Morrises. By 1935 you could even have a factory-fitted radio in your Minx, and an all-syncromesh gearbox became standard that year.

Zugpferd und Gezogener ...

Dieses Mitglied des Lake District Ski Club (oben) braucht weder Berge noch viel Schnee, solange die Standard-Nine-Limousine von etwa 1936 mit ihrem 1052-ccm-Vierzylinder zieht. Im Mai 1936 (unten) ist es hingegen das Auto, das gezogen wird – Monica, die Elefantenkuh im Liverpooler Zoo, zeigt an einem Hillman Minx, was sie kann. Hillmans bestverkauftes Modell war 1931 auf der Olympia Motor Show vorgestellt worden und galt als anspruchsvollere Alternative zu den Rivalen von Austin und Morris in der 10-Steuer-PS-Klasse. Seit 1935 konnte man den Minx sogar mit eingebautem Radio bestellen, und das voll synchronisierte Getriebe war von diesem Jahr an Standard.

Remorqués et remorqueurs ...

Il suffit d'un peu de neige, même en plaine, pour que ce membre du Lake District Ski Club (en haut) en profite pour se faire tracter par une berline Standard Nine 1 052 cm³ quatre cylindres de 1936. En mai, cette fois, c'est une Hillman Minx qui doit se faire remorquer par l'éléphante Monica du zoo de Liverpool (en bas) ; ce modèle Hillman, apparu à l'Olympia Motor Show de 1931, fut considéré comme une alternative haut de gamme à ses rivales Austin et Morris 10 ch et se vendit très bien. En 1935, il était même possible de disposer d'une Minx équipée d'une radio ; c'est cette année-là que la boîte à vitesses synchronisées devint la norme.

... towing and towed

In December 1932 a group of Cornishmen haul a rather battered Morris tourer (above) to safety from the edge of the cliffs at Land's End, after strong winter winds had blown it off the road. The Austin Seven, in this case a model probably built in 1929 (below) might not have had a lot of power – just 13bhp from its 750cc four-cylinder side-valve engine – but it was enough to tow this glider at Hanworth, Middlesex, in January 1931.

... Gezogener und Zugpferd

Im Dezember 1932 retten einige Männer in Cornwall (oben) einen recht angeschlagenen Morris, den die Winterstürme an den Rand der Klippen von Land's End geblasen hatten. Der Austin Seven, hier (unten) vermutlich ein Exemplar von 1929, war nicht gerade ein Kraftprotz – der seitengesteuerte 750-ccm-Vierzylinder gab 13 PS ab –, aber doch stark genug, um im Januar 1931 in Hanworth, Middlesex, dieses Segelflugzeug in die Höhe zu ziehen.

... remorqueurs et remorqués

En décembre 1932, ce groupe de Cornouaillais essaie de tirer d'un mauvais pas une Morris passablement abîmée (en haut), qu'une violente rafale de vent a fait sortir de la route près des falaises de Land's End. L'Austin Seven, ici un modèle datant probablement de 1929 (en bas), n'avait certes pas beaucoup de puissance – son moteur 750 cm³ à soupape latérale ne développant que 13 ch – mais était toutefois capable de tracter ce planeur de Hanworth (Middlesex) en janvier 1931.

Cars and stars ...

In the film star world of Hollywood in the 1930s, cars were a vital part of the glamorous, rakish image. Paramount star Charles Rogers (above left) poses outside his Beverly Hills home with his Du Pont Phaeton; singer and actress Elizabeth Arden's choice (below left) was a Rolls-Royce Sedanca, with cap; blonde bombshell Jean Harlow (below right) chose a similar body-style on an American classic, the Cadillac V12.

Cars and stars ...

Für die Hollywood-Filmstars der dreißiger Jahre gehörten große Autos zum Leben in Luxus und Glamour dazu. Der Paramount-Star Charles Rogers (oben) lässt sich zu Hause in Beverly Hills mit seinem Du Pont Phaeton ablichten; die Sängerin und Schauspielerin Elizabeth Arden (links unten) zog einen Rolls-Royce Sedanca mit offenem Führerhaus vor, Sexbombe Jean Harlow einen amerikanischen Klassiker vom gleichen Bautyp, den Cadillac V12.

Voitures et vedettes ...

Dans les années 1930, les automobiles étaient un élément essentiel de l'image glamour et désinvolte que les stars d'Hollywood voulaient donner d'elles-mêmes. Charles Rogers, une vedette de la Paramount (en haut à gauche), pose ainsi devant sa maison de Beverly Hills près de son phaéton Du Pont ; la chanteuse et actrice Elizabeth Arden (en bas à gauche) a choisi une Rolls-Royce Sedanca de Ville, un style de carrosserie qu'apprécie également la blonde Jean Harlow (en bas à droite) mais sur une voiture plus classiquement américaine, la Cadillac V12.

A universal problem

By the mid-1930s, motor cars were being produced in
their millions, in Europe as well as America, and when
they all came together they sometimes ground to a halt.
Traffic jams such as this, at the entrance to New York's
Holland Tunnel (left), and the one in May 1935 at Hyde
Park Corner in London during the Jubilee celebrations
(right), were a fact of life for motorised city-dwellers.

Ein weltweites Problem

In den dreißiger Jahren wurden Automobile in Europa
und Amerika bereits in Millionenstückzahlen produziert,
und wenn sie alle gleichzeitig unterwegs sein wollten,
kam der Verkehr bisweilen zum Erliegen. Staus wie jenen
am Eingang zum New Yorker Holland Tunnel (links)
oder am Londoner Hyde Park Corner im Mai 1935 bei
den Feiern zum silbernen Kronjubiläum Georgs V.
(rechts) waren für städtische Automobilisten Schicksal.

Un problème universel

Au milieu des années 1930, il existe déjà plusieurs millions
d'automobiles, en Europe comme aux États-Unis, dont
le flot ne cesse de provoquer des embouteillages dans
les grandes villes, comme ici à l'entrée du Holland Tunnel
de New York (à gauche) ou, à Londres en mai 1935, à
Hyde Park Corner pendant les célébrations du Jubilée
(à droite).

Gathered together

In August 1939, 500 1940-model Vauxhalls (top left) left the factory in a great 'drive-away' to dealers. In October 1938 these Vauxhalls (top right) went to Czechoslovakia with the British 'Peace Army'. In July 1936 a fleet of cars (above left) brought guests of honour to the Berlin Olympics. The world's first parking meter was installed in Oklahoma City in 1935; by 1938 Omaha, Nebraska, had rows of them (above right).

Gleich und Gleich

Im August 1939 verließen 500 Vauxhalls des neuen Modells (oben links) das Werksgelände zur Auslieferung an die Händler. Im Oktober 1938 kam eine Reihe von Vauxhalls (oben rechts) mit der britischen »Friedensarmee« in die Tschechoslowakei. Eine Wagenflotte (unten links) stand im Juli 1936 bei den Berliner Olympischen Spielen für die Ehrengäste bereit. Die erste Parkuhr der Welt wurde 1935 in Oklahoma City aufgestellt; 1938 gab es sie in Omaha, Nebraska, reihenweise (unten rechts).

Rassemblés

En août 1939, ce sont 500 Vauxhall modèle 1940 (ci-dessus, à gauche) qui quittent l'usine. En octobre 1938, « l'Armée de Paix » britannique doit conduire ces Vauxhall (en haut à droite) en Tchécoslovaquie. En juillet 1936, toute une flotte de voitures avec chauffeur (ci-dessus, à gauche) est à la disposition des invités d'honneur aux Olympiades de Berlin. Le premier parcmètre du monde fut installé à Oklahoma City en 1935 et ils se comptent déjà par dizaines en 1958 dans cette rue d'Omaha (Nebraska).

Winter sunshine

In March 1938, as fascism spread the threat of war across Europe, and Britain continued a rapid rearmament, wintry sunshine brought Londoners out to the Serpentine in Hyde Park, where their cars, including a Rolls-Royce, an Auburn, a Vauxhall and a Packard, several of them with chauffeurs in attendance, were lined up to enjoy the view.

Ein sonniger Wintertag

Im März 1938 hatte der Faschismus bereits große Teile Europas ergriffen, die Zeichen standen auf Krieg und die Aufrüstung Großbritanniens lief auf Hochtouren, doch der winterliche Sonnentag brachte die Londoner trotzdem hinaus an den Serpentine-Teich im Hyde Park; viele bewunderten die Landschaft vom geparkten Wagen aus, wie sie hier in langer Reihe stehen, darunter ein Rolls-Royce, ein Auburn, ein Vauxhall und ein Packard, etliche mit wartendem Chauffeur.

Soleil hivernal

En mars 1938, alors que la montée du fascisme accroît la menace de guerre sur l'Europe et que la Grande-Bretagne poursuit un réarmement rapide, le soleil hivernal a entraîné les Londoniens à Hyde Park, où ils contemplent la vue des rives de la Serpentine depuis leur voiture ; on reconnaît une Rolls-Royce, une Auburn, une Vauxhall et une Packard, certaines avec chauffeur.

Let the show begin

In London, October has long been Motor Show time. In 1931 (above) workers prepare a two-seater utility version of the Morris Minor 8hp for its debut, at the magic figure of £100. In 1932 MG's F-Type Magna and J-Type Midget (below) are about to go on show. In 1937, when the Show moved from Olympia to Earls Court (right) for the first time, there were still a huge number of independent companies.

Die Show kann beginnen

Der traditionelle Monat für die Londoner Motor Show ist der Oktober. 1931 (oben) wird ein zweisitziges Basismodell des 8-PS-Morris Minor, der zum magischen Preis von £ 100 verkauft werden soll, für seine Premiere auf Hochglanz gebracht. 1932 bereitet MG den Magna F-Type und den Midget J-Type zur Ausstellung vor (unten). 1937, als der Autosalon erstmals nicht mehr im Olympia, sondern in Earls Court stattfand (rechts), gab es noch eine große Zahl unabhängiger Marken.

Que le spectacle commence

Le mois d'octobre est traditionnellement celui du salon de l'Auto de Londres. Des ouvriers finissent de préparer la version utilitaire deux places de la Morris Minor 8 ch (en haut), vendue au prix magique de 100 £, qui sera présentée au salon de 1931. La Magna Type F et la Midget Type J de MG (en bas) seront dévoilées à celui de 1932. En 1937, il subsiste un grand nombre de firmes indépendantes lorsque le Salon déménage de Olympia à Earls Court (à droite).

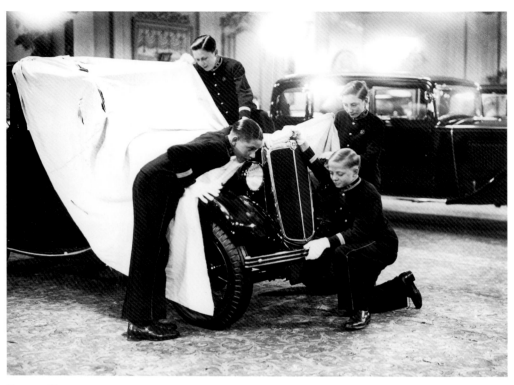

Guests of honour

In August 1934, bell-boys (above) take a sneak preview of the new Baby Morris, on show at the Grosvenor House Hotel, London, in the same year William Morris became Lord Nuffield and his company installed its first moving production lines. At an official dinner at Morris rivals the Standard Motor Company, in June 1936 (right), cars are the stars.

Ehrengäste

Im August 1934, als der Baby-Morris im Londoner Grosvenor House Hotel Premiere hat, werfen die Pagen schon einmal einen heimlichen Blick auf ihn (oben). Im selben Jahr wurde William Morris als Lord Nuffield geadelt, und seine Fabrik nahm das erste Fließband in Betrieb. Bei einem Empfang der Standard Motor Company, Morris' Rivalen, im Juni 1936 waren die Autos die Stars (rechts).

Invités d'honneur

La nouvelle Baby Morris est présentée en août 1934 au Grosvenor House Hotel de Londres (ci-dessus), l'année même où William Morris devient lord Nuffield et où sa firme installe sa première chaîne de fabrication mobile. Les voitures sont les vedettes lors de ce dîner officiel chez le rival de Morris, la Standard Motor Company, en juin 1936 (à droite).

Drawing the line

Road markings inevitably followed the spread of the automobile to control its movements, but it wasn't until October 1924 that the first central white line appeared on the road, in London's Whitehall. The white line changed shape to convey different messages, though the exact meaning of the warning given by this one on a perfectly straight road in Los Angeles in 1938 is a mystery.

Man muss einen Strich ziehen

Je mehr Autos auf die Straßen kamen, desto dringender wurden Markierungen erforderlich, die sie in Bahnen lenkten – auch wenn London sich bis zum Oktober 1924 Zeit ließ, bis in Whitehall die erste weiße Mittellinie gezogen wurde. Mit unterschiedlichen Markierungen konnte man dem Fahrer bestimmte Hinweise geben; was allerdings diese 1938 in Los Angeles aufgenommene Linie auf einer vollkommen geraden Straße ihm sagen wollte, bleibt ein Rätsel.

Une voie toute tracée

Le marquage des routes suit le développement de l'automobile mais ce n'est pas avant octobre 1924 qu'apparaît la première ligne blanche, à Whitehall à Londres. Si cette ligne blanche change de type selon les indications à fournir à l'automobiliste, la signification exacte de celle-ci, sur une route parfaitement droite de Los Angeles en 1938, reste mystérieuse !

Roads from the past, roads for the future

In October 1937 workmen are seen repainting the white lines on an English country road in Oxfordshire (above), with little traffic to disturb them. In 1934 Hitler had started a programme to build a network of auto-bahns in Germany, and this (below) is the opening of the first stretch of the Reichsautobahn from Munich to the Austrian border.

Alte Straßen, neue Straßen

Im Oktober 1937 erneuern Arbeiter auf einer englischen Landstraße in Oxfordshire den weißen Strich (oben), und der Verkehr, der sie dabei stört, ist kaum der Rede wert. In Deutschland hatte Hitler 1934 mit dem Bau von Autobahnen begonnen, und das Foto (unten) zeigt die Eröffnung des ersten Teilstücks der Reichsautobahn von München bis zur österreichischen Grenze.

Routes du passé et voies de l'avenir

En octobre 1937, ces ouvriers qui repeignent à la main la ligne blanche d'une route de campagne anglaise de l'Oxfordshire (en haut) ne sont pas vraiment gênés par la circulation automobile. C'est en 1934 que Hitler lance le programme de construction d'un vaste réseau d'autoroutes en Allemagne ; on voit ici (en bas) l'inauguration du premier tronçon de la Reichsautobahn, qui va de Munich à la limite du land de Bavière.

The people's car

As well as building roads to
stimulate the economy, Hitler
planned a car that could be
bought by all – the Volkswagen.
It was designed by Ferdinand
Porsche (opposite), showing a
model to Hitler and associates
(above) in April 1938. The real
thing appeared at the ceremony
in May 1938 (right) when Hitler
laid the foundation stone for
the factory where the VW would
be built.

Der Volkswagen

Die Nazis bauten, um die Wirtschaft in Gang zu bringen, nicht
nur Straßen, sondern dazu sollte
es auch einen Wagen geben, der
für jedermann erschwinglich
war. Der Konstrukteur Ferdinand
Porsche (gegenüber) führt Hitler
und einigen Funktionären im
April 1938 ein Modell vor (oben).
In Lebensgröße konnte man den
Volkswagen im Mai 1938 sehen,
als Hitler den Grundstein für das
Werk legte, in dem er gebaut
werden sollte (rechts).

La voiture du peuple

Faisant construire des autoroutes
pour stimuler l'économie, Hitler
veut également une voiture que
tout Allemand puisse acheter.
Cette Volkswagen, c'est-à-dire
« voiture du peuple », fut conçue
par Ferdinand Porsche (ci-contre),
qui en présente la maquette à
Hitler et ses affidés (ci-dessus)
en avril 1938. Cette voiture sera
présentée en mai 1938, lors de
la cérémonie d'inauguration de
l'usine où elle sera construite
(à droite).

On the road

In mid-1930s America, cars like this elderly truck with minimal bodywork and different types of wheel front and back were pure workhorses, kept on the road not by expensive new spare parts from the manufacturer but by those salvaged from outlets like this (above) in Atlanta, Georgia. Hitching a ride (right), near Vicksburg, Mississippi – an American way of life.

Immer auf Achse

Im Amerika der mittleren dreißiger Jahre waren die Fahrzeuge oft reine Arbeitspferde, wie etwa der alte Lastwagen mit minimalem Aufbau und unterschiedlichen Vorder- und Hinterrädern; sie wurden nicht mit neuen Ersatzteilen vom Hersteller in Gang gehalten, sondern mit dem, was sich in Werkstätten wie dieser (oben) in Atlanta, Georgia, zufällig fand. Anhalter bei Vicksburg, Mississippi (rechts) – in Amerika eine Selbstverständlichkeit.

Sur la route

Vers le milieu des années 1930, aux États-Unis, des véhicules comme ce camion, à carrosserie minimale et roues de types différents n'étaient pas rares. Ces automobiles circulent grâce non pas à des pièces détachées onéreuses venues de l'usine mais à celles que vendent des garages comme celui-ci (ci-dessus), d'Atlanta, Georgie. L'auto-stop (à droite), près de Vicksburg, Mississipi, est un mode de transport alors très américain.

230

Motorists of the future

Children from a public nursery in Tokyo preparing for a day's outing in what seems to be a Model T coach (above) around 1935, when the Japanese motor industry was also in its infancy. The Mitsubishi Shipbuilding Co. in Kobe had built some cars between 1917 and 1921 but the industry started properly with the arrival of Datsun (soon to become Nissan) in 1932 and Toyota in 1936. Around the same time, village children somewhere in Ghana (below) gather around a much used Morgan three-wheeler from the early 1920s.

Automobilisten der Zukunft

Kindergartenkinder in Tokio, bereit zu einem Ausflug mit dem Bus (oben), offenbar auf Model-T-Basis, aufgenommen um 1935, als die japanische Autoindustrie selbst noch in den Kinderschuhen steckte. Die Mitsubishi Shipbuilding Co. in Kobe hatte zwar zwischen 1917 und 1921 einige Wagen gebaut, doch wirklich in Gang kam die Industrie erst mit der Gründung von Datsun (bald in Nissan umbenannt), 1932, und Toyota, 1936. Etwa zur gleichen Zeit versammeln sich Dorfkinder in Ghana (unten) um ein arg strapaziertes Morgan-Dreirad aus den frühen Zwanzigern.

Les automobilistes du futur

Ces enfants d'une école maternelle de Tokyo préparent une sortie dans ce qui semble être un autocar Ford Model T (en haut), à une époque (vers 1935) où l'industrie automobile japonaise en est encore à ses débuts. La Mitsubishi Shipbuilding Co. de Kobe a bien construit quelques voitures entre 1917 et 1921 mais l'industrie automobile ne se développe véritablement qu'avec l'arrivée de Datsun (par la suite Nissan) en 1932 et de Toyota en 1936. Vers la même époque, les enfants d'un village du Ghana (en bas) se rassemblent autour d'un tricycle Morgan très fatigué datant du début des années 1920.

World travellers

In June 1936 two unemployed Czechoslovakian adventurers, Akos Balazs and Joseph Zahradnick, arrived in Manchester, England, and added another badge to the dozens already covering the 1926 Tatra T12 in which they were attempting to drive around the world. The T12 was a fine car for the trip, designed by the brilliant Hans Ledwinka and built in Czechoslovakia until 1933, with 7,525 made in some 11 body styles, of which this was one of the more sporting.

Weltreisende

Im Juni 1936 treffen die tschechoslowakischen Abenteurer Akos Balazs und Joseph Zahradnick im englischen Manchester ein, wo sie den zahlreichen Plaketten, mit denen die Motorhaube ihres 1926er Tatra T12 schon geschmückt ist, eine weitere hinzufügen. Die beiden Arbeitslosen waren zu einer Reise um die Welt aufgebrochen, und der T12 war ein guter Wagen dafür; vom Meisterkonstrukteur Hans Ledwinka entworfen, wurde er in der Tschechoslowakei bis 1933 gebaut, insgesamt 7525 Exemplare in elf Karosserievarianten, von denen dies eine der sportlicheren war.

Les grands voyageurs

En juin 1936, deux aventuriers tchécoslovaques au chômage, Akos Balazs et Joseph Zahradnick, arrivent à Manchester (Angleterre) et ajoutent un nouvel auto-collant à la douzaine de ceux qui couvrent déjà le capot de leur Tatra T12 de 1926 avec laquelle ils comptent effectuer le tour du monde. Voiture idéale pour ce genre de voyage, conçue par le brillant ingénieur Hans Ledwinka, la T12 fut construite en Tchécoslovaquie jusqu'en 1933 et produite à 7 525 exemplaires en 11 modèles différents (celui-ci est un des plus sportifs).

Starting young

Young Gwennie Beavor (above) has her pedal car fully loaded for a holiday trip in March 1931. Don Banks (below) in 1934, showing off what looks like an impressive replica of Sir Henry Segrave's Sunbeam record breaker of 1926. And a real record breaker (right) – Sir Malcolm Campbell's new Bluebird in January 1933, the basis of the car with which he finally broke the 300mph barrier in 1935. In the cockpit is his son Donald, who was destined to become holder of both land and water speed records.

Klein anfangen

Die junge Gwennie Beavor (oben) hat im März 1931 ihr Tretauto für die Urlaubsfahrt gepackt. Don Banks (unten) zeigt 1934 stolz seine eindrucksvolle Miniaturausgabe von Sir Henry Segraves Sunbeam-Rekordwagen von 1926. Und ein echter Rekordwagen (rechts) – Sir Malcolm Campbells neuer Bluebird vom Januar 1933, mit dessen Weiterentwicklung er 1935 erstmals die 300-Meilen-Grenze überschritt. Im Cockpit ist sein Sohn Donald zu sehen, der später selbst Geschwindigkeitsrekorde zu Land und zur See errang.

Commencer jeune

La jeune Gwennie Beavor (en haut) a lourdement chargé sa voiture à pédales pour partir en vacances, en mars 1931. En 1934, Don Banks (en bas) présente ce qui semble être une impressionnante réplique de la Sunbeam de sir Henry Segrave, avec laquelle il battit le record de vitesse en 1926. La nouvelle Bluebird de sir Malcolm Campbell – prototype de la voiture avec laquelle il franchira finalement la barrière des 482 km/h en 1935 – est présentée ici (à droite) en janvier 1933 par son fils Donald, futur détenteur des records de vitesse sur terre et sur l'eau.

Gentlemen and players

Pupils at Eton public school in October 1934 watching two friends (above) in Rytecraft Scootacars, tiny but fully roadworthy single-seat cars launched that year, with a 98cc single-cylinder two-stroke engine. In 1938, less privileged schoolboys play in a field (right) in their garage owner father's old Austin Seven.

Gentlemen und kleine Jungs

Schüler der Privatschule Eton haben sich im Oktober 1934 (oben) um zwei Freunde in Rytecraft Scootacars versammelt; die winzigen, doch durchaus gebrauchstüchtigen Einsitzer, angetrieben von einem 98 ccm-Einzylinder-Zweitaktmotor, waren in jenem Jahr auf den Markt gekommen. Weniger privilegierte Schuljungen spielen 1938 auf der Wiese (rechts) im alten Austin Seven ihres Vaters, eines Werkstattbesitzers.

Gentlemen et joueurs

Les élèves du collège d'Eton en octobre 1934 contemplent deux de leurs camarades (ci-dessus) au volant de Scootacar Ryte-craft, petites voitures monoplace équipées d'un moteur mono-cylindre deux temps de 98 cm³ lancées l'année même. En 1938, des collégiens moins privilégiés s'amusent à conduire (à droite) la vieille Austin Seven de leur père, propriétaire d'une station service.

Small scale

Another version of the Hanomag Kommissbrot two-seater (above left), a car advertised as 'cheaper than a third-class railway ticket' and on which Hanomag's success was founded. In September 1939 the pedal-powered Velocar (above right) addressed the coming problem of wartime petrol rationing, while the 1939 Scootacar (below left) claimed to do 80mpg. The tiny Studebaker (below right) was shown at the 1935 Schoolboys' Own Exhibition in London, and inspected by Britain's tallest man, Sergeant McCulloch. The Whitwood two-seater 'monocar' of 1954 (right) was yet another approach to compact motoring.

Kleinformat

Eine weitere Variante des Zweisitzers Hanomag Kommissbrot (oben links). Der Hanomag, beworben mit dem Slogan »Billiger als eine Bahnfahrkarte dritter Klasse«, war für die Firma der größte Erfolg. Das Velocar mit Pedalantrieb (oben rechts) lieferte im September 1939 schon die Lösung für die Benzinrationierungen des Krieges, doch auch der Scootacar aus demselben Jahr (unten links) sollte mit 3,5 Litern auf 100 Kilometer zufrieden sein. Der winzige Studebaker (unten rechts) war auf einer Schulausstellung in London 1935 zu sehen und wird hier vom größten Mann in Großbritannien inspiziert, Sergeant McCulloch. Das zweisitzige Whitwood-»Monocar« von 1954 (rechts) war ein weiterer Beitrag zum Thema Kompaktwagen.

Petite échelle

La publicité disait de cette voiture, une version deux places de la Kommissbrot Hanomag (en haut à gauche), qu'elle revenait « moins cher qu'un billet de chemin de fer en 3ᵉ classe », un argument sur lequel s'est fondé tout le succès de Hanomag. En septembre 1939, le Velocar à pédales (en haut à droite) semble parfaitement adapté au futur problème de rationnement en essence pendant la guerre, tout comme ce Scootacar de 1939 (en bas à gauche), qui n'aurait consommé que 3,5 l/100 km. Cette minuscule Studebaker (en bas à droite) fut présentée à la Schoolboys' Own Exhibition de Londres en 1935 et examinée par l'homme le plus grand de Grande-Bretagne à l'époque, le sergent McCulloch. Le « monocar » deux places Whitwood de 1934 (à droite) était une autre approche de l'automobile compacte.

Ancient and modern

Margaret Allen on the Brooklands banking in March 1936 in Richard Marker's stripped and streamlined 4.5-litre Bentley (above) – the archetypal British sports car of its day. In contrast, in October 1937 the state-sponsored German Grand Prix cars from Mercedes-Benz and Auto Union brought ultimate pre-war racing design to Donington Park. This (right) is an airborne Mercedes W125; the race was won by Bernd Rosemeyer's Auto Union.

Alt und neu

Margaret Allen im März 1936 in der Hochkurve von Brooklands (oben). Der Wagen ist Richard Markers gewichtsreduzierter und mit Strom-linienhaube versehener 4,5-Liter-Bentley – der Inbegriff des briti-schen Sportwagens jener Zeit. Die modernsten Rennwagenkonstruk-tionen der Vorkriegszeit kamen jedoch aus Deutschland, und im Oktober 1937 waren die staatlich finanzierten Grand-Prix-Wagen von Mercedes-Benz und Auto Union im Donington Park am Start. Der Mercedes W125 nimmt die Strecke im Flug (rechts), doch Sieger wurde Bernd Rosemeyer auf Auto Union.

Ancien et moderne

En mars 1936, on pouvait admirer Margaret Allen prendre le virage de Brooklands dans la Bentley 4,5 l profilée due à Richard Marker (ci-dessus) – archétype de la voiture de sport britannique de l'époque. En octobre 1937, les Mercedes-Benz et Auto Union qui participent au Grand Prix d'Allemagne, sponsorisé par l'État, présentent au public de Donington Park le dernier cri en matière de conception des voitures de course, avec notamment cette Mercedes W125 (à droite) ; la course fut remportée par l'Auto Union de Bernd Rosemeyer.

Demonstration models

In 1936, JT Griffin (above) of Castleford, Yorkshire, demonstrates a system of rollers below the radiator designed to stop pedestrians falling under the car. In 1932, strongman J Rolleano (below left) has a Citroën drive over his chest; in contrast, learner Winnie Collins (below right) only drives over the kerbstones. The 'gunman' (opposite) is showing the effectiveness of bullet-proof glass on an American Chrysler Airflow, with gun ports, tested by police in London in 1937.

Experimente

Im Jahr 1936 führt J. T. Griffin aus Castleford, Yorkshire, seine rollenden Stoßstangen vor (oben), die verhindern sollen, dass Fußgänger unter ein Auto geraten. Der Muskelprotz J. Rolleano lässt sich 1932 einen Citroën über die Brust fahren (unten links); die Fahrschülerin Winnie Collins (unten rechts) übt noch an Bordsteinkanten. Der »Ganove« (gegenüber) führt die Wirksamkeit des kugelsicheren Glases an einem amerikanischen Chrysler Airflow vor; die mit Schussrohren versehenen Wagen wurden 1937 von der Londoner Polizei getestet.

Inventions et démonstrations

En 1936, J. T. Griffin, de Castleford (Yorkshire), fait la démonstration d'un système à rouleaux fixé sous le radiateur et destiné à empêcher les piétons de passer sous la voiture (en haut). En 1932, tandis que J. Rolleano fait passer une Citroën sur sa poitrine (en bas à gauche), l'apprentie conductrice Winnie Collins (en bas à droite) semble ne savoir rouler que sur les bordures de trottoir. En 1937, ce faux gangster de la police de Londres (ci-contre) prouve l'efficacité du verre antiballes monté sur une Chrysler Airflow américaine, équipée de hublots de tir.

Directing traffic

A young policeman (above) leads a traffic awareness game at school in Lancashire in 1936. Real traffic policemen around the world in the 1930s had their own styles – the Parisian with his cape and baton (opposite, top left), the London bobby with his white sleeves (opposite, top right), the Malay with his semaphore board, and the Boston cop trying to keep warm with his stove (opposite, below left and right).

Große und kleine Ordnungshüter

Ein jugendlicher Polizist (oben) ist der Anführer in einem Verkehrserziehungsspiel in einer Schule in Lancashire, 1936. Bei echten Verkehrspolizisten hatte in den Dreißigern jedes Land seinen eigenen Stil – in Paris (gegenüber, oben links) mit Umhang und Stock, der Londoner Bobby (oben rechts) mit weißen Ärmeln, ein Malaie (unten links) mit umgeschnalltem Anzeigebrett und (unten rechts) ein Polizist in Boston, der auf seinem Stand ein Öfchen hat, damit ihm nicht kalt wird.

Circulez !

Les agents de la circulation des années 1930 ont un style différent selon les pays : l'hirondelle de Paris, avec sa cape et son bâton (ci-contre, en haut à gauche), le bobby de Londres avec ses manchettes blanches (ci-contre, en haut à droite), le policier colonial malais avec sa planche sémaphore (ci-contre, en bas à gauche) ou le cop de Boston dont la guérite est équipée en hiver d'un petit poêle (ci-contre, en bas à droite). En 1936, ce jeune policier du Lancashire (ci-dessus) règle la circulation de son école.

Signs of the times

A young boy in his pedal car racer (opposite, left) looking at one of the new speed limit signs in Bristol in 1935; a mother in 1937 (opposite, right) giving a bit more protection to her cyclist son; young and old demonstrators in 1937 (above) encouraging their local authorities to impose a 30mph speed limit and save lives; and final stages in the production of hundreds of new road signs for Britain's roads in 1935 (below).

Zeichen der Zeit

Ein junger Automobilist im Tretrennwagen begutachtet eins der neuen Geschwindigkeitsbegrenzungsschilder in Bristol, 1935 (gegenüber links); eine Mutter nimmt 1937 die Sicherheit ihres Fahrrad fahrenden Sohnes selbst in die Hand (gegenüber rechts); Jung und Alt protestieren 1937 gemeinsam (oben) für mehr Verkehrssicherheit durch ein 30-Meilen-Tempolimit; und die letzten Retuschen an Hunderten von neuen Schildern, die 1935 an britischen Straßen aufgestellt wurden (unten).

Signes des temps

Des panneaux de signalisation divers, peints à la main (en bas) fleurissent sur le bord des routes britanniques vers 1935 et suscitent parfois des interrogations chez certains, comme ce panneau de limitation de vitesse, installé à Bristol (ci-contre, à gauche). En 1937, cette jeune mère préfère évidemment prévenir – « S'il vous plaît, M. l'automobiliste, faites attention à moi ! » – face aux dangers de la route que doit affronter son fils (ci-contre, à droite). La vitesse des voitures devient effectivement un problème comme en témoignent ces manifestants, jeunes et vieux (en haut), incitant les autorités locales à imposer une limitation à 30 miles/h.

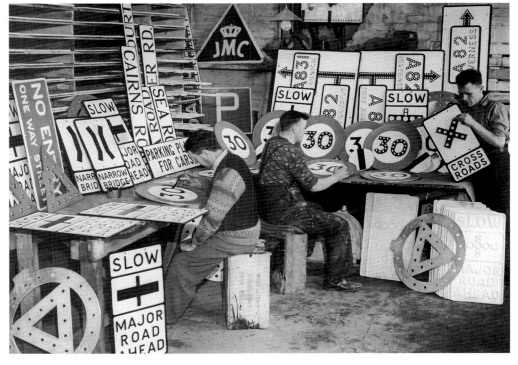

Innovators and inventors

In 1931 at the International Exhibition of Inventions in London, ED Sykes (above) showed his system of signals controlled from the steering column. Shatterproof windscreen glass with chemically strengthened inner panes (below left) was demonstrated in 1938. The automatic traffic-arm signal of 1934 (below right) was meant for night-time, when use of the horn was not permitted. Sir Dennistoun Burney was the designer of the R100 airship, and the Burney Streamline (right), a strange looking but technically advanced car with all-independent suspension and rear-mounted Alvis engine, which was launched in 1930.

Neuerer und Erfinder

1931 stellt E. D. Sykes (oben) auf der Internationalen Erfindermesse in London seinen Richtungsanzeiger mit Schalter an der Lenksäule vor. Sicherheitswindschutzscheiben mit chemisch verstärkter Innenschicht (unten links) sah man 1938. Der automatische Winker von 1934 (unten rechts) war für Nachtfahrten gedacht, wo das Hupen verboten war. Neben dem Luftschiff R100 konstruierte Sir Dennistoun Burney auch den Burney Streamline (rechts); das seltsam anzusehende, doch technisch fortschrittliche Gefährt mit einzeln aufgehängten Rädern und einem Alvis-Motor im Heck kam 1930 auf den Markt.

Novateurs et inventeurs

E. D. Sykes propose son système de signaux optiques commandés depuis la colonne de direction lors de l'International Exhibition of Inventions de Londres de 1931 (en haut). Un pare-brise à verre sécurit avec panneaux intérieur renforcés chimiquement (en bas à droite) est présenté en 1938. En 1934, une fausse main adaptée à la portière permet de signaler automatiquement les changements de direction la nuit, où l'usage de l'avertisseur est interdit (en bas à gauche). Sir Dennistoun Burney, le concepteur du dirigeable R100, est l'inventeur de la Burney Streamline (à droite), une voiture d'étrange allure mais techniquement avancée, lancée en 1930, qui dispose d'une suspension entièrement indépendante et d'un moteur Alvis à l'arrière.

The end of the road

Nowadays, recycling of motor cars
that have outlived their usefulness
is a sophisticated process dictated
by laws and surrounded by politics.
In February 1935, in a scrapyard
in the Tottenham area of north
London, the idea of recycling parts
held good, but the methods were
much simpler.

Ende der Fahrt

Heute ist das Recycling von aus-
gemusterten Fahrzeugen eine
Wissenschaft für sich, mit gesetz-
lichen Richtlinien und politischen
Vorgaben. Die Idee, Altteile weiter-
zuverwerten, gab es jedoch auch
schon im Februar 1935, als dieses
Foto von einem Schrottplatz im
Nordlondoner Stadtteil Tottenham
entstand – nur die Methoden
waren weitaus einfacher.

Le bout de la route

Le recyclage des automobiles et la
récupération des pièces détachées
sont aujourd'hui soumis à une
législation complexe et sévèrement
contrôlés. Ce n'était pas encore le
cas en février 1935 dans cette casse
automobile des environs de
Tottenham, au nord de Londres.

251

Small car fashions

Hanomag eventually replaced the old Kommissbrot 'army loaf' with more conventional looking small cars, such as (above) the front-engined, four-cylinder 800cc 3/16PS Kleinwagen, which was introduced in 1928. Like many European small cars of the time, it owed much of its philosophy to the car that had set the pattern for motoring for the masses on this side of the Atlantic back in the early 1920s – the hugely successful Austin Seven (right), of which this is a 1932 example.

Klein, aber fein

Die Nachfolger des »Kommissbrot« waren bei Hanomag wieder konventionellere Kleinwagen, etwa dieses 1928 vorgestellte Modell; der Vierzylinder war nun vorn eingebaut und leistete 3/16 PS aus 800 ccm (oben). Wie viele europäische Kleinwagen der Zeit folgte auch er der Grundform, die diesseits des Atlantiks Anfang der zwanziger Jahre für das billige Massenauto gefunden worden war – mit dem äußerst erfolgreichen Austin Seven (rechts), hier das Modell von 1932.

La mode des petites voitures

Hanomag remplaça finalement son ancienne Kommissbrot par une voiture d'allure plus conventionnelle, comme cette Kleinwagen 3/16PS à moteur quatre cylindres de 800 cm³ placé à l'avant (ci-dessus), commercialisée en 1928. À l'instar de nombreuses petites voitures européennes de l'époque, elle devait beaucoup à l'Austin Seven, dont on voit ici un modèle de 1932 (à droite), une voiture très réussie qui a défini le style de l'automobile populaire en Europe au milieu des années 1920.

Powerful men; helpless victims

Hermann Göring (above) leaving Berlin Cathedral on his wedding day in April 1935, in the inevitable Mercedes – the elegant and sporty 540K. Lenin liked Rolls-Royces, but Joseph Stalin (below) chose the home-grown product, the large official saloon closely modelled on American cars of the time. In 1933 the AMO car factory in Moscow was renamed Zavod Imieni Stalina in his honour, and the cars became ZISs – and the long-time choice of Russian leaders. The dark side of 1930s fascism (right): tired troops, broken cars in 1936, at the height of the Spanish Civil War.

Mächtige Männer, wehrlose Opfer

Hermann Göring (oben) verlässt im April 1935 nach seiner Hochzeit die Berliner Kathedrale, natürlich im Mercedes – dem eleganten und sportlichen 540K. Lenin fuhr gern Rolls-Royce, doch für Joseph Stalin (unten) musste es etwas Heimisches sein, wobei die schwere Staatslimousine sich eng an amerikanische Vorbilder der Zeit anlehnte. 1933 wurden die AMO-Werke in Moskau ihm zu Ehren in Zawod Imieni Stalina umbenannt; die Wagen hießen nun SIS und fuhren über lange Jahre die sowjetischen Staatsoberhäupter. Die Schattenseite des Faschismus der dreißiger Jahre (rechts): erschöpfte Truppen und zerstörte Fahrzeuge auf dem Höhepunkt des Spanischen Bürgerkrieges, 1936.

De la gloire à la défaite

Le jour de son mariage (avril 1935), Hermann Göring quitte la cathédrale de Berlin dans l'élégante et sportive Mercedes 540K, symbole de réussite et quasi « voiture d'État » (en haut). Si Lénine aimait les Rolls-Royce, Joseph Staline préférait ce genre de vaste berline, très inspirée des voitures américaines de l'époque mais construite en URSS (en bas). C'est en 1933 que l'usine automobile AMO de Moscou fut rebaptisée en son honneur Zavod Imieni Stalina, qui donna ainsi naissance à la marque ZIS des voitures officielles soviétiques. Le fascisme n'épargne ni les hommes ni les automobiles, comme ici en 1936 pendant la guerre d'Espagne (à droite).

Preparing for war – again

Through much of the 1930s it was clear war was coming and this time the car would be in the front line. There were early experiments (above) with wireless communications, as on this Morris Tourer, and with portable bridges (above right), while the King's Own Royal Regiment in Lancashire in 1936 (opposite) used vehicles as a recruiting aid. Even the Rytecraft found another role (below right).

Rüstung für den nächsten Krieg

Im Laufe des Jahrzehnts wurde immer deutlicher, dass ein Krieg unvermeidlich war, und es war keine Frage, dass diesmal Automobile an vorderster Front stehen würden. Es gab frühe Experimente mit Funkwagen wie diesem Morris Tourer (oben) und mit transportablen Brücken (rechts oben); das King's Own Royal Regiment warb 1936 in Lancashire mit Wagenparaden Rekruten an (gegenüber), und selbst der Rytecraft fand eine neue Rolle (rechts unten).

La guerre, encore !

Pendant les années 1930, tout le monde s'attend à ce que la guerre éclate et l'automobile sera cette fois en première ligne. On procède à des expériences de télécommunication sans fil, ici sur une Morris Tourer (ci-dessus), ou de ponts transportables (en haut à droite). En 1936, le King's Own Royal Regiment utilise ses véhicules pour le recrutement des volontaires au Lancashire (ci-contre) alors que certaines unités de défense passive se servent du Scootacar Rytecraft (en bas à droite).

6
Back to War:
The Forties under Fire

As the 1940s dawned, Europe was at war again, private motoring was seriously curtailed, production
of private cars effectively stopped. Even Hitler's
project to build a 'People's Car' was on hold – at
least so far as the civilian market was concerned.

In different circumstances, it would have provided a spectacular entrance for the motoring democracy into the new
decade. Way back in 1934, opening the Berlin Motor Show, the
new Chancellor had laid out his plans. 'It is a bitter thought',
he said, 'that millions of good and industrious people are
excluded from the use of a means of transport that, especially
on Sundays and holidays, could become for them a source of
unknown joy. The problem is one that must be tackled with
courage, boldness and resolution. What cannot be achieved in
one year will, perhaps, be taken for granted in ten ...'

'Germany', he went on, ' has only one automobile for each
100 inhabitants, France has one for each 28 and the United
States one for each six. That disparity must be changed ...
I would like to see a German car mass-produced so that it can
be bought by anyone who can afford a motorcycle. Simple,
reliable, economic transportation is needed. We must have a
real car for the German people – a Volkswagen'.

It was the first time he had used the word Volkswagen in a
public speech, and he meant it literally as 'a car for the people'.
It was a real vision. Hitler never learned to drive but he was
obsessed with the idea of giving the ordinary German previously unheard of mobility. Imprisoned in Landsberg in the
1920s, he had read Henry Ford's book, *My Life and Work*, and
he made no secret of his admiration for Ford's ideas. In its way
his own vision was an extension of the dreams of the earliest
pioneers, and if Hitler also saw the political power inherent in
it, the underlying principle of a people's car remained.

In May 1934 he had presented his main criteria for the car
to the man most likely to design it, Dr Ferdinand Porsche. It
had to be capable of cruising at 100kph (60mph) on the new
autobahns, while delivering more than 33mpg; it had to
accommodate four to five people; it had to be air-cooled for
reliability and it had to be easy to maintain and repair. And the
punchline? It had to sell for less than 1,000 Reichsmarks –
barely half what Ford's Model T had sold for in its heyday. The
rest of the German car industry could see the task was impossible, but in June 1934 Dr Porsche accepted the contract.

The development story was long and complex, and the later
plan to sell the car through a stamp-savings scheme added
further complications but Porsche showed Hitler his first two
prototypes in June 1936, and thirty more were completed by
early 1937, for endurance testing by selected SS officers. In May
1938, with Porsche's part in the project completed, Hitler laid
the foundation stone for a vast new factory, and a town to support it. Two days later he ordered troops to prepare for the
invasion of Czechoslovakia, but the work continued.

In April 1938 the first machinery was installed, and stamp
investors were promised cars would be ready by 1940. Some
335,000 Germans had subscribed to the scheme by the time the
war began, but the only people who ever drove the pre-production cars were high-ranking Nazi officers. Soon, the factory, like car factories across Europe, was switched to war work.
It made munitions, repaired aircraft and built two military
vehicles hastily adapted from the Volkswagen, the Kubelwagen
staff car and the amphibious Schwimmwagen.

Early in 1940, Britain was forced to abandon a huge proportion of its already fairly sparse supply of military vehicles
in Dunkirk, and the British industry began to work flat out to
replace them and to manufacture all the other necessities of
war, from aircraft to tanks, boats to tractors, armoured cars
and rocket launchers to ambulances. For their efforts, of
course, they became a prime target for the enemy bombers.

In America, there were no bombs and, in the beginning, no
direct involvement in the war. Civilian car production, for the
interim, continued almost unabated, America building around
3.7 million cars a year through 1940 and 1941, while again supplying significant volumes of military hardware to the Allies.
And in general the American cars of the period were fine
things, stylish, substantial, powerful and well equipped, with
Chevrolet comfortably heading Ford in the sales race.

In 1942 all that changed as Detroit joined the rest of
America on a national war footing. Virtually everyone built
trucks, most built a lot more. Chrysler made, among many
other things, aircraft engines and fuselages, rockets, tanks,
marine engines and boats; General Motors, the biggest con-
tributor of all, built entire aircraft, guns, torpedoes, armoured
cars, tanks and much else; other manufacturers had their own
specialities, from Packard's version of the Rolls-Royce Merlin
aero engine to Hudson's B-29 bomber components, and
Studebaker's radial aircraft engines. Henry Ford, as in the first
war, maintained his position of pacifism and neutrality, but his
company nonetheless built Liberator bombers, Sherman tanks,
armoured personnel carriers, and gliders.

In the end, the American car makers would produce some $29 billion-worth of war materials and perhaps the best known of them was a motor vehicle – the Jeep. The four-wheel-drive 'General Purpose' vehicle (the initials GP supposedly gave it its name) was produced first by Bantam, the company that had built the American Austin Seven, but its production was soon farmed out to bigger companies who could build the vast numbers needed for the war effort, amongst them Ford, but most notably Willys. The Jeep without doubt became one of the war's most vital, most versatile tools; afterwards it became a civilian vehicle, and it started an entire off-road movement.

When the world war ended in 1945, America was still fighting in the Far East, and Europe was in a parlous state – not least its car factories, many of which had been bombed almost out of existence because of their strategic importance over the past few years. Materials were in short supply, fuel and oil would be rationed into the 1950s, and again, economies had been crippled. For the motor industry, the remainder of the 1940s would be a limbo period, but it was a sign of the industry's resilience that even now they were looking ahead.

For now, survival was the priority, and the British watchword was 'export or die'; exports alone could earn the foreign currency, notably dollars, to buy the materials to keep industry moving. The availability of new cars on the home market was severely restricted (and heavily taxed) by a new socialist government which (in a new show of establishment antipathy) didn't have the private motorist high on its list of priorities. And although they were far more expensive than they had been immediately before the war, the 'new' cars of the early post-war years were really no more than old models with token updating. It wouldn't be until the London Motor Show of 1948 that anything genuinely new appeared, but then the British industry (which was now the most prolific in Europe) introduced dozens of newcomers – from the prosaic Morris Minor and Hillman Minx to the sporty Jaguar XK120.

The industry was reborn. Even the export drive worked, with the vast majority of British cars being sent abroad, including many to America, whose homecoming troops were particularly keen to import the kind of small, very British sports cars they had come to know during their time in Europe – to the huge benefit of companies like MG, and later Triumph. America, too, however, had manufacturing restrictions, and in Europe outside of Britain, reconstruction would largely be based on small economy models such as the 2CV from Citroën

and the 4CV from Renault in France, or the Topolino in Italy. A full return to normality was coming but it would still take time.

Amid the reconstruction, there was one notable survivor. At the end of the war, the factory Hitler had created to build his Kraft-durch-Freude, KdF-Wagen (the 'Strength through' Joy car), was heavily damaged, the savings scheme abandoned, the car still in effect little more than a prototype. What remained was taken over first by American troops then the British military, and in 1945 the town of KdF-Stadt was renamed Wolfsburg and the car Volkswagen. The project was offered to several manufacturers as war reparations; all of them, from Ford to engineers from the Rootes Group, rejected it (car design included) as of no possible value. In the absence of any other taker, VW was managed for a while by a British officer, Major Ivan Hirst, who resumed production late in 1945, originally building cars purely for military use. In 1948 the company was returned to German administration, and in 1949 two Beetles, as the car had been nicknamed, were exported to America. They were the first of many millions, as the Beetle eventually overtook the Model T as the biggest selling car of all time.

Als die vierziger Jahre ins Land zogen, herrschte in Europa von neuem Krieg; private Autofahrten unterlagen strikten Beschränkungen, und die Produktion von Fahrzeugen für den privaten Gebrauch war fast zum Erliegen gekommen. Selbst Hitlers Traum vom Volkswagen lag auf Eis – zumindest, was den zivilen Markt betraf.

Dabei hätte das Projekt unter anderen Umständen der motorisierten Demokratie einen spektakulären Eintritt ins neue Jahrzehnt verschaffen können. Schon 1934 hatte der frisch gewählte Reichskanzler bei der Eröffnung des Berliner Autosalons seinen Plan mit den folgenden Worten skizziert: »Es erfüllt mich mit Schmerz, dass Millionen von guten und fleißigen Menschen ein Verkehrsmittel verwehrt bleibt, das vor allem an Sonn- und Feiertagen für sie ein Quell ungeahnter Freude sein könnte. Das ist eine Herausforderung, der wir mit Mut, Kühnheit und Entschlossenheit begegnen müssen. Was in einem Jahr nicht gelingen kann, ist in zehn Jahren vielleicht schon Selbstverständlichkeit ...«

»In Deutschland«, fuhr er fort, »gibt es nur einen einzigen Wagen auf hundert Einwohner, in Frankreich ist das Verhältnis 1 zu 28 und in Amerika sogar nur 1 zu 6. Dieses Missverhältnis gilt es auszugleichen ... Ich will erleben, wie ein deutsches Fahrzeug in Massenproduktion geht, ein Fahrzeug, das für jeden erschwinglich ist, der sich ein Motorrad leisten kann. Was wir brauchen, ist ein einfaches, zuverlässiges, sparsames Transportmittel. Wir brauchen ein echtes Fahrzeug für das deutsche Volk – einen Volkswagen.«

Damals sprach Hitler zum ersten Mal in einer öffentlichen Rede vom Volkswagen, und er meinte es durchaus wörtlich, als Wagen für das ganze Volk. Hitler lernte selbst nie Auto fahren, aber er war besessen von der Idee einer bis dahin unvorstellbaren Mobilität für das deutsche Volk. Als er in den zwanziger Jahren in Landsberg inhaftiert war, hatte er Henry Fords Buch *Mein Leben und Werk* gelesen, und er machte keinen Hehl aus seiner Bewunderung für Fords Ideen. In gewisser Hinsicht setzte seine eigene Vision die Träume der Autopioniere fort, und auch wenn natürlich politische Motive dahinter steckten, blieb doch der Grundgedanke einer Wohltat für das Volk intakt.

Im Mai 1934 hatte er seine Hauptkriterien für ein solches Fahrzeug dem Mann vorgelegt, der als dessen geeignetster Konstrukteur galt: Dr. Ferdinand Porsche. Es sollte auf den neuen Autobahnen mit einer Geschwindigkeit von 100 km/h fahren können, bei einem Verbrauch von 8,5 Litern auf 100 Kilometer; es sollte Platz für vier bis fünf Personen haben; der größeren Zuverlässigkeit wegen sollte es luftgekühlt sein, und es sollte leicht zu warten und zu reparieren sein. Und das Wichtigste? Es sollte weniger als 1000 Reichsmark kosten – knapp die Hälfte dessen, was Fords Model T in seinen besten Zeiten gekostet hatte. Obwohl der Rest der deutschen Automobilindustrie das für eine unlösbare Aufgabe hielt, unterschrieb Porsche im Juni 1934 den Vertrag.

Die Geschichte der Entwicklung war lang und kompliziert, und der erst später hinzugekommene Gedanke, das Auto über einen Sparplan zu verkaufen, schuf weitere Komplikationen. Dennoch führte Porsche im Juni 1936 Hitler die ersten beiden Prototypen vor, und Anfang 1937 wurden weitere 30 Wagen fertig gestellt und für Belastungstests an ausgewählte SS-Offiziere übergeben. Im Mai 1938, als Porsche seinen Teil der Arbeit getan hatte, legte Hitler den Grundstein für eine riesige neue Fabrik mit eigener Stadt. Zwei Tage später ordnete er den Einmarsch in die Tschechoslowakei an, doch die Arbeiten am Automobilwerk beeinträchtigte das zunächst nicht.

Im April 1938 wurden die ersten Maschinen installiert, und die Käufer von Sparmarken erhielten die Zusage, dass die ersten Wagen 1940 vom Band laufen würden. Bei Kriegsausbruch beteiligten sich rund 335 000 Deutsche an der Aktion, aber die Einzigen, die je mit Vorserienexemplaren fahren durften, waren hohe Naziofiziere. Schon bald ging die Fabrik wie Automobilwerke überall in Europa zur Produktion von Kriegsgütern über. Sie stellte Munition her, reparierte Flugzeuge und baute zwei Militärfahrzeuge, die man in aller Eile auf der Grundlage des Volkswagens entwickelt hatte: den Kübelwagen und den amphibischen Schwimmwagen.

Anfang 1940 mussten die Briten einen großen Teil ihres ohnehin knappen militärischen Geräts in Dünkirchen zurücklassen, und die britische Industrie arbeitete auf Hochtouren, um die Lücken zu füllen und die vielen anderen kriegsnotwendigen Güter zu produzieren, von Flugzeugen über Panzer und Schiffe bis hin zu Traktoren, Raketenwerfern, Panzer- und Krankenwagen. Damit wurden die Werke natürlich zu einem Hauptziel feindlicher Bombenangriffe.

In Amerika gab es keine Bomben und zunächst auch keine aktive Beteiligung am Krieg. Die zivile Autoproduktion ging fast unbeeinträchtigt weiter, und zwischen 1940 und 1941 liefen dort jährlich rund 3,7 Millionen Fahrzeuge vom Band; gleichzeitig wurde auch diesmal in großem Umfang militärisches Gerät für die Alliierten produziert. Die amerikanischen Automobile dieser Zeit waren meist elegante, komfortable, große

In 1942 Field Marshal Erwin Rommel directs German troops of the 15th Panzer division in North Africa from his staff car.

Im Jahr 1942 führt Feldmarschall Erwin Rommel in Nordafrika die 15. deutsche Panzerdivision von seinem Kommandowagen aus.

En 1942, le maréchal Erwin Rommel dirige depuis son véhicule d'état-major les troupes allemandes de la division du 15ᵉ Panzer stationnées en Afrique du Nord.

Wagen, hatten starke Motoren und eine gute Ausstattung; bei den Verkaufszahlen rangierte Chevrolet deutlich vor Ford.

Das änderte sich 1942 – von da an stand die Produktion in Detroit wie im ganzen Land im Zeichen des Krieges. Fast alle bauten Lastwagen, die meisten noch vieles andere. Chrysler produzierte unter anderem Flugzeugmotoren und -rümpfe, Raketen, Panzer, Schiffsmotoren und Schiffe. Den größten Beitrag leistete General Motors: Dort entstanden ganze Flugzeuge, Kanonen, Torpedos, Panzerwagen, Panzer und vieles mehr. Andere Hersteller spezialisierten sich; Packard baute eine eigene Version des Rolls-Royce Merlin-Flugzeugmotors, Hudson fertigte Teile für den B29-Bomber, und Studebaker produzierte Sternmotoren für Flugzeuge. Wie schon im Ersten Weltkrieg wahrte Henry Ford auch diesmal seine Neutralität und pazifistische Einstellung, was seine Firma jedoch nicht daran hinderte, Liberator-Bomber, Sherman-Panzer, gepanzerte Truppentransporter und Gleitflugzeuge zu bauen.

Insgesamt produzierten die amerikanischen Autohersteller Rüstungsgüter im Wert von rund 29 Milliarden Dollar, und das vielleicht bekannteste darunter war ein Motorfahrzeug, der Jeep. Dieses vierradgetriebene Allzweckfahrzeug (seinen Namen verdankt es angeblich den Anfangsbuchstaben GP von General Purpose, dem englischen Ausdruck für »Allzweck«) wurde zunächst bei Bantam gefertigt, wo zuvor die amerikanische Variante des Austin Seven entstanden war, aber schon bald verlagerte man die Produktion in größere Firmen, die eher die für den Krieg benötigten Stückzahlen liefern konnten, unter anderem Ford, vor allem aber Willys. Binnen kurzem zählte der Jeep zu den wichtigsten, vielseitigsten Fahrzeugen im Feld. Später entstanden zivile Versionen, und er wurde zum Vorreiter der Off-road-Bewegung.

Als der Zweite Weltkrieg 1945 zu Ende ging, kämpften die Amerikaner immer noch im Fernen Osten, und Europa lag in Trümmern – nicht zuletzt die Automobilfabriken, die wegen ihrer strategischen Bedeutung in den Jahren zuvor zum großen Teil in Grund und Boden gebombt worden waren. Material war knapp, Treibstoff und Öl sollten bis in die fünfziger Jahre rationiert bleiben, und wieder musste die Wirtschaft ganz von vorn anfangen. Es sollte noch den Rest des Jahrzehnts dauern, bis die Autoindustrie sich halbwegs erholt hatte, und es zeugt von der Zähigkeit dieses Industriezweigs, dass man selbst in jenen schwierigen Zeiten in die Zukunft blickte.

Zunächst einmal ging es jedoch ums nackte Überleben, und in Großbritannien lautete die Devise »Exportieren oder untergehen«; nur mit Exporten ließen sich Devisen ins Land holen, vor allem

Dollars, mit denen man die nötigen Rohstoffe kaufen konnte, um die Produktion in Gang zu halten. Die neue Labour-Regierung, in deren demonstrativ gegen das Establishment gerichteter Politik der private Autofahrer keinen hohen Stellenwert hatte, begrenzte die Zahl der Neuwagen für den heimischen Markt und belegte sie mit hohen Steuern. Und obwohl sie weit mehr kosteten als unmittelbar vor dem Krieg, waren die »neuen« Autos der ersten Nachkriegsjahre in Wirklichkeit nicht mehr als alte Modelle mit ein paar halbherzigen Neuerungen. Erst beim Londoner Autosalon von 1948 gab es etwas wirklich Neues, und die britische Industrie (inzwischen die produktionsstärkste in Europa) stellte Dutzende von Neuheiten vor – von Alltagswagen wie dem Morris Minor und dem Hillman Minx bis zum sportlichen Jaguar XK120.

Die Automobilindustrie war wie neugeboren. Der Export hatte Erfolg, und die Mehrzahl der britischen Autos ging ins Ausland, nicht zuletzt nach Amerika, wo die Kriegsheimkehrer ein lebhaftes Interesse an den kleinen, sehr britischen Sportwagen zeigten, die sie in Europa kennen gelernt hatten – zur großen Freude von Firmen wie MG und später Triumph. Doch auch in Amerika gab es Produktionsbeschränkungen, und im übrigen Europa stützte sich der Wiederaufbau vor allem auf kleine, sparsame Modelle wie den Citroën 2CV und den Renault 4CV in Frankreich oder den Fiat Topolino in Italien. Zwar zeichnete sich die Rückkehr zur Normalität ab, aber es sollte noch eine Zeit lang dauern.

Ein Überlebender spielte beim Wiederaufbau eine ganz besondere Rolle. Am Ende des Krieges war die Fabrik, in der Hitler seinen Kraft-durch-Freude-Wagen bauen wollte, schwer beschädigt, der Sparplan aufgegeben, und das Auto war noch immer kaum mehr als ein Prototyp. Was blieb, wurde zunächst von amerikanischen Truppen, später vom britischen Militär übernommen, und im Jahr 1945 erhielt die KdF-Stadt den Namen Wolfsburg, das Auto hieß nun offiziell Volkswagen. Das Projekt wurde verschiedenen Firmen als Reparationsleistung angeboten, doch alle, von Ford bis zu den Ingenieuren der Rootes-Gruppe, gaben ihm (und dem Fahrzeug) nicht die geringste Chance. Da sich kein anderer dafür interessierte, wurde VW eine Zeit lang von dem britischen Offizier Major Ivan Hirst geleitet, der Ende 1945 die Produktion wieder aufnahm und anfangs ausschließlich Militärfahrzeuge baute. Von 1948 an stand die Fabrik wieder unter deutscher Leitung, und 1949 wurden zwei »Käfer«, wie man sie mittlerweile nannte, nach Amerika exportiert. Sie waren die Ersten von vielen Millionen, und der Käfer löste schließlich das Model T als meistverkauftes Auto aller Zeiten ab.

When the freedom to travel returned, the private motorist would be able to explore exciting new possibilities, including the first car-carrying air-ferries.

Als nach Kriegsende das Reisen wieder möglich wurde, gab es für den privaten Autofahrer manch aufregende Neuerung, zum Beispiel solche Transportflugzeuge, die speziell für das Übersetzen von Automobilen eingerichtet waren.

Les automobilistes profitent du retour de la liberté de circulation pour inaugurer les nouvelles possibilités de voyager au loin qu'offrent par exemple les premiers avions-cargo transporteurs de voitures.

L'Europe est à nouveau entraînée dans la guerre à l'aube des années 1940. L'usage privé de l'automobile est ralenti et la production de voitures particulière stoppée. En Allemagne, le développement de la « voiture du peuple » voulue par Hitler est même interrompu, du moins en ce qui concerne les applications civiles.

En d'autres circonstances, l'aboutissement de ce projet, qui ouvrait la voie à la démocratisation de l'automobile, aurait été un progrès formidable. C'est à l'occasion de l'inauguration du Salon de l'Auto de Berlin, en 1934, que le nouveau Chancelier allemand a exposé son ambition pour la première fois. « Il est regrettable, dit-il, que les millions d'ouvriers laborieux et de braves citoyens du peuple allemand se voient privés d'un moyen de transport qui, notamment le dimanche et en vacances, pourrait leur être une source de joies jusqu'alors inconnues. Ce problème est de ceux auxquels il faut s'attaquer avec courage, audace et résolution. Et ce qui ne peut pas être accompli en une année sera sans doute devenu tout naturel dans dix ans ... »

« L'Allemagne, poursuit-il, ne dispose que d'une automobile pour 100 habitants alors que la France en compte une pour 28 et qu'il y a une voiture pour six Américains. Cette disparité doit s'effacer ... J'aimerais qu'une voiture allemande soit produite en masse de telle sorte que quiconque capable d'acheter une motocyclette puisse également l'acquérir. Il faut que ce soit un moyen de transport simple, fiable et économique. Nous devons offrir une vraie voiture au peuple allemand – une Volkswagen ».

C'est la première fois qu'il emploie le mot « Volkswagen » dans un discours public, et c'est dans son acception littérale de « voiture pour le peuple » qu'il l'utilise. Hitler ne sait pas conduire mais est obsédé par l'idée d'offrir aux Allemands ordinaires une mobilité qu'ils ne connaissent pas. Admirant les idées de Henry Ford, dont il a découvert l'autobiographie, *Ma Vie et mon Œuvre*, au cours de sa captivité à Landsberg dans les années 1920, son ambition d'une voiture pour tous rejoint en ce sens les aspirations des pionniers de l'automobile, même si ce projet de voiture du peuple a pour lui également l'intérêt d'être un argument de politique intérieure.

C'est en mai 1934 qu'il présente les principaux critères de la voiture qu'il désire à l'homme le plus apte à la concevoir, Dr Ferdinand Porsche. Ce cahier des charges prévoit qu'elle soit capable de rouler à 100 km/h sur les nouvelles autoroutes qu'il fait construire et consomme moins de 8,5 l aux 100 km ; qu'elle puisse transporter quatre ou cinq personnes ; qu'elle soit refroidie par air pour garantir une meilleure fiabilité et soit facile à entretenir et à réparer ; enfin, elle doit être vendue moins de 1 000 marks – c'est-à-dire près de la moitié de ce que coûtait le Model T de Ford à son âge d'or. Alors que l'industrie automobile allemande juge la tache impossible, Porsche accepte de relever le défi en juin 1934.

Le développement de la Volkswagen, dont le nom de code est alors KdF-Wagen, ou « voiture Kraft-durch-Freude » (la Force par la Joie), se complique du fait qu'il est prévu de vendre la voiture par souscription de plans de timbres-épargne. Porsche présente ses deux premiers prototypes à Hitler en juin 1936, et en achève trente autres qui seront essayés début 1937 lors de tests d'endurance conduits par des officiers SS soigneusement sélectionnés. La première machine est installée en avril 1938 et Hitler inaugure le mois suivant la vaste nouvelle usine qui doit assembler les voitures et la ville où seront logés ses ouvriers. Deux jours plus tard, il ordonne à ses troupes de se préparer à envahir la Tchécoslovaquie.

Mais, alors qu'on a promis aux 335 000 Allemands ayant souscrit à l'achat que les premières automobiles seraient prêtes en 1940, les seuls qui aient jamais conduit les voitures de pré-production furent des officiers nazis. Pendant la guerre, l'usine automobile, comme toutes celles d'Europe, est convertie à l'armement pour fabriquer des munitions et réparer des avions ; elle ne construit que deux véhicules à usage militaire, hâtivement adaptés de la Volkswagen : la Kübelwagen (véhicule de liaison) et la Schwimmwagen (véhicule amphibie).

En 1940, après que la Grande-Bretagne a dû abandonner à Dunkerque une grande partie de ses effectifs de véhicules militaires, l'industrie britannique tourne à plein pour les remplacer et fabriquer toutes les équipements et matériels nécessités par la guerre – des avions aux chars d'assaut, des navires aux tracteurs, des voitures blindées et des lance-roquettes aux ambulances – au prix évidemment de devenir la cible privilégiée des bombardements ennemis.

Aux États-Unis, qui ne subissent pas ces bombardements et, au début tout au moins, ne sont même pas impliqués directement dans la guerre, la production de véhicules civils se poursuit au même rythme : près de 3,7 millions de voitures seront construites par an entre 1940 et 1941, avec Chevrolet largement en tête des ventes devant Ford. Les automobiles américaines de cette époque sont en général de belles et élégantes voitures, grandes, puissantes et bien équipées. Comme lors de la Première Guerre mondiale, l'Amérique assure toute-

One legacy of the war in big cities, as here in London's Piccadilly in 1943, was bright road and kerb markings designed to be visible in low light during the black-outs.

Ein Kriegserbe in den großen Städten, wie hier am Londoner Piccadilly, blieben die Leuchtmarkierungen an Straßen und Bordsteinkanten, die auch bei dem schwachen Scheinwerferlicht, das bei Verdunkelung erlaubt war, noch zu sehen waren.

Le marquage au sol des grandes voies et des bordures de trottoir, facilite la circulation dans les grandes villes pendant les black-out, comme ici sur Piccadilly à Londres en 1943.

fois aux Alliés un important approvisionnement en matériel militaire.

Tout change en 1942 lorsque Detroit (capitale de l'automobile américaine) participe avec tout le pays à l'effort de guerre. Si toutes les usines produisent des camions, la plupart construisent en plus d'autres matériels. Chrysler fabrique notamment des moteurs et des fuselages d'avion, des fusées, des chars d'assaut, des machines pour bateaux et des navires. Au premier rang de tous vient la General Motors, qui construit des avions, des canons, des torpilles, des véhicules blindés, des tanks et bien d'autres choses. Certains constructeurs se spécialisent : Packard produit la version aviation du moteur Rolls-Royce Merlin, Hudson assemble des éléments du bombardier B-29, Studebaker construit des moteurs d'avion en étoile. Henry Ford conserve la même position pacifique et neutre adoptée pendant la Première Guerre mondiale mais permet néanmoins à son entreprise de construire les bombardiers Liberator et les chars Sherman, ainsi que des transports de troupes blindés et des planeurs.

À la fin de la guerre, les constructeurs automobiles américains auront produit pour près de 29 milliards de dollars de matériels et de véhicules militaires, dont le plus connu fut sans doute la Jeep. Ce véhicule « tous usages » (General Purpose, dont l'acronyme GP donnera Jeep) à quatre roues motrices fut d'abord construit par la firme Bantam, qui avait réalisée l'Austin Seven américaine, puis par Ford et surtout Willys, des entreprises plus importantes et capables d'assurer le rythme de production nécessité par l'effort de guerre. C'est la Jeep qui va lancer la mode du tout-terrain une fois rendue à la vie civile, après s'être auréolée de gloire pendant une guerre où elle fut certainement l'un des véhicules les plus indispensables et les plus polyvalents de tous.

Lorsque la Seconde Guerre mondiale se termine en 1945, l'Europe en général est en ruines et plus particulièrement les usines d'automobiles, dont la plupart ont été pratiquement rasées par les bombardements en raison de leur importance stratégique. La fin des années 1940 est une période de mise en sommeil pour l'industrie automobile, même si quelques signes montrent qu'elle se tourne déjà vers l'avenir.

Pour l'heure, l'industrie britannique n'a qu'une priorité, survivre, et son mot d'ordre est « exporter ou disparaître ». Seule l'exportation peut lui rapporter les devises étrangères, notamment des dollars, nécessaires pour acheter les matières premières indispensables à la poursuite de ses activités. La

vente de nouvelles voitures sur le marché intérieur est sévèrement limitée (et lourdement taxée) par le nouveau gouvernement socialiste qui, faisant une nouvelle fois la preuve de l'antipathie des gouvernants britanniques à l'égard de l'establishment, ne place pas la voiture en tête de liste de ses priorités. Bien qu'elles soient plus chères que juste avant la guerre, les « nouvelles » voitures qui sortent alors ne sont rien de plus que d'anciens modèles légèrement modernisés. Ce n'est pas avant 1948, lors du Salon de l'Auto de Londres, que l'industrie automobile britannique (désormais la plus prolifique d'Europe) sort de véritables nouveautés, depuis les prosaïques Morris Minor ou Hillman Minx jusqu'à la sportive Jaguar XK120.

L'industrie renaît peu à peu de ses cendres en Grande-Bretagne. La grande majorité des voitures sont expédiées à l'étranger, et notamment aux États-Unis. Les soldats américains apprécient particulièrement de pouvoir importer – pour le plus grand bénéfice de marques comme MG puis Triumph – ces petites voitures sportives très anglaises qu'ils avaient eu l'occasion de conduire pendant leur séjour en Europe. Si les États-Unis connaissent aussi quelques restrictions de production, la reconstruction en Europe continentale va s'appuyer essentiellement sur de petits modèles économiques comme la 2cv Citroën et la 4cv Renault en France, ou la Fiat Topolino en Italie. Le retour complet à la normale va prendre encore quelque temps.

En Allemagne, l'usine que Hitler avait créée pour construire la Volkswagen est très endommagée, les plans d'épargne souscrits avant-guerre abandonnés et la voiture est à peine plus aboutie qu'un prototype. En 1945, après le passage des troupes américaines, les militaires britanniques, qui administrent la région, reprennent l'usine et renomment la ville Wolfsburg. Le projet de voiture, rebaptisée Volkswagen, est alors proposé à plusieurs constructeurs en guise de réparations de guerre ; tous, de Ford aux ingénieurs du Rootes Group, le refusent, conception de la voiture comprise, comme sans aucun intérêt. En l'absence de tout autre repreneur, les ateliers VW sont alors gérés pendant quelque temps par le major Ivan Hirst, un officier britannique qui fait repartir la production fin 1945 en se contentant au départ de construire uniquement des véhicules à usage militaire. En 1948, l'entreprise revient sous administration allemande et exporte aux États-Unis l'année suivante deux « Beetle » (équivalent anglophone de Coccinelle), rapidement suivies par plusieurs millions d'autres. Le succès de la Coccinelle est si grand qu'elle détrône finalement le Model T de Ford de la place de voiture la plus vendue de tous les temps.

Designs for the future, such as this early rendering of a post-war Morris, began with sketches, sculptures like this in clay, and scale models long before the real car was built.

Ein neuer Wagen, wie hier ein Morris der Nachkriegszeit, nahm mit Zeichnungen und Tonmodellen Gestalt an, und bevor über den Bau entschieden wurde, entstanden original große Modelle.

Les ingénieurs et les designers développent après la guerre de nouveaux concepts automobiles, qu'ils matérialisent d'abord par le dessin, une maquette en glaise – ici la première ébauche de la nouvelle Morris – puis grandeur nature bien avant que la véritable voiture n'entre en fabrication.

Back to the front
German troops advancing along a country road in Poland in the early days of the war (above) still present a mixture of motor transport – both saloon and purpose-built troop carrier – and horses. Manpower was still important, too, when the mud was too heavy even for the new, four-wheel-drive Jeep (right).

Und wieder an die Front
Deutsche Truppen rücken in den Anfangstagen des Krieges auf einer polnischen Landstraße vor (oben), teils noch mit Pferden, teils motorisiert mit Personenwagen und speziellen Truppen-transportern. Muskelkraft war nach wie vor gefragt, wenn der Schlamm selbst für den neuen Jeep mit Vierradantrieb zu tief wurde (rechts).

De retour au front
Les troupes allemandes, que l'on voit ici sur une route de la campagne polonaise dans les premiers jours de la guerre (ci-dessus), utilisent des véhicules très variés – berlines, engins mi-auto mi-camion de transport de troupe ou voitures de commandement – ainsi que des chevaux. Il arrivait parfois que la boue soit trop épaisse et trop profonde pour la nouvelle Jeep américaine à quatre roues motrices (à droite).

Adapting to survive

As wartime limited the use of petrol
or oil, motorists tried other fuel,
such as coal gas (left), as stored in
the bag on this van. Because of
the black-out, kerbs were painted
(above) to help visibility. In October
1940, London cleans up (right);
the Humber is beyond salvation.

Man muss sehen, wie man durchkommt

Da Benzin und Öl während des
Kriegs streng rationiert waren, wurden
Fahrzeuge auf andere Brennstoffe
umgestellt, unter anderem Leuchtgas, das dieser Lieferwagen (links)
in einem großen Ballon speicherte.
Da die Straßenlampen verdunkelt
waren, wurden die Bordsteine
markiert (oben), um die Orientierung
zu erleichtern. Im Oktober 1940
beginnen im Londoner Stadtteil
Piccadilly nach einem Bombarde-
ment die Aufräumarbeiten (rechts),
doch die Humber-Limousine ist
nicht mehr zu retten.

S'adapter pour survivre

Pendant la guerre, l'essence et l'huile
étant fournies en quantité limitée,
les automobilistes durent s'accommoder de carburants de substitution,
dont le gaz de charbon, stocké ici
sur ce camion de livraison (à gauche).
L'éclairage public des villes s'éteig-
nant le soir, il fallut peindre les
bordures de trottoir pour qu'elles
restent visibles (ci-dessous). Cette
Humber, malheureusement station-
née dans Piccadilly en octobre 1940
est désormais irrécupérable (à droite).

YOU ARE ENTERING
GERMANY.
AN ENEMY COUNTRY.
KEEP ON THE ALERT

On different fronts

In May 1944 US Army Signal Corps personnel cross from Belgium into Germany (left) in a Jeep. The four-wheel-drive Jeep, short for General Purpose vehicle, went into production in 1940, was built by several companies including Ford and Willys, and was one of the most important designs of the war. Cars provide shelter (above) from German snipers after Paris was liberated by the Americans in 1945. In 1940, Berliners (below) had their own way of coping with transport shortages.

Gefährliches Terrain

Fernmelder der U.S. Army überqueren (links) im Mai 1944 in einem Jeep die Grenze von Belgien nach Deutschland. Die Produktion des vierradgetriebenen Jeeps, dessen Name sich von »General Purpose vehicle« (Allzweckfahrzeug) herleitet, lief seit 1940 bei verschiedenen Firmen vom Band, darunter Ford und Willys, und sollte zu einem der wichtigsten Fahrzeugtypen des Krieges werden. 1945, nachdem die Amerikaner Paris befreit hatten, boten Autos auch Deckung vor deutschen Scharfschützen (oben). Die Berliner des Jahres 1940 (unten) hatten ihre eigene Art, mit dem Mangel an Transportmitteln fertig zu werden.

Sur différents fronts

En mai 1944, des membres de l'U.S. Army Signal Corps franchissent la frontière entre la Belgique et l'Allemagne à bord de leur Jeep (à gauche). La Jeep (acronyme de General Purpose ou GP), l'une des créations automobiles les plus importantes de la guerre, fut construite à partir de 1940 par plusieurs firmes, dont Ford et Willys. Ces automobiles (en haut) offrent un abri relatif aux FFI contre les snipers allemands pendant les combats de la Libération, à Paris en 1945. En 1940, les Berlinois se regroupent pour faire face aux problèmes de transport (en bas).

Life goes on

Before America entered the war, after Pearl Harbor in December 1941, it combined production of military materials for the Allies with civilian auto production for the domestic market. The last year in which new models were made was 1941, when this Pontiac station wagon was built – a time when real wood trim was still most definitely the thing for the American market. Through the war, the Pontiac division of General Motors made buses for the civilian market.

Das Leben geht weiter

Bevor die Vereinigten Staaten nach dem Angriff auf Pearl Harbor im Dezember 1941 in den Krieg eintraten, blieb dort neben der Produktion von Rüstungsgütern für die Alliierten die zivile Kraftfahrzeugproduktion für den heimischen Markt bestehen. 1941 war das letzte Jahr, in dem neue Modelle vorgestellt wurden, darunter dieser Pontiac-Kombiwagen – damals galt in Amerika das Holzdekor für Kombis noch als ausgesprochen schick. Während des Krieges baute die Pontiac-Division von General Motors Autobusse für den Zivilbereich.

La vie continue

Avant que les États-Unis n'entrent en guerre à la suite de l'attaque de Pearl Harbour en décembre 1941, les véhicules militaires pour les Alliés étaient produits en même temps que les automobiles civiles destinées au marché domestique. Les derniers nouveaux modèles civils sortirent en 1941, l'année où fut commercialisé ce Pontiac break (ou station wagon, dit aussi « canadienne » en France), à une époque où les parements exécutés en bois véritable étaient du dernier cri sur le marché américain. Pendant la guerre, la division Pontiac de la General Motors construisit des autobus civils.

Badge engineering

America made badge engineering an art, big manufacturers building closely related models for subtly different markets, with different badges. In 1940, within the Ford family, there were more similarities than differences between the V8s from Ford (right) and Mercury (above) – a badge introduced in 1939 to bridge the gap between utilitarian Ford and luxury Lincoln.

Ein Auto, viele Marken

Die großen amerikanischen Hersteller machten aus dem Trick, eine Karosserieform für bestimmte Zielgruppen unter verschiedenen Markennamen anzubieten, eine Kunst. Die Ähnlichkeit zwischen dem Ford V8 (rechts) und dem Mercury (oben) von 1940 ist nicht zu übersehen. Ford hatte die Marke Mercury 1939 ins Leben gerufen und auf halbem Wege zwischen den Alltagsmodellen von Ford und den Luxuswagen von Lincoln angesiedelt.

Déclinaisons automobiles

Les États-Unis ont fait du « badge engineering » un art, les fabricants construisant des modèles proches les uns des autres mais commercialisés sous des marques différentes pour s'adapter plus étroitement à un marché particulier. Dans la gamme Ford de 1940, il y a plus de ressemblances que de différences entre les V8 de Ford (à droite) et de Mercury (ci-dessus) – une sous-marque introduite en 1939 pour combler le segment entre les Ford, des voitures plutôt utilitaires, et les Lincoln, plus luxueuses.

Back to business

In a Europe dogged by materials shortages and financial hardship it took a while for the industry to recover, but London's first post-war motor show (above), opening at Earls Court in September 1948, finally saw the launch of many completely new models, rather than the upgraded pre-war designs that had filled the gap. The Hillman Minx, shown off in ghost form (below) was one of them, the Morris Minor another. The Austin A40 on sale in a New York showroom in 1948 (right) was a symbol of the industry's rallying cry – export or die.

Zurück zum Geschäft

In Europa dauerte es eine Weile, bis die Industrie sich von Materialknappheit und Finanznot erholt hatte, doch als der erste Londoner Nachkriegs-Autosalon im September 1948 eröffnete (oben), war doch eine ganze Reihe komplett neuer Modelle zu sehen, die an die Stelle der nur leicht überarbeiteten Vorkriegswagen treten sollten, die zuvor die Lücke gefüllt hatten. Einer davon war der Hillman Minx, der sich in einem durchsichtigen Modell präsentierte (unten), ein anderer der Morris Minor. Der Austin A40, der 1948 in einem New Yorker Schaufenster angeboten wird (rechts), war Ausdruck des Schlachtrufs der britischen Automobilindustrie: Exportieren oder untergehen.

Les affaires reprennent

Il fallut du temps avant que l'industrie automobile ne retrouve un rythme normal dans une Europe que frappaient les restrictions matérielles et les difficultés financières. Le premier Salon de l'Auto londonien d'après-guerre, qui se tint à Earl's Court en septembre 1948 (en haut), fut l'occasion de lancer plusieurs modèles totalement nouveaux, et non pas seulement des améliorations de véhicules d'avant-guerre, comme la Hillman Minx, présentée en « éclaté » (en bas), ou la Morris Minor. L'Austin A40 exposée en 1948 dans ce show room de New York (à droite) est la manifestation du nouveau mot d'ordre de l'industrie automobile britannique : « exporter ou disparaître ».

Just testing

As cars became more complex and customers more demanding, pre-production testing and proving became more sophisticated and more high-profile. In 1948 the new Morris Oxford (above) was put through the freeze test, at minus 40° for five days, and still started at the second attempt. In America in 1947, the steel-bodied Ford V8 (and passenger) survives three million volts of artificial lightning (right). In 1949 American Gary Davis designed a strange front-engined three-wheeler (opposite), claimed to drive in a 13-foot circle at 55mph without skidding, but only 17 were built.

Härtetests

Je komplizierter die Wagen wurden und je höher die Ansprüche der Kunden, desto anspruchsvoller wurden die Testverfahren und desto mehr wurden sie auch für Werbezwecke eingesetzt. 1948 absolvierte der Morris Oxford (oben) den Kältetest; fünf Tage lang stand er bei minus 40° C und sprang trotzdem noch beim zweiten Versuch an. Jenseits des Atlantiks übersteht 1947 die Ganzstahlkarosserie des Ford V8 und der Fahrer einen künstlichen Blitzschlag von drei Millionen Volt. Der Amerikaner Gary Davis stellte 1949 einen kuriosen Drei-radwagen mit Frontmotor vor (gegenüber), der einen 4-Meter-Kreis mit 90 km/h fahren konnte, ohne zu kippen, doch nur 17 Stück fanden einen Käufer (rechts).

De simples essais

Les essais effectués en pré-production s'appuient sur des critères plus durs et plus précis à mesure qu'augmentent la complexité des voitures et l'exigence des clients. En 1948, la nouvelle Morris Oxford (ci-dessus) passe un test de réfrigération qui nécessite qu'elle reste cinq jours en chambre froide à –40° C et puisse redémarrer dès la seconde tentative. En 1947, aux États-Unis, la Ford V8 à carrosserie en acier (et son passager) doit subir la décharge d'un éclair artificiel de 3 millions de volts (à droite). Cet étrange tricycle à moteur avant (ci-contre), dessiné en 1949 par l'Américain Gary Davis, peut braquer sur un rayon de 4 m de diamètre à 90 km/h sans déraper ; mais seuls 17 exemplaires furent cependant construits.

From East 42nd to the East End

In spite of following the one-way arrows (left), this was a spectacularly bad piece of parking on New York's East 42nd Street. On Cable Street in the heart of London's East End in 1947 (right), there were jobs and entertainment on offer, but bomb damage and post-war poverty were still in evidence, and the large 4.1-litre-engined Humber Snipe saloon would still have been subject to strict petrol rationing – until 1950 in fact, when rationing was abolished in Britain but fuel taxes doubled. Humbers had been a popular choice of staff car during the war, and famously included an open Super Snipe tourer known as Old Faithful, used by Field Marshall Montgomery in North Africa.

Von der 42. Straße zum East End

Auch wenn er sich immerhin an die Einbahnstraßenschilder hielt, war dieser Wagen auf der New Yorker East 42nd Street doch ausgesprochen unglücklich geparkt (links). Auf der Cable Street im Herzen des Londoner East End, 1947 (rechts), versprechen die Plakate zwar Arbeitsplätze und Unterhaltung, doch Bombenschäden und die Armut der Nachkriegszeit sind noch deutlich zu sehen, und die große Humber Snipe 4,1-Liter-Limousine hatte noch mit Benzinrationierungen zu kämpfen – die in Großbritannien erst 1950 endeten, und das mit einer Verdoppelung der Brennstoffsteuern. Die Humber-Wagen waren im Krieg bei den Offizieren beliebt gewesen, am berühmtesten darunter ein offener Super Snipe mit dem Spitznamen »Old Faithful«, der Feldmarschall Montgomery in Nordafrika als Kommandowagen diente.

De la 42ᵉ Rue Est à l'East End

Il n'est pas sûr que cet automobiliste ait bien compris les indications des flèches de sens unique (à gauche) pour se garer dans la East 42nd Street de New York. En 1947, cette grosse limousine Humber Snipe 4,1 l ne semble pas tout à fait à sa place dans Cable Street, au cœur du quartier de l'East End de Londres (à droite), où les dommages dus aux bombardements et l'apparente pauvreté des habitants sont manifestes. Le rationnement d'essence est encore en vigueur à cette époque en Grande-Bretagne – il le sera jusqu'en 1950, date à laquelle les taxes sur l'essence seront doublées. La Humber était la voiture préférée des états-majors, la plus célèbre étant une torpédo décapotable Super Snipe appelée Old Faithful, utilisée par le maréchal Montgomery en Afrique du Nord.

Shaking up the industry

In 1949 the British export drive faced a slump in orders, leaving cars like these Standard Vanguards (above) stockpiled. After the war, Allied car makers declined to take on Volkswagen even as war reparations, but the Allies put the factory back to work (below left): the rest is history. The new Morris Oxford in 1948, getting ready to face the ravaged road surfaces of post-war Britain (below right).

Erste Turbulenzen

1949 erlebte die britische Exportoffensive einen Rückschlag, und manche Wagen wie diese Standard Vanguards (oben) standen auf Halde. Nach dem Krieg wollten die Automobilfabriken der Alliierten den Volkswagen nicht einmal als Reparationsleistung haben, und so brachten die Militärs die Fabrikation wieder in Gang (unten links): Der Rest ist Geschichte. Der neue Morris Oxford, 1948 vorgestellt, war stabil gebaut, denn er musste mit den im Krieg vernachlässigten britischen Straßen zurechtkommen (unten rechts).

Secouer l'industrie

En 1949, l'industrie automobile britannique doit faire face à une chute de ses commandes à l'exportation ; les parkings des usines sont alors encombrés de voitures, comme ces Standard Vanguard (ci-dessus), en attente de client. Malgré le refus de certains constructeurs automobiles alliés de reprendre Volkswagen (même au titre des réparations de guerre), les Britanniques remettent en route l'usine (en bas à gauche). En 1948, la nouvelle Morris Oxford est prête à affronter les routes défoncées de la Grande-Bretagne d'après-guerre (en bas à droite).

Cultural shifts

At the beginning of the 1940s, the African-American family (above) leaving Florida during the Great Depression genuinely relied on the car for their everyday lives. A decade later (right) middle America had come to rely on the car for even the shortest journey. The 1938 Chevrolet Master Series De Luxe and the 1936 Studebaker President (foreground) were typical of the previous generation; the fastback Buick in the centre was the latest in styling directions, and the car just turning towards the camera has the look of an early hot rod.

Neue Lebensgewohnheiten

Die afroamerikanische Familie, die in den vierziger Jahren der Armut in Florida entfliehen will (oben), ist für das tägliche Leben auf ihren Wagen angewiesen. Zehn Jahre später war es für den Durchschnittsamerikaner schon zur Selbstverständlichkeit geworden, dass er auch den kürzesten Weg mit dem Auto zurücklegte (rechts). Der 1938er Chevrolet Master Series De Luxe und der Studebaker President von 1936 (Vordergrund) waren typisch für die vorige Wagengeneration; der Fließheck-Buick in der Bildmitte zeigt die neuesten Stiltendenzen, und das Exemplar, das links auf die Kamera zufährt, hat etwas von einem frühen Dragster.

Changements culturels

Cette famille afro-américaine (ci-dessus) quitte la Floride pendant la Grande Dépression du début des années 1940 avec leur voiture pour tout bien de valeur. Dix ans plus tard (à droite), l'Américain moyen utilise sa voiture même pour effectuer les plus petits trajets. La Chevrolet Master Series De Luxe de 1938 et la Studebaker President de 1936 du premier plan sont caractéristiques de la génération automobile précédente ; en revanche, la Buick à hayon au centre est du dernier cri en matière de style tandis que la voiture en train de tourner a des allures de « hot rod » (ci-contre).

7

A New Order –
And Conspicuous Consumption

A New Order – and Conspicuous Consumption

Previous page: The gathering pace of modern life. In a typical 1959 rush-hour, cars stream along a three-lane highway in New York City. In America, 1955 had seen the industry reach an all-time record output, but the middle of the decade saw American sales in decline, and Europe hit by oil shortages.

Vorherige Seite: Das moderne Leben gewinnt an Tempo. In einer typischen Rush-hour des Jahres 1959 strömen die Wagen dreispurig über einen New Yorker Highway. 1955 war für die amerikanische Industrie ein Rekordjahr gewesen, doch danach gingen die Zahlen zurück, und Europa hatte in jenen Jahren mit Benzinknappheit zu kämpfen.

Page précédente : la vie moderne à l'ère de l'automobile, en 1959, ce sont ces files de voitures les unes derrière les autres à l'heure de pointe sur une autoroute à trois voies de New York. Aux États-Unis, si l'année 1955 voit la production automobile atteindre des records, le milieu de la décennie est marqué par le déclin des ventes américaines et les restrictions pétrolières en Europe.

Of all the more recent periods in the history of the automobile, the 1950s are often seen as the most flamboyant, the most creative and the most exciting – an era of fins and chrome, reflecting the prosperity and optimism of the rock 'n' roll, baby-boom Fifties. And the decade had all those things in its motoring make-up; but as ever, it wasn't that simple.

It's appropriate to look at America first, because at the time nowhere shouted louder about the new order than Detroit, which had become, since the early years of the century, the spiritual home of the motor industry. There were still military and political problems in the Pacific but, for now, America could reasonably celebrate its role in winning the world war and was determined to do so. The American people were feeling good about life, optimistic for the future, and they were looking forward to the prospect of peace with growing prosperity. Material possessions for the American family of the 1950s were an expression of success. Conspicuous consumerism wasn't frowned upon, it was celebrated, and for the 1950s American in the street, few consumer goods were more conspicuous than the motor car.

In America as in Europe, civilian car production had eventually been stopped by the war during the mid-1940s, and at the end of that previous decade materials shortages in particular and investment cash shortages in the wider picture had restricted genuinely new models exactly as it had in Europe, leading to a period of modestly (and cheaply) upgraded prewar models masquerading as the next latest thing, while not really having very much to offer.

If that built a certain amount of frustration it also built a lot of expectation, and all those expectations were brilliantly fuelled by the industry's massive efforts to go into the 1950s with new freedom, new confidence, and new products.

In 1950 America became embroiled in a conflict in Korea which would last for more than three years, and began a military aid programme to the new 'state' of Vietnam which would have repercussions lasting far longer than that; but there was always the glamour of the automobile to take America's mind off the worst of its problems. Inevitably, a lot of smaller manufacturers had disappeared over recent, troubled years, but the ones who had survived – and in some cases made unaccustomed profits through their wartime contributions – were actually among the first to hit the market with new designs. They were brave while the big corporations were still cautious, but although that prompted some remarkable new cars it also precipitated several more downfalls, as companies who had risked investing in brave new designs could ill afford to change them when the market didn't take to them with the expected enthusiasm. Not least among those was the ambitious Tucker Corporation, whose revolutionary saloon with its rear-mounted flat-six engine (derived from a Bell helicopter unit), its all-independent rubber-sprung suspension, all-disc brakes and its spectacular streamlined looks, was launched in 1948 but was dead, amid huge debts and claims of fraud, by the time the 1950s arrived.

The longer established big guns were more conservative but they were also stronger and that was the combination that worked, especially when their conservatism was more about corporate matters and finance than about design, as was fast proving to be the new trend.

This became the age of the stylist, and to a lesser extent the age of the engineer, flamboyantly promoted by the advertising man. The stylists were now the aristocrats of the industry, and men like Harley Earl, Virgil Exner and Bill Mitchell had the power to change the look at the stroke of a pen, and did so year on year, creating a demand driven by the stigma of being seen for too long in last year's model. So Cadillac created fins at the beginning of the decade and they simply grew bigger and more ludicrously overstated as time went on, as did the toothy chrome grins and the dripping brightwork that virtually every American car of the 1950s couldn't survive without.

Big was definitely beautiful. Everything grew bigger, while the big manufacturers balanced the books by making many variants on essentially similar underpinnings, with little more than engine sizes, equipment levels and badges actually to distinguish between what were ostensibly similar makes, like Ford and Mercury in the Ford stable, Chrysler, De Soto and Plymouth at Chrysler, and Chevrolet, Pontiac and Buick at GM.

But there was substance under some of the flashy clothes. Performance continued to increase as the V8 engine became the American standard, and overhead valves replaced side valves. Automatic transmissions, notably improved by General Motors, were also becoming the overwhelming preference, and suspension, steering and brakes all made strides to keep up – in the advertising copy if not always in reality.

New materials and new manufacturing methods, not to mention new economies of scale, continued to bring real prices down and to push value for money up, and with it bring big increases in production volumes. In 1955 the industry had its all-time record year and in 1956 a new Federal Highway Act initiated a long-term programme for more than 40,000 miles of new interstate highways, in a country still remarkably lacking in really good roads.

That, however, was the high spot, and just as so many times before the bust was lining up behind the boom, as depression loomed yet again. In 1957 and 1958, unemployment soared, sales plummeted, and the embarrassing total flop of Ford's new marque, the Edsel, somehow became a symbol of the problem – all glitter and little substance. Yet it's impossible now to look back on the 1950s and not think of cars like these.

Their designs were even reflected in Europe, inevitably perhaps given the close relationships between the various branches of Ford, General Motors and to a lesser extent Chrysler in America and Europe. Inevitably, too, given the fact that many Europeans in the 1950s saw everything in America, from rock 'n' roll to Coca-Cola, denim jeans to Davy Crockett hats, as the height of style and modern living.

The reality for the motorist, unfortunately, was rather different, and it was governed inescapably by one factor that would have a massive influence on the European industry through the decade, and beyond it. That factor was fuel prices, and the reality was that in America big cars with big engines worked because the price of gasoline was (and always had been) minimal, while in Europe it was many, many times as high, mainly due to large taxes, but also because virtually all of it had to be bought in from outside. That, in the end, was what brought about the biggest changes in European motoring in this still unsettled decade, as the good times began to falter on this side of the Atlantic, too.

In Europe, where unlike America the physical damage from the war had been severe, the decade started with austerity, went through a period of increasing prosperity and ended with renewed crisis in the Middle East. Wartime petrol rationing officially ended in May 1950 and brought record traffic jams. In November, King Farouk of Egypt demanded 'total and immediate' evacuation of British troops from the Suez Canal Zone. The Canal was the route via which virtually all oil from the Arab oil fields came to Europe.

The dispute dragged on until in 1956, after British troops had withdrawn, Colonel Nasser, president of the new Arab Republic of Egypt, seized control of the Canal, nationalised it and cut the oil supply route. By October the Suez War had

started and the Canal was blocked, starting a period when Europe's oil supplies from the Middle East were severely restricted by the need to ferry them half-way around the world, via the Cape of Good Hope.

In Britain, petrol was rationed again and across Europe the bubble car and the microcar came into being to react to the shortages. They were horrible cars, hardly cars at all, with minimal room, tiny, usually smoky two-stroke engines, embarrassingly meagre performance and often very ugly looks. The then boss of the British Motor Corporation, Sir Leonard Lord, particularly hated them and he asked his Chief Engineer, Alec Issigonis, to build a 'real' small car to drive them off the roads.

Issigonis (later Sir Alec) was the genius who had taken BMC into the 1950s with the big-selling Morris Minor; now he gave the world the Mini. It was launched in August 1959, had a slow start until it was latched onto by the smart set and the motor sporting fraternity, but once it had become accepted it stood the motoring world on its ears.

It was the forerunner of a modern genre of small front-drive cars, a fashion icon, a prolific winner in races and rallies, another new kind of 'people's car' to rival the Model T and the Volkswagen. It is still in production at the turn of the millennium and was only just pipped to the post by the Model T as an international jury's choice of 'Car of the Century'. In 1959 it was the culmination, yet in a way the antithesis, of everything that had gone before in these early years of the automobile. Most of all, it was the gateway to the next generation.

Die Fünfziger gelten oft als das extravaganteste Jahrzehnt der jüngeren Automobilgeschichte, als das kreativste, aufregendste – die Zeit von Chrom und Heckflossen, Ausdruck von Wohlstand und Optimismus der Baby-Boom- und Rock 'n' Roll-Ära. All das prägte die Dekade tatsächlich, aber wie so oft waren die Dinge komplizierter, als sie scheinen.

Es ist nur angemessen, wenn wir den Blick zuerst nach Amerika richten, denn nirgends wurde lautstärker der Anbruch einer neuen Zeit verkündet als in Detroit, wo schon seit Anfang des Jahrhunderts das Herz der Automobilindustrie schlug. Zwar schwelten noch militärische und politische Auseinandersetzungen im pazifischen Raum, doch die Vereinigten Staaten konnten sich zu Recht als Sieger des Zweiten Weltkriegs fühlen und waren fest entschlossen, den Sieg auch zu feiern. Die Nation blickte froh und optimistisch in eine Zukunft, die ihr Frieden und wachsenden Wohlstand versprach. Materieller Besitz war für eine amerikanische Familie der fünfziger Jahre der Maßstab allen Erfolgs. Konsum um seiner selbst willen galt noch nicht als anstößig, man kaufte mit Gusto, und kaum ein anderes Konsumgut war für den Durchschnittsamerikaner jener Jahre so verlockend wie das Automobil.

Wie in Europa war auch in den Vereinigten Staaten die zivile Fahrzeugproduktion Mitte der vierziger Jahre zum Erliegen gekommen, und wie dort hatten auch in Amerika Materialknappheit und fehlende Geldmittel nach dem Krieg die Konstruktion wirklich neuer Modelle verhindert; notdürftig (und billig) aktualisierte Vorkriegstypen wurden als letzter Schrei angepriesen, obwohl sie in Wirklichkeit längst alte Hüte waren.

Das mochte zunächst enttäuschend sein, baute jedoch immer höhere Erwartungen auf, angefeuert durch eine Industrie, die fest entschlossen war, das neue Jahrzehnt mit neuer Freiheit und neuem Mut zu begrüßen – und mit neuen Modellen.

1950 begann der Koreakrieg, der sich über mehr als drei Jahre hinziehen sollte, und die Vereinigten Staaten leisteten ihre erste Militärhilfe an das neue Regime in Südvietnam, ein Akt, dessen Folgen das Land noch lange beschäftigen sollten; aber die Attraktion der neuesten Automodelle war stets groß genug, um die Mehrzahl der Amerikaner von den Schattenseiten der neuen Ära abzulenken. Eine Reihe kleinerer Hersteller hatte in den ersten Nachkriegsjahren das Handtuch werfen müssen, doch diejenigen, die überlebten – und die in einigen Fällen durch Kriegsproduktion mehr Gewinn gemacht hatten als je in Friedenszeiten –, zählten nun auch zu den Ersten, die mit neuen Entwürfen auf den Markt kamen. Die Kleinen hatten den Mut zum Risiko, wo die Großen noch abwarteten, und das brachte eine Reihe hochinteressanter Wagen hervor, wurde aber etlichen Firmen zum Verhängnis, denn wenn ein kleiner Hersteller in ein Modell investierte, das beim Publikum keinen Anklang fand, fehlte oft das Geld zu einem zweiten Versuch. Ein gutes Beispiel dafür ist die ehrgeizige Tucker Corporation, deren revolutionäre Limousine mit Sechszylinder-Boxermotor im Heck (auf Basis eines Hubschraubermotors von Bell), unabhängig aufgehängten Rädern mit Gummifederung, Scheibenbremsen und einer spektakulären Stromlinienkarosserie 1948 auf den Markt kam; doch die Firma, hoch verschuldet und des Betrugs angeklagt, war schon am Ende, als die Fünfziger begannen.

Die großen Konzerne, die schon länger im Rennen waren, waren konservativer und hatten dazu das dickere Finanzpolster, und das war eine Kombination, die sich auszahlte, besonders da, wo die konservative Einstellung sich auf Firmenpolitik und Finanzen beschränkte und den Designern freie Hand ließ – denn was von nun an zählte, war das Äußere der Autos.

Die neue Ära war eine Ära des Designers, nicht mehr in erster Linie des Konstrukteurs, und hinter ihm stand die ganze Kraft des Marketing. Die Karosseriegestalter waren die neuen Aristokraten der Industrie, und Männer wie Harley Earl, Virgil Exner und Bill Mitchell hatten die Macht, das Äußere der Wagen mit einem einzigen Bleistiftstrich zu ändern, und taten es auch Jahr für Jahr; wer sich zu lange im Vorjahresmodell sehen ließ, auf den schauten die anderen herab, und das war die Triebkraft des Marktes. So kam es, dass Cadillac zu Anfang des Jahrzehnts Schwanzflossen aufbrachte, die von Jahr zu Jahr größer und auffälliger wurden, und so erklären sich auch der grinsende Chromgrill und all der Zierrat, ohne den kein amerikanischer Wagen der Fünfziger bestehen konnte.

Je größer, desto besser, lautete die Devise. Alles wuchs, und damit die Produktionskosten nicht mitwuchsen, brachten die Konzerne aus denselben Grundformen zahlreiche Varianten auf den Markt, die sich außer in Motorisierung, Ausstattung und Markennamen kaum unterschieden; so hatte Ford weitgehend identische Wagen als Ford und Mercury im Programm, Chrysler verkaufte seine Palette als Chrysler, De Soto und Plymouth, GM ihre als Chevrolet, Pontiac und Buick.

Doch zumindest manche hatten auch etwas unter der glitzernden Haube. V8-Motoren mit immer größerer Leistung wurden zum amerikanischen Standard, und kopfgesteuerte

European fuel shortages in the wake of the Suez crisis created the bubble car boom, and strange designs like this front access two-seater at the Dornier works.

Nach der Suezkrise war überall in Europa das Benzin knapp, und das brachte eine Welle von Kleinstwagen hervor, seltsame Geschöpfe wie dieser Dornier mit Fronteinstieg.

Les restrictions pétrolières en Europe à la suite de la crise de Suez ont provoqué un véritable boom des mini-voitures et l'apparition de modèles étranges, comme cette voiture deux places à porte avant de Dornier.

Maschinen ersetzten die seitengesteuerten. Automatikgetriebe, deren Entwicklung General Motors weit vorangetrieben hatte, verdrängten die manuellen, und Fahrwerk, Steuerung und Bremsen machten allesamt Fortschritte, um mit der höheren Leistung mitzuhalten – zumindest in der Reklame, wenn auch nicht immer in Wirklichkeit.

Neue Materialien und Herstellungsverfahren, ganz abgesehen von bis dahin ungekannten Verkaufszahlen, drückten die Preise; das Preis-Leistungs-Verhältnis wurde immer besser, und das führte wiederum zu noch größeren Stückzahlen. 1955 war das absolute Rekordjahr der Industrie, und zudem beschloss die amerikanische Regierung 1956 ein Langzeitprogramm zum Bau von über 40 000 Meilen Interstate Highways – denn noch immer fehlte den Vereinigten Staaten ein echtes Fernstraßennetz.

Damit war jedoch der Höhepunkt des Booms erreicht, und wie so oft folgten den fetten die mageren Jahre. 1957 und 1958 schnellten die Arbeitslosenzahlen in die Höhe, der Verkauf ging rapide zurück, und das Debakel der neuen Ford-Marke Edsel wurde zum Symbol der ganzen Krise: alles Schau und nichts dahinter. Und doch sind genau das die Wagen, die für uns zum Inbegriff der Fünfziger geworden sind.

Amerikanisches Design blieb auch in Europa nicht ohne Einfluss, vielleicht zwangsläufig, denn die europäischen Filialen von Ford und General Motors waren eng an die Mutterhäuser gebunden waren (der Einfluss von Chrysler war geringer). Zwangsläufig auch deswegen, weil für viele Europäer Amerika zum Inbegriff des modernen Lebens geworden war, von Rock'n'Roll über Coca-Cola und Blue Jeans bis hin zur Waschbärmütze.

Für den Autofahrer sah die Realität anders aus, und sie wurde von einem Faktor beherrscht, der entscheidenden Einfluss auf die Dekade und noch weit über sie hinaus gewinnen sollte. Dieser Faktor war der Treibstoffpreis, und während in den Vereinigten Staaten große Wagen mit großen Motoren möglich waren, weil der Preis für Benzin so niedrig war, dass er kaum ins Gewicht fiel, betrugen in Europa die Benzinpreise ein Vielfaches dessen, hauptsächlich der hohen Steuern wegen, aber auch weil das Öl fast durchweg importiert werden musste. Das sollte in dem orientierungslos gewordenen Jahrzehnt schließlich die größten Veränderungen für die europäischen Autofahrer mit sich bringen, denn auch auf dieser Seite des Atlantiks waren die fetten Jahre vorüber.

Anders als in Amerika hatte in Europa die Infrastruktur im Krieg schwere Schäden erlitten, und zunächst waren die Fünfziger ein Jahrzehnt des Mangels; dann folgten einige Jahre des Aufschwungs, doch nach den Ereignissen im Nahen Osten endete das Jahrzehnt wiederum mit einer Krise. In Großbritannien wurde die Benzinrationierung offiziell im Mai 1950 aufgehoben, und die Verkehrsstaus der ersten Tage sind Legende. Doch schon im November forderte König Faruk von Ägypten den »vollständigen und sofortigen« Abzug der britischen Truppen am Suezkanal, durch den fast alle Lieferungen von den arabischen Ölfeldern nach Europa kamen.

Die Auseinandersetzungen zogen sich bis 1956 hin, dem Jahr, in dem die Stationierung endete; danach verstaatlichte der zum Präsidenten der neuen Arabischen Republik Ägypten aufgestiegene Oberst Nasser den Kanal und sperrte ihn für Ölschiffe. Im Oktober begann der Suezkrieg, die Tanker mit dem Öl für Europa mussten den langen Umweg um das Kap der Guten Hoffnung in Kauf nehmen, und binnen kurzem war Öl Mangelware.

Treibstoff war knapp und teuer, und in Europa kamen sparsame Kleinwagen auf den Markt. Die meisten davon waren jämmerliche Konstruktionen, kaum als Auto anzusehen, sie waren winzig und eng, fuhren meist mit qualmenden Zweitaktmotoren, hatten Fahrleistungen, dass man sich schämen musste, und waren oft noch hässlich. Sir Leonard Lord, damals der mächtigste Mann bei der British Motor Corporation, hatte eine tiefe Abneigung gegen diese Wagen und gab seinem Chefingenieur Alec Issigonis den Auftrag, einen »echten« Kleinwagen zu bauen, der sie von der Straße fegen sollte.

Issigonis (später Sir Alec) war der Mann, dem die BMC mit dem Morris Minor schon ihren ersten großen Erfolg der fünfziger Jahre zu verdanken hatte – nun wurde er zum genialen Konstrukteur des Mini. Der Wagen kam im August 1959 auf den Markt und verkaufte sich anfangs nur schleppend; erst als Mode und Motorsport ihn für sich entdeckten, kam auch das Publikum – doch als er sich erst einmal durchgesetzt hatte, stellte er die ganze Motorwelt auf den Kopf.

Er war der Vorreiter eines neuen Bautyps mit Quermotor und Frontantrieb, es galt als schick, ihn zu fahren, er gewann Rennen und Rallyes und stieg zu einem neuen »Volkswagen« auf, der dem Model T und dem Wolfsburger Käfer den Rang abzulaufen drohte. Auch heute, zu Beginn des neuen Jahrtausends, wird er noch gebaut, und als kürzlich eine internationale Jury das »Auto des Jahrhunderts« wählte, verwies ihn das T-Modell nur knapp auf den zweiten Platz. Als der Mini 1959 auf die Straßen kam, war er nicht nur der Gegenpol, sondern auch die Summe dessen, was in den ersten 75 Jahren Automobilbau erarbeitet worden war. Vor allem aber war er das Sprungbrett in die nächste Generation.

—— 7 ——

Un nouvel ordre
économique :
l'ère de la consommation

Les années 1950 sont souvent considérées comme la période la plus flamboyante, la plus créative et la plus excitante de toute l'histoire de l'automobile, une époque où les ailerons et les chromes sont le reflet de cette prospérité et de cet optimisme retrouvés qu'expriment autrement le rock'n'roll et le baby-boom des Fifties.

Il convient de se tourner en premier lieu vers les États-Unis où Detroit, devenue le foyer de l'industrie automobile mondiale depuis le début du siècle, appelle de ses vœux un nouvel ordre. Bien que les problèmes militaires et politiques ne soient pas tous résolus dans le Pacifique, l'Amérique se glorifie raisonnablement de son rôle victorieux au cours de la dernière guerre. Les Américains trouvent la vie belle, sont optimistes pour leur avenir et se réjouissent à l'avance des perspectives de paix et de prospérité croissante. La réussite personnelle et professionnelle des Américains s'exprime ouvertement par la quantité et la qualité des biens matériels que possède la famille et on favorise au plus haut point un consumérisme particulièrement ostentatoire. Pour l'Américain moyen des années 1950, rien n'est alors plus désirable qu'une belle automobile.

Après que la guerre ait interrompu la production de véhicules civils, aux États-Unis comme en Europe, la pénurie de matières premières et la frilosité des investisseurs freine particulièrement tout élan éventuel de commercialisation de nouveaux modèles. À la place, comme ils n'ont pas encore grand chose à offrir, les constructeurs ressortent, en les modernisant à peine (et à moindre coût), des modèles datant d'avant-guerre qu'ils essaient de faire passer pour du tout dernier cri.

Si cela provoque alors une certaine frustration, auprès du public comme des constructeurs, cela génère aussi beaucoup d'espoirs, fondés sur les importants efforts de l'industrie pour entrer dans les années 1950 avec plus de liberté et de confiance mais, surtout, en présentant plus de nouveaux modèles.

Bien que les États-Unis se trouvent alors entraînés en Corée dans un conflit qui allait durer plus de trois ans et lancent un programme d'aide militaire au nouvel « État » du Vietnam, dont les répercussions se prolongeront bien au-delà des années 1950, les Américains demeurent suffisamment fascinés par l'automobile pour oublier les pires problèmes.

Alors que la guerre a inévitablement entraîné la disparition d'un grand nombre des constructeurs les plus faibles, ceux d'entre eux qui ont survécu – et dont certains ont réalisé des profits inhabituels grâce à leur contribution à l'effort de guerre – sont en réalité parmi les premiers à oser présenter et proposer au public des automobiles de conception et de ligne nouvelles alors que les grandes compagnies restent prudentes. Si cela permet de voir apparaître plusieurs magnifiques et remarquables voitures, cela précipite aussi la faillite de quelques indépendants qui, ayant investi à risque sur des modèles audacieux, n'ont plus les moyens financiers de modifier leur gamme si leurs nouvelles créations ne rencontrent pas l'enthousiasme attendu de la part du marché. L'ambitieuse Tucker Corporation est à cet égard exemplaire ; la berline révolutionnaire et délirante, d'une ligne spectaculaire, équipée d'un moteur six-cylindres à plat monté à l'arrière (dérivé d'un moteur d'hélicoptère Bell), d'une suspension indépendante à ressorts caoutchouc et de quatre freins à disque qu'elle lance en 1948 tombe assez rapidement dans l'oubli.

Les grandes firmes, souvent établies depuis plus longtemps, se montrent plus conservatrices – en réalité surtout sur des questions d'entreprise et financière que la conception – mais, étant également plus puissantes, peuvent se permettre de se lancer à leur tour dans cette nouvelle tendance.

En effet, les années 1950 sont la grande époque du stylisme et de l'ingénierie automobile, dont les résultats sont promus par les publicitaires. Des stylistes comme Harley Earl, Virgil Exner et Bill Mitchell deviennent les aristocrates de l'industrie automobile, capables de modifier d'un coup de crayon la silhouette d'une automobile pour créer chaque année des modèles différents que tout Américain voudra posséder par souci de prestige et de crainte d'être vu trop longtemps au volant d'un modèle démodé – celui de l'année précédente ! C'est ainsi que les ailerons dont Cadillac affuble ses modèles au début de la décennie atteignent des dimensions aussi ridicules que démesurées, tout comme les calandres à dents de requin surchargées de chromes rutilants, ou les colorations agressives auxquelles aucune voiture américaine digne de ce nom ne peut échapper.

« Big is beautiful » est le slogan de ce temps. Les grands constructeurs cherchent aussi à rentabiliser leurs investissements en hommes et en matériel en déclinant à partir d'une base commune des modèles de voiture dont seuls la puissance des moteurs, le niveau d'équipement ou la désignation permet de les distinguer les unes des autres. C'est ainsi qu'apparaissent chez Ford les gammes Ford et Mercury, chez Chrysler les noms De Soto, Chrysler et Plymouth, et à la General Motors les déclinaisons Chevrolet, Pontiac et Buick.

Ces carrosseries tapageuses dissimulent aussi des mécaniques en proportion des ambitions qu'elles affichent, notamment le gros moteur V8 qui devient bientôt la norme américaine, les soupapes en tête remplaçant les soupapes latérales. La transmission automatique, améliorée notamment par General Motors, devient également la référence incontournable, tandis que les suspensions, la direction et le freinage se modernisent pour rester à la pointe de la technologie – en tout cas dans la publicité sinon dans la réalité.

Des matériaux et des méthodes de fabrication nouveaux, sans parler des économies d'échelle, permettent de faire baisser le coût réel des voitures et d'augmenter le rapport qualité-prix, tout en provoquant une forte croissance des volumes de production qui, en 1955, conduit l'industrie automobile américaine à battre tous ses records. Cet envolée des ventes sera facilitée par l'adoption en 1956 de la loi fédérale dite Federal Highway Act qui, dans un pays où des routes véritablement viables font encore défaut, lance un programme à long terme de construction de plus de 64.000 km de nouvelles voies inter-états.

Malheureusement, comme toujours, le spectre de la dépression se profile une fois encore et le déclin économique s'amorce en 1957–1958 : le chômage s'accélère, les ventes plongent. Cette période de marasme est illustrée symboliquement par l'embarrassant échec de l'Edsel, nouveau nom décliné par le groupe Ford et pur produit de marketing : tout de brillant mais sans véritable substance. Ce sont cependant des voitures comme celle-ci qui marquent les années 1950.

Le style américain est même exporté en Europe. Le phénomène semble inévitable non seulement en raison des liens étroits qui existent entre les différentes branches américaines et européennes de Ford, de General Motors et, dans une moindre mesure, de Chrysler, mais aussi parce que nombre d'Européens considèrent alors tout ce qui provient des États-Unis – du rock'n'roll au Coca-Cola, et des jeans denim à la toque de Davy Crockett – comme le nec plus ultra de la modernité.

La réalité est malheureusement assez différente pour l'automobiliste européen, qui se trouve confronté à un facteur économique qui allait avoir une influence majeure sur l'industrie de cette décennie et au-delà : le prix du pétrole. Alors que l'essence est (et a toujours été) bon marché aux États-Unis, son prix est beaucoup plus élevé en Europe, non seulement en raison des taxes qui y sont ajoutées mais aussi parce que la grande majorité du pétrole doit être importé. Ce facteur déterminant va finalement entraîner les plus grands bouleversements de l'automobile européenne au cours de la décennie.

En Europe, où, à la différence des États-Unis, les dommages subis consécutivement à la guerre sont importants, les années 1950 commencent dans l'austérité puis connaissent une période de prospérité croissante et se terminent par une nouvelle crise au Moyen-Orient. Alors que le rationnement de l'essence a officiellement cessé en Grande-Bretagne en mai 1950 (1949 en France), le roi Farouk d'Égypte exige en novembre 1950 l'évacuation « totale et immédiate » des troupes britanniques de la zone du canal de Suez, voie privilégiée par laquelle transite en direction de l'Europe pratiquement tout le pétrole extrait des champs pétroliers arabes.

Le conflit traîne jusqu'à l'évacuation des troupes britanniques en 1956. Le colonel Nasser, président de la nouvelle République arabe d'Égypte, nationalise alors le canal et coupe la route d'approvisionnement du pétrole, déclenchant ainsi en octobre la crise de Suez. Le canal étant bloqué, l'approvisionnement de l'Europe en pétrole du Moyen-Orient est considérablement gêné par l'obligation qu'ont les navires de faire le tour de l'Afrique par le cap de Bonne-Espérance.

L'essence étant de nouveau rationnée en Grande-Bretagne et dans presque toute l'Europe, les constructeurs automobiles sortent alors en réaction des voiturettes et des microcars, ou « pots de yaourt ». Ces voitures (à peine s'agit-il d'automobiles), souvent très laides, offrent une habitabilité minimum, des moteurs minuscules à deux-temps qui fument généreusement et ont des performances particulièrement faibles. Le patron de la British Motor Corporation (regroupement de Morris, Austin, Riley et Wolseley), sir Leonard Lord, qui les détestait singulièrement, demanda alors à son ingénieur en chef Alec Issigonis de lui dessiner une « vraie » petite voiture.

Issigonis (qui sera anobli par la suite) est ce génie qui, dans les années 1950, a offert un énorme succès à Morris grâce à la Minor. La Mini, le trait de génie du siècle a-t-on dit, est lancée en août 1959 mais connaît des débuts difficiles jusqu'à ce que la mode s'en empare et que les pilotes de course l'adoptent.

Précurseur des modernes petites voitures à traction avant, victorieuse dans nombre de courses et de rallyes, ce nouveau type de « voiture du peuple » concurrence le Model T et la Coccinelle. Toujours en production aujourd'hui, elle a été devancée de justesse par le Model T de Ford au titre de « Voiture du Siècle », décerné par un jury international. En 1959, elle marque l'apogée – et d'une certaine manière l'antithèse – de tout ce qui avait été construit depuis les premières années de l'automobile et ouvre toutes grandes les portes de l'avenir à la génération suivante d'automobiles.

The man who burst the bubble car's bubble and took motoring into a new era - Alec Issigonis with his revolutionary design, the Mini, launched in 1959 and still on sale.

Der Mann, der den Kabinenrollern den Garaus machte und ein neues Kapitel der Automobilgeschichte einläutete – Alec Issigonis mit seinem revolutionären Mini, 1959 vorgestellt und heute noch gebaut.

Voici l'homme qui créa les petites voitures et fit entrer l'automobile dans une nouvelle ère : Alec Issigonis, inventeur de la révolutionnaire Mini, lancée en 1959 et toujours commercialisée.

Wide open spaces

The motor car gave ordinary people the chance to go to places that were previously way beyond their reach, places that were once only for explorers and adventurers. A shaft of light breaks through the dark skies above a lone car on the road through the White Sands Desert in New Mexico in 1952.

Endlose Weiten

Durch das Auto bekamen einfache Menschen die Chance, an Orte zu fahren, die zuvor unerreichbar für sie gewesen waren und an die sich nur Forscher und Abenteurer gewagt hatten. Ein Sonnenstrahl bricht durch die dunklen Wolken über dem einsamen Wagen, der 1952 die White-Sands-Wüste in Neumexiko durchquert.

Les grands espaces

L'automobile a donné aux gens ordinaires la possibilité d'aller dans des endroits qui leur étaient auparavant hors d'atteinte, des lieux qui ne convenaient qu'aux explorateurs et aux aventuriers. Un rayon de soleil perce les cieux menaçants au-dessus d'une voiture solitaire dans le désert de White Sands au Nouveau Mexique en 1952.

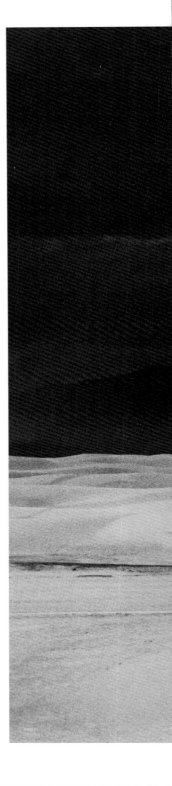

Streams of consciousness
A night-time view (left) of city traffic in the early 1950s, as cars weave their way up Park Avenue, New York. The view is looking north from the home of one of the automobile's rivals, from the clock tower over the Grand Central Railway terminal. Just the straight flat open road ahead (right) for the driver of this hardtop coupé – a body style introduced by most of America's image-conscious manufacturers right at the start of the 1950s – on one of America's sparsely populated desert highways.

Man strömt dahin
Eine Nachtaufnahme des Stadtverkehrs in den frühen fünfziger Jahren (links), wo die Wagen ihre geschlängelten Bahnen über die New Yorker Park Avenue ziehen. Die Kamera blickt nordwärts vom Sitz eines damals noch großen Rivalen des Automobilverkehrs, vom Uhrenturm des Bahnhofs der Grand Central Railway. Nur das schnurgerade Band der Straße hat der Fahrer dieses Hardtop-Coupés (rechts) vor sich – ein Karosserietyp, den die meisten modischeren US-Hersteller Anfang der fünfziger Jahre in ihr Programm aufgenommen hatten –, unterwegs auf einem der fast menschenleeren amerikanischen Wüstenhighways.

Flux et reflux
Au début des années 1950, l'incessant défilé nocturne des voitures sur Park Avenue, à New York, vue vers le Nord depuis la tour de l'horloge dominant la gare de chemin de fer de Grand Central (à gauche), contraste avec l'immense solitude de ce coupé hard-top – un style de carrosserie inauguré à l'époque par la plupart des fabricants américains – sur l'une des autoroutes du désert les moins peuplées des États-Unis (à droite).

Going nowhere fast

In 1957, striking taxi drivers (above) paralysed city traffic in Kingsway, Delhi. Most of the cars are either Fiats or Morrises. From Riley to Simca to the boxy rear-engined, water-cooled two-cylinder Rovin runabout, built in the old Delaunay-Belleville works in Paris from around 1947 to 1954, there is huge variety on the Champs-Élysées (right) in mid-1950s Paris.

Nichts geht mehr

Streikende Taxifahrer haben 1957 den Verkehr von Delhi mit einer Blockade des Kingsway lahm gelegt (oben). Die meisten Wagen stammen von Fiat oder Morris. Im Gedränge der Champs-Élysées (rechts) ist Mitte der fünfziger Jahre neben Simca und Riley auch ein Rovin-Cabriolet zu sehen. Die kantigen Kleinwagen mit dem wassergekühlten Zweizylinder-Heckmotor entstanden von etwa 1947 bis 1954 in der ehemaligen Delaunay-Belleville-Fabrik in Paris.

Nulle part très vite

En 1957, les chauffeurs de taxi de Delhi (Inde), la plupart équipés de Fiat ou de Morris, sont en grève et paralysent la circulation sur Kingsway (ci-dessus). Au milieu des années 1950, les Champs-Élysées semblent le point de rencontre de toutes les marques automobiles : Riley, Simca ou, au premier plan, ce runabout Rovin à moteur bi-cylindre arrière refroidi par eau, construit dans les anciens ateliers parisiens Delaunay-Belleville entre 1947 et 1954 (à droite).

Even in Moscow ...

Very few Russians, not even city-dwelling Moscovites, owned private cars in 1956, but there were more than enough Pobeda taxis (one of the biggest selling Russian cars of its day), and a few more upmarket limousines, to cause these jams on the day of a major football match in Moscow's Dynamo Stadium.

Sogar in Moskau ...

Nur die wenigsten Sowjetbürger, nicht einmal die Haupt-städter in Moskau, hatten 1956 einen eigenen Wagen, doch es gab mehr als genug Pobeda-Taxis (seinerzeit eins der meistverkauften sowjetischen Modelle) und auch ein paar größere Limousinen, um für einen solchen Verkehrsstau zu sorgen, wenn im Moskauer Dynamo-Stadion ein wichtiges Fußballspiel stattfand.

Même à Moscou ...

En 1956, très peu de Russes, même parmi les Moscovites, possèdent un véhicule privé. Il y a toutefois bien assez de taxis Pobeda (l'un des véhicules soviétiques les plus vendus à l'époque) et de quelques limousines haut de gamme pour provoquer des embouteillages à l'heure d'un grand match de football au stade du Dynamo de Moscou.

Following the signs

Along the Alaskan Highway in 1955 (left), homesick motorists created their own signposting system at the remote beauty spot of Watson Lake, 3,200 miles from Pittsburgh, 3,500 miles from Montreal. Around the same time, motorists on the turnpike from the Washington Bridge to the Delaware Memorial Bridge (opposite, left) had only one important sign to worry about. The trusty van (opposite, above right) is headed down a highway in Uta;, the rusty skeleton (opposite, below right) is going nowhere in the Australian outback.

Man muss nur den Schildern folgen

Auf dem Alaska-Highway (links), aufgenommen 1955, haben Reisende am schönen, doch entlegenen Watson Lake – 3200 Meilen von Pittsburgh, 3500 von Montreal – ihre eigene Art gefunden, ihr Heimweh zum Ausdruck zu bringen. Wer dagegen, etwa zur gleichen Zeit, auf der Schnellstraße von der Washington Bridge zur Delaware Memorial Bridge fuhr, hatte nur dies eine Schild (gegenüber, links), um das er sich kümmern musste. Der tapfere Lieferwagen (gegenüber, rechts oben) ist auf einer Fernstraße in Utah unterwegs; das verrostete Wrack (gegenüber, rechts unten) hat seine letzte Ruhe in der australischen Einöde gefunden.

Des indications à suivre

À voir ces panneaux, ici en 1955 (à gauche), on pourrait croire que chacun des automobilistes qui a emprunté l'Alaskan Highway a voulu marquer son passage près du lac Watson, situé à 5 200 km de Pittsburgh et 5 700 km de Montréal. Vers la même époque, les automobilistes qui circulent sur l'autoroute à péage entre le Washington Bridge et le Delaware Memorial Bridge (ci-contre, à gauche) n'ont à s'occuper que d'un seul panneau de limite de vitesse. C'est sans doute plus lentement encore que ce fidèle van (ci-contre, en haut à droite) descend vers l'Utah par l'autoroute ; une chance que n'a plus cette carcasse oubliée dans le désert australien (ci-contre, en bas à droite).

Away from it all

Out of the city rush, in February 1948, vacationers drive through the Everglades National Park (above), Florida, in a Chevrolet Fleetmaster Cabriolet convertible not unlike the one that was Pace Car for the Indianapolis 500 in 1948. Around 1955, with the Dezadeash mountains rising in the background (right), the driver of the late-1940s Ford two-door coupé sedan follows the simple signposting of the Alaskan Highway – one of America's last great roadbuilding projects.

Die Ferne lockt

Urlauber fahren im Februar 1948 mit einem Chevrolet Fleetmaster-Cabriolet im Everglades-Nationalpark in Florida spazieren (oben); ein ähnliches Modell führte auch die Aufwärmrunde der 500 Meilen von Indianapolis im selben Jahr an. Um 1955 ist die zweitürige Ford-Coupé-Limousine aus den späten Vierzigern auf dem Alaska-Highway unterwegs, einem der letzten großen Straßenbauprojekte Amerikas. Im Hintergrund erheben sich die Dezadeash Mountains.

Loin de tout

Ces vacanciers traversent l'Everglades National Park en février 1948 (ci-dessus) dans un cabriolet décapotable Chevrolet Fleetmaster peu différent de celui qui servit de pace car aux 500 Miles d'Indianapolis de 1948. Vers 1955, avec les montagnes de Dezadeash dominant l'arrière-plan (à droite), le conducteur de cette limousine coupé deux portes Ford de la fin des années 1940 suit les panneaux de l'Alaskan Highway, l'un des derniers plus grands projets de construction routière des États-Unis.

Designing the future

The transparent Morris Oxford (above) appeared at the 1951 London Motor Show. In the same year Austin chairman Leonard Lord and stylist Dick Burzi (opposite, above left) study a clay model of the new A30, while General Motors' styling guru Harley J Earl (opposite, below left) looks at a full-size mock-up of his more flamboyant Buick Le Sabre. By 1955 another generation was on the drawing board (opposite, right).

Entwürfe für die Zukunft

Der transparente Morris Oxford (oben) war auf dem Londoner Autosalon von 1951 zu sehen. Im selben Jahr begutachten Austin-Chef Leonard Lord und der Designer Dick Burzi (gegenüber, oben links) ein Modell des neuen A30, während Harley J. Earl, der Styling-Guru von General Motors, schon ein lebensgroßes Modell seines extravaganten Buick Le Sabre bewundern kann (gegenüber, unten links). 1955 (gegenüber, rechts) entstand bereits eine neue Generation auf den Zeichenbrettern.

Dessiner l'avenir

Cette Morris Oxford transparente (ci-dessus) est apparue au salon de l'Auto de Londres de 1951. La même année, le président d'Austin Leonard Lord et le styliste Dick Burzi (ci-contre, en haut à gauche) étudient une maquette en glaise de la nouvelle A30 tandis que Harley J. Earl de la General Motors (ci-contre, en bas à gauche) examine une maquette de la flamboyante Buick Le Sabre. En 1955, la nouvelle génération d'ingénieurs planche déjà sur les futurs modèles (ci-contre, à droite).

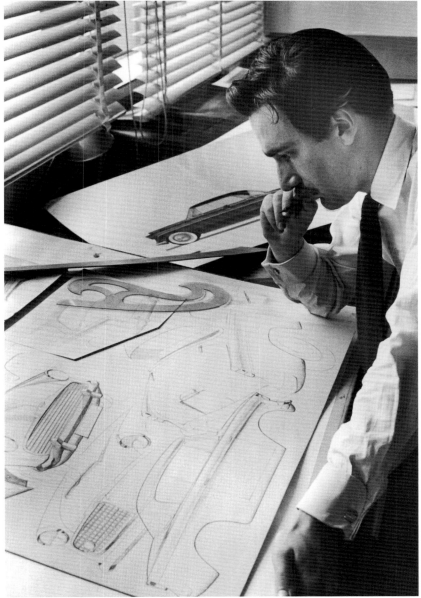

That's show business

Concept cars have long shared the limelight with the real thing. Harley Earl's 1951 Le Sabre (opposite) did the rounds, as did General Motors' futuristic, gas-turbine powered Firebird II in 1956 (above left). The Simca Aronde, shown in cutaway form (top right) at the 1956 Paris Show, and the technically advanced Citroën DS-19, seen in Paris in 1955 (bottom right), were real production models.

Showbusiness muss sein

Designstudien teilten sich oft mit echten neuen Modellen das Rampenlicht. Harley Earls 1951er Le Sabre (gegenüber) war überall zu sehen, ebenso wie im Jahr 1956 der futuristische, von einer Gasturbine getriebene Firebird II von General Motors (links). Der Simca Aronde (rechts oben), auf dem Pariser Salon von 1956 in angeschnittener Form präsentiert, und der fortschrittliche Citroën DS-19 (rechts unten), erstmals 1955 in Paris gezeigt, waren dagegen tatsächlich zu kaufen.

Du spectacle !

Les « concept car » ont longtemps partagé les feux de la rampe avec les « véritables » automobiles. Cette Le Sabre 1951 due au crayon de Harley Earl (ci-contre) a fait beaucoup d'envieux, tout comme la futuriste Firebird II à turbine à gaz de 1956 (ci-dessus, à gauche). La Citroën DS-19, exposée à Paris en 1955 (ci-dessus, en bas à droite), et la Simca Aronde (ci-dessus, en haut à droite) au salon de l'Auto de Paris en 1956 étaient en revanche de véritables automobiles de production.

Style and styling

The fashion model (left) showing off a day-suit for *Vogue* in 1952 is leaning against a Buick, its sculpted sides showing off the heavily moulded shapes characteristic of American styling of the period, echoed by the toothy grin of the Pontiac in the background. The line of cars parked in a street in downtown New York (right) around 1955 shows another American styling theme that started in the 1940s and just about made it into the 1950s – the fastbacked, streamlined look, in this case from GM.

Stil und Styling

Das Mannequin, das 1952 für *Vogue* ein Kostüm präsentiert (links), steht an einen Buick gelehnt, dessen üppige Rundungen typisch für das amerikanische Styling der Zeit sind, ebenso wie beim Pontiac im Hintergrund der Kühlergrill, der die Zähne zeigt. Die Wagen, die um 1955 an einer Straße der New Yorker Innenstadt geparkt stehen (rechts), zeigen ein andereres amerikanisches Stylingthema, das in den vierziger Jahren aufkam und sich bis Anfang der Fünfziger hielt – das fließende Coupéheck mit Stromlinienanklängen, hier bei einem GM-Modell.

Style et stylisme

Posant pour *Vogue* en 1952, ce mannequin est appuyé contre une Buick, dont les flancs sculptés montrent des formes accentuées, caractéristiques du style américain de l'époque et que l'on retrouve dans la calandre agressive et surchargée de la Pontiac à l'arrière-plan (à gauche). Les voitures en stationnement dans cette rue de New York vers 1955 (à droite) présentent un autre aspect du style américain né dans les années 1940 qu'adopte encore le public des années 1950 : le coupé à « dos rond » (« fast back ») profilé, adopté ici par la GM.

Chrome classics

The Fifties was the era of fins and chrome in the USA, and every car had its excesses. Cadillac started the fins fashion as the Forties ended, and by 1952 (above) Cadillacs were dripping chrome, too. At the 1956 Paris Motor Show, there was chrome on everything – the Cadillac Eldorado Brougham (opposite, top left), the Dodge Custom Royal (opposite, top right and below left), even the Italian Maserati (opposite, below right).

Chrom-Klassiker

In den USA waren die Fünfziger die Zeit von Heckflossen und Chrom, und jedes neue Modell zeigte neue Extreme. Cadillac hatte die Heckflossenmode Ende der vierziger Jahre aufgebracht, und 1952 (oben) blitzten die Cadillacs auch vor Chrom. Der Pariser Autosalon von 1956 zeigt Chrom im Überfluss – am Cadillac Eldorado Brougham (gegenüber, oben links), am Dodge Custom Royal (oben rechts und unten links) und sogar am italienischen Maserati (gegenüber, unten rechts).

Classicisme des chromes

Les Fifties sont marquées aux États-Unis par la profusion des chromes. Cadillac lance les ailes surdimensionnées vers la fin des années 1940 pour aboutir, en 1952, à des modèles de Cadillac où flamboient les chromes (ci-dessus). Au salon de l'Auto de Paris de 1956, le chrome règne en maître sur la Cadillac Eldorado Brougham (ci-contre, en haut à gauche), la Dodge Custom Royal (ci-contre, en haut à droite et en bas à gauche) et même sur la Maserati italienne (ci-contre, en bas à droite).

The most tragic race

The 1955 Le Mans 24-Hour race saw the worst racing tragedy of all, when the Mercedes of Pierre Levegh crashed into the startline stands, killing Levegh and more than 80 spectators. Mike Hawthorn (in D Type Jaguar number 6) was involved in the accident but won the race after a classic battle with Juan Manuel Fangio's Mercedes (number 19) was ended by Mercedes' withdrawal from the race.

Das schlimmste Rennen

Die 24 Stunden von Le Mans des Jahres 1955 waren vom schwersten Rennunfall aller Zeiten überschattet; Pierre Levegh raste mit seinem Mercedes in die Starttribüne, und er selbst und über 80 Zuschauer fanden den Tod. Mike Hawthorn (im Jaguar D-Type, Startnummer 6) war ebenfalls in den Unfall verwickelt, gewann jedoch trotzdem das Rennen nach einem klassischen Zweikampf mit Juan Manuel Fangio im Mercedes (Nummer 19), der erst endete, als Mercedes sich vom Rennen zurückzog.

La course tragique

L'édition de 1955 des 24 Heures du Mans est sans doute la course la plus tragique de tous les temps, marquée par l'accident de la Mercedes de Pierre Levegh qui s'écrase dans les tribunes, tuant le pilote et plus de 80 spectateurs. Également impliqué dans l'accident, Mike Hawthorn, à bord de la Jaguar Type D numéro 6 – que l'on voit ici à la lutte avec la Mercedes de Juan Manuel Fangio (numéro 19) – remporte cependant la course après le retrait total de Mercedes de la compétition.

On two continents

Strictly speaking, the Redex Trial around Australia wasn't a race or even a rally in the modern sense but Duck Anderson, in the Australian GM-built 2.1-litre six-cylinder Holden FJ (left) in around 1955, wasn't holding back on the dirt roads. Italy's long-distance classic, the Mille Miglia, on the other hand, was definitely a real race, and in 1950 it was won by Giannino Marzotto (above) in his works Ferrari 195S Berlinetta – becoming, at the age of 22, the race's youngest winner.

Auf zwei Kontinenten

Das Redex Trial rund um Australien war kein Rennen im heutigen Sinne, nicht einmal eine Rallye, aber das war für Duck Anderson, hier (links) etwa 1955 zu sehen, noch lange kein Grund, auf den Staubpisten vom Gas zu gehen. Er fährt einen 2,1-Liter-Sechszylinder FJ von Holden, der australischen GM-Tochter. Der italienische Langstreckenklassiker Mille Miglia war dagegen in jeder Hinsicht ein echtes Rennen; 1950 hieß, auf einem Werks-Ferrari 195S Berlinetta, der Sieger Giannino Marzotto (oben) – mit seinen 22 Jahren der Jüngste, der je das Rennen gewann.

Sur deux continents

À strictement parler, le Redex Trial n'était ni une course ni même un rallye au sens moderne du terme ; cela n'empêcha pas Duck Anderson, sur une Holden FJ six-cylindres 2,1 l construite par la GM Australie (à gauche) de foncer sur les routes poussiéreuses d'Australie vers 1955. En remportant l'édition de 1950 des Mille Miglia, la classique italienne de l'endurance, sur une Ferrari 195S Berlinetta d'usine, Giannino Marzotto devint ainsi, à l'âge de 22 ans, le plus jeune vainqueur de la course (ci-dessus).

Summer and winter sports

In America motor racing has always had branches of its own, quite different from the circuit racing that dominates in Europe. In the 1950s, drag racing (right, opposite, above left) a head-to-head straight line acceleration contest, usually over a quarter of a mile, started as an unsanctioned sport, growing out of the craze for hot rods (opposite, below left) but soon became big business. And when the weather changed, you could always fit your hot rod with tyre chains (opposite, below right) and go ice racing (opposite, above right).

Sommer- und Wintersport

In den Vereinigten Staaten hat es von Anfang an Spielarten des Motorsports gegeben, die gänzlich anders sind als die Rundstreckenrennen, die den Sport in Europa bestimmen. Drag Racing (rechts und gegenüber oben links) entwickelte sich in den fünfziger Jahren als reiner Beschleunigungswettkampf, meist über eine Viertelmeile; ursprünglich war es ein Amateursport, der von der Leidenschaft für frisierte Hot Rods (unten links) her kam, aber mittlerweile werden mit diesen Rennen große Geschäfte gemacht. Und wenn das Wetter umschlägt, kann man bei seinem Hot Rod immer noch Schneeketten aufziehen (unten rechts) und zum Eisrennen antreten (oben rechts).

Sports d'hiver et d'été

Alors que la course sur circuit domine en Europe, il existe aux États-Unis des types de compétition automobile très divers. C'est dans les années 1950 que sont inaugurées les courses de dragsters (ci-contre, en haut à gauche et sur cette page), des bolides qui s'affrontent deux par deux sur une ligne droite de 400 m environ, dérivées des courses de « hot rod » (ci-contre, en bas à gauche). En hiver, il est alors possible d'adapter des chaînes aux roues des « hot rod » (ci-contre, en bas à droite) pour courir sur glace (ci-contre, en haut à droite).

Supreme Soviet

When Soviet premier Nikita Kruschev attended the Paris summit meeting in May 1960 he brought his own official car, the massive ZIL 111 cabriolet. The ZIL company grew out of the ZIS company, when its name was changed in 1956 from Zavod Imieni Stalina to the less politically sensitive Zavod Imieni Likhatcheva, after a former minister of roads and transport. The 6-litre V8 powered 111 was in production for dignitaries like Mr Kruschev from 1959 until 1970.

Der Oberste Sowjet

Als der sowjetische Ministerpräsident Nikita Chruschtschow im Mai 1960 zum Pariser Gipfeltreffen kam, brachte er seine eigene Staatskarosse mit, das imposante SIL-111-Cabriolet. SIL war 1956 aus den vormaligen SIS-Werken entstanden, als man das inzwischen verfänglich gewordene Sawod Imieni Stalina nach einem ehemaligen Verkehrsminister in das neutralere Sawod Imieni Likhatschewa umbenannte. Der von einem 6-Liter-V8 angetriebene 111 wurde für hohe Politiker wie Chruschtschow von 1959 bis 1970 gebaut.

Le Suprême Soviet

Lorsque le premier Soviétique, Nikita Khrouchtchev, assiste au sommet de Paris en mai 1960, il vient avec sa voiture officielle, le massif cabriolet ZIL 111. La marque ZIL est issue de la ZIS (Zavod Imieni Stalina), qui fut débaptisée en 1956 pour devenir la Zavod Imieni Likhatcheva (du nom d'un ministre des transports), une désignation moins marquée politiquement. La ZIL 111 à moteur V8 de 6 l fut produite de 1959 à 1970 à l'intention quasi exclusive des hauts dignitaires du régime soviétique.

Of princesses and presidents

In April 1956, after their wedding in Monaco Cathedral, Princess Grace and Prince Rainier of Monaco (above) drove through the streets of Monte Carlo in their open Rolls-Royce. After the ceremony marking his inauguration in January 1953, the 34th president of the United States, Dwight D Eisenhower, headed the celebration parade through Washington, DC (below), in his flamboyant open-topped Cadillac Eldorado – a true American icon.

Fürstinnen und Präsidenten

Nach ihrer Hochzeit in der Kathedrale von Monaco im April 1956 fahren Fürstin Gracia und Fürst Rainier in ihrem offenen Rolls-Royce durch die Straßen von Monte Carlo (oben). Dwight D. Eisenhower wurde im Januar 1953 als 34. Präsident der Vereinigten Staaten vereidigt; nach der Zeremonie führt er im prachtvollen offenen Cadillac Eldorado – Inbegriff des American way of life – die Parade durch Washington, D.C., an (unten).

Princesses et présidents

Après leur mariage dans la cathédrale de Monaco, en avril 1956, la princesse Grace et le prince Rainier de Monaco (en haut) parcourent les rues de la principauté dans leur Rolls-Royce décapotable. Après la cérémonie marquant son intronisation en janvier 1953, le 34ᵉ président des États-Unis, Dwight D. Eisenhower, traverse Washington, D.C., à bord d'une flamboyante Cadillac Eldorado découverte – véritable symbole de l'Amérique (en bas).

School days

In 1953 students at Brooklyn High School, New York (above), could learn to handle the controls of a car in simulated traffic, using a screen in the classroom. In 1955 an American insurance company was also sponsoring driving simulators like the Drivotrainer (right) in driving schools, in an attempt to reduce the number of accidents connected with learner drivers.

Wer fahren will, muss lernen

1953 konnten die Schüler der Brooklyn High School, New York, die Grundbegriffe des Autofahrens vor einer Projektionswand im simulierten Verkehr erlernen (oben). Eine amerikanische Versicherung finanzierte 1955 Simulatoren wie den »Drivotrainer« (rechts) in den Fahrschulen, um die Zahl der Unfälle zu reduzieren, die beim Fahrunterricht geschahen.

À l'école

En 1953, les étudiants de la Brooklyn High School de New York (ci-dessus) peuvent apprendre à conduire à l'aide d'un simulateur automobile. En 1955, une compagnie d'assurance américaine sponsorise également des simulateurs de conduite comme le « Drivotrainer » (à droite) dans les auto-écoles afin de diminuer le nombre d'accidents imputables aux jeunes conducteurs.

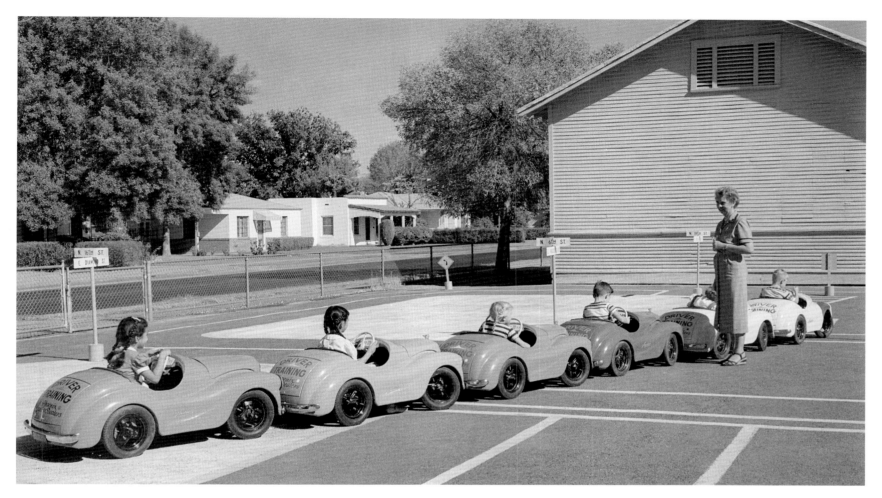

Young hands on the wheel

In the mid-1950s, children in many American schools, such as here at Garfield Elementary School in Phoenix, Arizona (above), were taught about traffic safety. At the other end of the scale, budding racing drivers (right), with last minute advice from their fathers, could compete in midget racers on oval circuits.

Früh übt sich …

Mitte der fünfziger Jahre bekamen die Kinder in vielen amerikanischen Grundschulen Unterricht in Verkehrssicherheit, hier in der Garfield Elementary School in Phoenix, Arizona (oben). Schneller ging es bei den zukünftigen Rennfahrern zu (rechts), die noch letzte Ratschläge von ihren Vätern bekommen, bevor sie zum Wettkampf auf dem Go-Kart-Kurs starten.

Des enfants au volant

Au milieu des années 1950, les enfants de nombreuses écoles américaines, comme à la Garfield Elementary School de Phoenix (Arizona) suivent des cours de code et de conduite (ci-dessus). À un niveau plus élevé, ces jeunes pilotes de course peuvent s'affronter sur circuit ovale à bord de Midget de compétition (à droite).

That feminine touch

In October 1955 the Rootes Group added glamour to the new Sunbeam Rapier (above). Porsche did the same with the Reutter-bodied 356 coupé (opposite, above left) in 1954. In 1958 English film star Diana Dors (opposite, above right) posed in her Cadillac. Open Austins (opposite, below left) lined up for the Concours d'Élégance in Brighton in 1950, while Mrs Nahum showed off her Daimler (opposite, below right) in Cannes in 1951.

Der feminine Touch

Im Oktober 1955 setzte die Rootes-Gruppe den neuen Sunbeam Rapier effektvoll in Szene (oben). Mit dem gleichen Mittel warb Porsche 1954 für das von Reutter karossierte 356-Coupé (gegenüber, oben links). 1958 posierte die englische Filmschauspielerin Diana Dors (oben rechts) im Cadillac. Austin-Cabriolets nehmen 1950 zum Concours d'Élégance in Brighton Aufstellung (unten links), und Mrs. Nahum zeigt 1951 in Cannes stolz ihren Daimler (unten rechts).

Ce petit plus féminin

Au concours d'Élégance de Brighton en 1950 sont présentées des Austin décapotables (ci-contre, en bas à gauche), meilleur marché que la Daimler de Mme Nahum, ici à Cannes en 1951 (ci-contre, en bas à droite). En 1954, Porsche lance le coupé 356 à carrosserie Reutter (ci-contre, en haut à gauche), imité en octobre 1955 par le Rootes Group pour la nouvelle Sunbeam Rapier (ci-dessus). Aux États-Unis, en 1958, l'actrice anglaise Diana Dors pose dans une Cadillac (ci-contre, en haut à droite).

Drive-in culture

By the mid-1950s in America in particular, urban life
had been dramatically changed by some people's almost
total reliance on the motor car, for even the shortest of
journeys. And because so many people no longer walked
to shops, restaurants or whatever, but almost invariably
took the car, an entire 'drive-in' culture began to appear
in towns all across the country.

Drive-in-Kultur

Mitte der fünfziger Jahre waren viele schon so abhängig
von ihrem Automobil geworden, dass sie selbst den
kürzesten Weg nicht mehr zu Fuß zurücklegten, und
besonders in Amerika hatte das dramatische Veränderungen
im städtischen Leben zur Folge. Da so viele nun nicht
einmal mehr zu Läden und Restaurants zu Fuß gingen,
war in Städten im ganzen Land eine regelrechte »Drive-
in-Kultur« entstanden.

La culture du drive-in

Au milieu des années 1950, l'automobile occupe une place
de plus en plus considérable dans la vie quotidienne des
gens, notamment aux États-Unis, et entraîne un assez
profond changement des mentalités. Des drive-in sont
créés dans les villes de tout le pays pour ceux qui ne se
rendent plus à pied ni dans les magasins, ni au restaurant
ou à leur banque mais utilisent leur voiture en toutes
circonstances, même pour effectuer de très courts trajets.

Please remain seated
The logical conclusion of drive-in convenience was that eventually you didn't even have to get out of your seat. In a drive-in burger restaurant in Hollywood in 1951 you could select your own space (above), order by remote control (middle), and take delivery (below), all from the wheel. Even when delivery wasn't totally automated (right) the waiter would never be far away.

Bleiben Sie sitzen
Es war nur eine Frage der Zeit, bis die Drive-in-Bequemlichkeit so weit getrieben wurde, dass man nicht einmal mehr den Fahrersitz verlassen musste. In einem Drive-in-Restaurant in Hollywood, 1951, fuhr man in eine Parkbucht (oben), bestellte per Fernbedienung (Mitte) und fand das Gewünschte hinter einer Klappe (unten), alles vom Steuer aus. Anderswo (rechts) war die Bedienung noch nicht ganz so automatisiert.

Veuillez rester assis
Le côté « pratique » du drive-in est qu'il n'est même plus besoin de sortir de voiture pour accomplir certaines tâches quotidiennes ! En 1951, dans ce snack d'Hollywood, vous pouvez ainsi choisir votre place (en haut), commander à distance (au milieu) et recevoir le repas que vous désirez (en bas) sans quitter le volant. Et si le service n'est pas automatisé (à droite), le personnel se fait une joie de vous apporter votre repas à « domicile ».

Drive-in for God ...

In America the automobile could even be a substitute for a church pew. The preacher (above) is addressing his mobile flock in Massachusetts in 1951, with piano accompaniment. The word of the Lord was relayed via in-car speakers (right), which could be clipped over the door to bring you your own private sermon.

Drive-in für Gott ...

In Amerika konnte das Auto sogar als Kirchenbank dienen. Der Prediger (oben) predigt seiner mobilen Gemeinde 1951 in Massachusetts mit Klavierbegleitung. Die frohe Botschaft wurde per Lautsprecher in jeden Wagen übertragen (rechts); das Kästchen klemmte man ans Fenster, und jeder konnte das Gefühl haben, der Prediger spreche nur zu ihm.

Drive-in de Dieu ...

L'automobile est à ce point omniprésente aux États-Unis qu'aucune église n'est plus nécessaire ! Quelques places de parking, une estrade et un lot de haut-parleurs à accrocher à la portière de la voiture des fidèles (à droite) suffit pour diffuser la parole de Dieu, comme ici en 1951 dans le Massachusetts (ci-dessus).

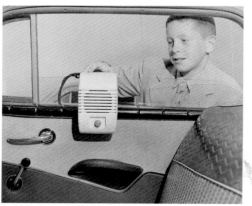

... and Mammon

Before long, there was almost nothing that you couldn't drive into or through – movies (right), churches, restaurants, even automated banks (above). With planning you could probably enjoy a whole day out, eat, drink, take in a show, shop and pay for it, all without setting a foot on the ground outside the car.

... und Mammon

Binnen kurzem gab es kaum etwas, wo man nicht hinein- oder hindurch-fahren konnte – Kinos (rechts), Kirchen, Restaurants, sogar auto-matische Banken (oben). Wer es gut plante, konnte einen Ausflug machen – essen, trinken, sich einen Film an-sehen, einkaufen und dafür zahlen –, ohne einen einzigen Schritt vor die Wagentür zu tun.

... et du Diable

Aux États-Unis, il n'y a rien que vous ne puissiez faire en voiture – voir un film au cinéma (à droite), assister à la messe, manger au restaurant et même retirer de l'argent à la banque automatique (ci-dessus). En prévoyant bien votre journée, vous auriez sans doute pu passer la journée entière dehors à manger, boire, assister à un spectacle, faire vos courses et les régler, sans jamais sortir de votre voiture.

Poverty and style

By the mid-1950s it seemed that no matter how poor or run-down the district, the street would be lined with cars. Puerto Rican immigrants use both parked cars and front steps as meeting places (left) outside tenement blocks in one of the poorest areas in New York in the early-1950s. Meanwhile, in the city, the sharply styled Plymouth (right) is the perfect library chair for the snappily dressed urban reader.

Ob arm, ob reich

Mitte der fünfziger Jahre konnte ein Stadtviertel noch so verarmt und heruntergekommen sein, die Straßen standen trotzdem voller Autos. Bei den Puertoricanern in einer der ärmsten Gegenden New Yorks Anfang der Fünfziger dienen nicht nur die Treppen vor den Mietshäusern, sondern auch die geparkten Wagen als Treffpunkt für einen Plausch (links). In der City bietet derweil der chromblitzende Plymouth diesem nicht minder eleganten Leser (rechts) den perfekten Sitzplatz.

Pauvreté et style

Au milieu des années 1950, les rues des villes sont pratiquement toutes bordées de voitures malgré le délabrement d'un quartier ou la pauvreté de ses habitants. Pour ces immigrants portoricains de l'un des quartiers les plus pauvres de New York, les calandres et les pare-chocs des voitures en stationnement remplacent avantageusement la chaise installée sur le trottoir où l'on se réunit pour bavarder (à gauche) à l'extérieur de son immeuble. Ailleurs en ville, cette élégante Plymouth est un fauteuil idéal pour ce chic amateur de lecture (à droite).

Putting on the ritz

It wasn't only in Hollywood that style ruled in the early-Fifties, but in Tinsel Town, at the heart of the movie industry, cars did make a statement and every manufacturer had a styling signature. For Buick it was the toothy grin and gunsight hood ornament carried over from this 1948 Roadmaster leading the pack, and for Ford it was the central bullet in the grille, as on the big-selling V8-powered Custom convertible tailing the Buick.

Nur nicht knausern

Hollywood war zwar nicht die einzige Stadt der frühen Fünfziger, wo der neue Stil regierte, aber in der Metropole der Filmindustrie hatten schicke Autos einen besonders hohen Stellenwert. Jede Marke hatte ihr Erkennungsmerkmal: Beim Buick war es der grinsende Kühlergrill und das vom 1948er Roadmaster, der hier das Feld anführt, übernommene, an das Korn einer Flinte erinnernde Ornament auf der Haube, bei Ford die Kugel im Mittelpunkt des Grills wie dahinter beim V8-Custom-Cabriolet, einem sehr erfolgreichen Modell.

Le jeu du luxe

Au début des années 1950, chaque constructeur automobile veut laisser son empreinte sur la décennie en offrant un style particulier à chacun de ses modèles de voiture. La signature de Buick est la calandre en « dents de requin » et la mascotte en forme de mire sur le capot de la Roadmaster de 1948 ; chez Ford, c'est l'enjoliveur central en forme d'ogive au centre de la calandre que l'on distingue sur la Custom 1500 décapotable à moteur V8 garée derrière la Buick.

Town and country in the city

The Parisian girls in high-fashion jeans (above) in 1954 are admiring a Chrysler Town & Country convertible; powered by a straight-eight engine it was one of the most glamorous cars in the Chrysler range until production stopped in 1950, as fashions changed again. Still in Paris, but now in 1955 and rather more in the European idiom, the Reyonnah (below) was a tandem two-seater compact car designed by a Monsieur Hannoyer, with front wheels which could be tucked in to let the car pass through narrow gaps, even doorways.

Eine Landpartie in die Stadt

Die beiden Pariserinnen in ihren hochmodischen Jeans (oben) bewundern 1954 ein Chrysler Town & Country-Cabriolet. Der Reihen-Achtzylinder gehörte zu den auffälligsten Modellen im Chrysler-Programm, wurde jedoch 1950 eingestellt, als andere Formen in Mode kamen. Ebenfalls in Paris, diesmal 1955 und deutlich europäischer, ist der Reyonnah-Kompaktwagen mit zwei hintereinander liegenden Sitzen zu sehen (unten). Das von einem Monsieur Hannoyer entwickelte Gefährt hatte einziehbare Vorderräder, so dass es durch enge Passagen und sogar durch Türen fahren konnte.

Ville et campagne à la ville

En 1954, ces jeunes Parisiennes en jeans (en haut) admirent une décapotable Chrysler Town & Country ; mue par un moteur huit-cylindres en ligne, ce fut l'une des voitures les plus élégantes de la gamme Chrysler jusqu'à la fin de sa production en 1950. L'année suivante à Paris et plus dans l'esprit européen, cette Reyonnah conçue par M. Hannoyer était une deux-places compacte, dont les roues avant pouvaient se replier vers l'intérieur de la carrosserie pour lui permettre de se faufiler dans les espaces les plus étroits (en bas).

For richer, for poorer

Children in a poor area of Bristol pose with their battered pedal car in 1954 (left), and probably just as proudly as the rather better-off Alvin and Lilly Fuller, pictured (right) outside their new home in Palm Beach, Florida, with their Mercedes-Benz 190SL sports car. The 190SL, launched in 1955 as a smaller, less expensive cousin to the legendary 300SL 'Gullwing', was one of the most fashionable of the European sporting imports at a time when upmarket America much preferred imported sports cars to home-grown ones.

Am anderen Ende der Skala

Kinder in einem Armenviertel von Bristol (links) posieren 1954 mit ihrem ramponierten Tretauto, und vermutlich nicht weniger stolz als am anderen Ende der sozialen Leiter Alvin und Lilly Fuller (rechts) mit dem Mercedes-Benz 190SL vor ihrem Haus in Palm Beach, Florida. Der 190SL, im Jahr 1955 als kleiner und preisgünstiger Vetter des legendären 300SL-Flügeltürers auf den Markt gebracht, war einer der gefragtesten europäischen Sportwagen zu einer Zeit, als die wohlhabenderen Amerikaner Importe den heimischen Produkten vorzogen.

Pour les plus riches et les plus pauvres

Ces enfants d'un quartier pauvre de Bristol (Angleterre) posent en 1954 avec leur vieille voiture à pédales (à gauche) et en sont apparemment aussi fiers que Alvin et Lilly Fuller, largement plus favorisés, que l'on voit ici dans leur nouvelle maison de Palm Beach (Floride) près de leur Mercedes-Benz 190SL (à droite). La 190SL, un cabriolet de sport lancé en 1955 pour faire le pendant en plus petit et en moins cher de la légendaire 300SL à « ailes de papillon », fut l'un des plus grands succès à l'importation aux États-Unis d'une voiture de sport européenne à une époque où la clientèle du haut de gamme américain préférait ce genre de voiture plutôt que celles produites aux États-Unis.

Cars for all seasons

In October 1955 the new Sunbeam Rapier emerges from
an extended test in the low temperature chamber (left)
at the Rootes Group factory in Coventry where the
Rapier was built, in successive model generations, from
1955 until the mid-1970s. In warmer climes in the same
year, American high school vacationers on the beach
at Bonita Springs, Florida (right), use the station wagon
as its designers intended – to carry six people and
everything needed for a summer picnic.

Wagen für jedes Wetter

Im Oktober 1955 kommt der neue Sunbeam Rapier
(links) nach einem längeren Test aus der Kältekammer
der Rootes-Werke in Coventry, wo der Rapier in
mehreren Modellgenerationen von 1955 bis in die Mitte
der siebziger Jahre gebaut wurde. Deutlich wärmer ist
es am Strand von Bonita Springs, Florida (rechts), wo
im selben Jahr amerikanische Highschool-Absolventen
den Kombiwagen genau so einsetzen, wie seine
Schöpfer es sich vorgestellt hatten – zum sommerlichen
Picknickausflug für sechs, samt allem, was sie dazu
brauchen.

Voitures des quatre saisons

La nouvelle Sunbeam Rapier sort d'une série de tests
complets réalisés en octobre 1955 en chambre froide dans
l'usine Rootes Group de Coventry (à gauche) où seront
construites plusieurs générations de ce modèle entre
1955 et le milieu des années 1970. Bénéficiant d'un meilleur climat, ces étudiants américains en vacances sur
la plage de Bonita Springs (Floride) utilisent le « station
wagon » (dit break en Europe) comme son concepteur
l'a souhaité : c'est-à-dire transporter six personnes et
tout le nécessaire pour un pique-nique estival (à droite).

Living with the motor car

Around 1955, a Fiat driver is directed by an Italian traffic policeman (left) in Rome. In 1956 a London motorist uses one of the new parking meters (opposite, above left) recently installed in the West End, while Mrs Szenden demonstrates a safety harness (opposite, above right) which she developed after a friend was injured by being thrown against the dashboard. The very first belts appeared in a Baker racing car in 1902; on the road, they were popularised by Nash in the early 1950s, became an option on European Fords in 1955 and would be fitted by Volvo as standard equipment in 1957. The police officer is testing for alcohol (opposite, below left), the psychologist testing a traffic offender's field of vision (opposite, below right) at a traffic safety school in New York in 1955.

Man gewöhnt sich daran

Der Fiat-Fahrer (links) bekommt um 1955 von einem italienischen Verkehrspolizisten in Rom seine Anweisungen. In London füttert eine Automobilistin 1956 eine der im West End frisch aufgestellten Parkuhren (gegenüber, oben links), und Mrs. Szenden demonstriert den Sicherheitsgurt (oben rechts), den sie entwickelt hatte, nachdem eine Freundin bei einem Unfall ans Armaturenbrett geschleudert worden war. Die ersten Gurte hatte es schon 1902 an einem Baker-Rennwagen gegeben; für den Alltagsgebrauch hatte Nash sie Anfang der fünfziger Jahre populär gemacht, als Zusatzausstattung waren sie ab 1955 bei europäischen Fords zu haben, und seit 1957 baute Volvo sie serienmäßig ein. Ein Verkehrssünder wird auf Alkohol untersucht (unten links), bei einem anderen testet ein Psychologe einer New Yorker Schule für Verkehrssicherheit 1955 das Gesichtsfeld (unten rechts).

Vivre avec l'automobile

Vers 1955, un policier italien de Rome indique son chemin au chauffeur d'une Fiat (à gauche). En 1956, cette automobiliste s'astreint à utiliser l'un des parcmètres tout récemment installés dans le quartier londonien de West End (ci-contre, en haut à gauche). En 1956, Mrs Szenden présente le modèle de ceinture de sécurité (ci-contre, en haut à droite) qu'elle a conçu après qu'un de ses amis se soit grièvement blessé en heurtant violemment le pare-brise. Les toutes premières ceintures de sécurité sont apparues en 1902 dans une Baker de course ; sur la route, elles furent popularisées par Nash au début des années 1950, furent posées en option sur les Ford fabriquées en Europe en 1955 et équipèrent en série les Volvo à partir de 1957. L'officier de police fait passer un test d'alcoolémie à un conducteur suspect d'ébriété (ci-contre, en bas à gauche) tandis que ce psychologue vérifie le champ de vision d'un contrevenant (ci-contre, en bas à droite) dans une des écoles de sécurité routière de New York en 1955.

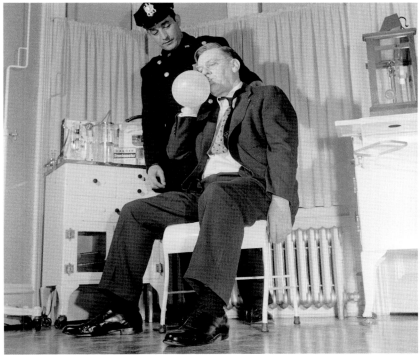

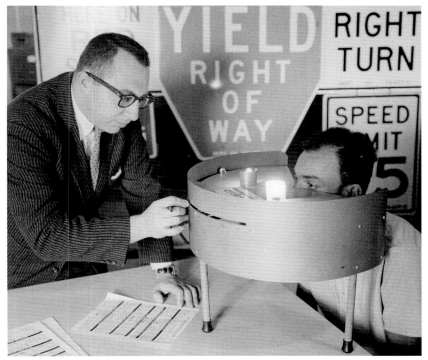

Stranger moments

The suburban couple (right) preparing to leave for a picnic in 1955 demonstrate the essential simplicity of the hugely popular Morris Minor – a wheel at each corner plus a spare in the back, a wheel for the driver, a simple four-cylinder side-valve engine in the front and what passed for impact absorbing bumpers, in the days before safety legislation began to proliferate. The real car waits behind, while the pampered poodle and chauffeur (opposite) can only look on in amazement.

Kuriose Augenblicke

Das Paar aus der Vorstadt, das hier (rechts) zu einem Picknick aufbricht, demonstriert, wie einfach der äußerst erfolgreiche Morris Minor gebaut ist – an jeder Ecke ein Rad, ein Reserverad hinten, ein Steuerrad für den Fahrer, vorn ein einfacher seitengesteuerter Vierzylinder und das, was als Stoßstange galt, bevor die heutigen Sicherheitsbestimmungen kamen. Das fertige Produkt wartet hinten, und da können der verwöhnte Pudel und sein Chauffeur (gegenüber) nur staunen.

D'étranges moments

Ce jeune couple de 1955 (à droite) illustre la grande simplicité mécanique de la très populaire Morris Minor que l'on voit derrière eux : quatre roues plus une de secours dans le coffre à l'arrière, un volant, un simple moteur quatre-cylindres à soupapes verticales à l'avant et des semblants de pare-chocs (à une époque où les lois sur la sécurité routière n'étaient pas aussi strictes que maintenant). Ce caniche et son chauffeur (ci-contre) sont sans doute dans une voiture d'une toute autre classe !

The bubble car boom

The Suez crisis brought petrol rationing to Europe and bubble cars and microcars had their day, although they were rather small for Prime Minister Harold Macmillan (above right).
In 1959 there was the single-cylinder, two-stroke, two-seater, three-wheeler Scootacar (above), in 1957 the BMW Isetta (below right), and in 1956 the Messerschmitt Kabinenroller (opposite) – an ideal advertising vehicle.

Die Zeit der Mikro-Autos

Die Suezkrise führte in ganz Europa zu Benzinrationierungen, und die Stunde der Kleinstwagen war gekommen – auch wenn sie für Fahrer wie den britischen Premier Harold Macmillan (rechts oben) doch ein wenig zu winzig geraten waren. 1959 kam der Scootacar (oben) auf den Markt, ein dreirädriger Zweisitzer mit Einzylinder-Zweitaktmotor, 1957 die BMW Isetta (rechts unten), 1956 der Messerschmitt-Kabinenroller (gegen-über), immerhin ein guter Werbeträger.

La vogue des « minis » et des « micros »

La crise de Suez ayant entraîné le rationnement de l'essence en Europe, les mini-voitures et les micro-cars connaissent un regain d'intérêt de la part du public ; évidemment, elles ne conviennent pas forcément à tout le monde, notamment au Premier ministre britannique Harold Macmillan (en haut à droite). C'est en 1959 qu'apparaît le Scootacar monocylindre, deux vitesses, deux places et trois roues (ci-dessus), en 1957 la BMW Isetta (ci-dessus, à droite) et, en 1956, la Kabinenroller Messerschmitt (ci-contre).

Motoring for the millions

Crises apart, the 1950s did see economies recovering
from the war years and the motor car enjoying growing
sales, especially for 'people's' cars. The Volkswagens (right)
awaiting export from the Wolfsburg factory in 1956 were
Germany's bestseller; Fiat two-door exports arrived in
Copenhagen in 1955 (above); and the British Ford Anglia
with its distinctive rear window (opposite) was introduced
in 1959.

Motorisierung für Millionen

Bei allen Krisen erholte sich doch die Wirtschaft in den
Fünfzigern weltweit vom Krieg, und die Verkaufszahlen
für Automobile stiegen immer weiter, gerade bei den
Massenmodellen. Der meistverkaufte deutsche Wagen
war der Volkswagen, der hier (rechts) 1956 beim Wolfsburger Werk auf Auslieferung wartet; zweitürige Fiat-
Exportmodelle kamen 1955 in Kopenhagen an (oben),
und der britische Ford Anglia (gegenüber) mit seiner
unverwechselbaren Heckpartie erschien 1959.

Des millions d'automobiles

Si l'on excepte la crise de Suez, les années 1950 voient
repartir l'économie et les ventes d'automobiles remonter
en flèche, notamment dans la gamme des voitures dites
« populaires ». Si ces Fiat deux-portes sont nombreuses
à Copenhague (ci-dessus) en 1955, les Volkswagen (à droite),
en attente d'exportation au parking de l'usine de Wolfsburg, représentent les meilleures ventes d'automobiles
de l'Allemagne. Commercialisée en 1959 et construite
en Grande-Bretagne, la Ford Anglia est reconnaissable
grâce à sa lunette arrière (ci-contre).

New directions

Alongside the bubble cars and the microcars, the end of
the 1950s saw a new generation of smaller 'real' cars,
with room for the family and few of the bubble cars'
freakish design features. Not that they didn't have their
own technical innovations, as in the twin-cylinder, rear-
engined, rear-drive Fiat Nuova 500 of 1957 (right), or
most of all in the incredible transverse-front-engined,
front-wheel-drive Mini (opposite), launched in 1959 and
still in production more than forty years later.

Neue Impulse

Neben Kleinstwagen und Kabinenrollern kamen in den
fünfziger Jahren auch »echte« Kleinwagen auf, die einer
ganzen Familie Platz boten und nicht ganz so eigenwillig
gestylt waren. Was nicht heißen soll, dass sie nicht
fortschrittlich waren, etwa der Fiat Nuova 500 von 1957
mit seinem Zweizylinder im Heck (rechts) und allen
voran der unglaubliche Mini (gegenüber) mit Quermotor und Frontantrieb, 1959 vorgestellt und nach über
vierzig Jahren noch heute im Programm.

De nouvelles directions

La fin des années 1950 voit émerger, outre des « micro »
et des « mini », une nouvelle génération de « vraies »
petites voitures, moins étranges que les « voitures bulle »
(bubble car) et qui offre suffisamment de place pour
toute une (petite) famille. La simplicité de leur conception n'exclut pas l'innovation technique, comme pour
cette Fiat Nuova 500 de 1957 (à droite), à moteur arrière
bi-cylindre, ou pour cette Austin Mini (ci-contre) à roues
avant motrices et moteur transversal, lancée en 1959 et
toujours commercialisée plus de quarante ans plus tard.

The future starts here

Alec Issigonis's small car masterpiece, the Mini, was launched in 1959 and became an icon of the 1960s. It has survived into the 21st century while all others have come and gone. It was an outstanding design, not only for its packaging but also for its performance, a small family car that became a prolific race and rally winner, worldwide, and the blueprint for generations of small cars to come. The sight of Timo Mäkinen 'yumping' his rallying Mini in 1967 is a perfect bridge between the dawn of the motoring era and the present day.

Der Sprung in die Zukunft

Alec Issigonis' Kleinwagen-Meisterwerk, der Mini, kam 1959 auf den Markt und wurde zum Inbegriff der Sechziger. Er hat den Sprung ins 21. Jahrhundert geschafft, während alle anderen längst Geschichte sind. Er war ein faszinierendes Auto, nicht nur im Äußeren, sondern auch in seinen Leistungen, ein kleiner Familienwagen, der doch auf allen Rennstrecken der Welt und bei den großen Rallyes zu Hause war, und das Vorbild für ganze Generationen kleinerer Wagen, die nach ihm kamen. Das Bild von Timo Mäkinen, wie er mit seinem Rallye-Mini über eine Bergkuppe gehüpft kommt, spannt perfekt den Bogen zwischen den Anfangstagen des Automobils und dem heutigen Tag.

Un bond vers l'avenir

La Mini, chef-d'œuvre de conception dû à Alec Issigonis, fut lancée en 1959 et devint rapidement le symbole des années 1960. C'est une des rares voitures à être entrée dans le XXIᵉ siècle presque sans une ride alors que bien d'autres sont déjà oubliées. Elle doit beaucoup non seulement à sa carrosserie particulière passe-partout qui a servi de modèle à plusieurs générations de petites voitures mais aussi à son potentiel de performances qui lui a permis de se faire connaître avec succès dans le monde entier comme voiture de course et de rallye. Cette photographie de la bondissante Mini de rallye pilotée par Timo Mäkinen en 1967 est un merveilleux symbole pour annoncer l'ère future de l'automobile.

gettyimages

This book was created by Getty Images, 21-31 Woodfield Road, London W9 2BA

Pictures in this book have been taken exclusively from Getty Images.